A History of the French & Indian Wars, 1689-1766

FRENCH AND INDIAN WAR

MAP OF THE SCENE OF OPERATIONS.

A History of the French & Indian Wars, 1689-1766

The Conflicts between Britain and France for the Domination of North America

ILLUSTRATED

A History of the French War
Rossiter Johnson

The Ohio Indian War
Thomas Guthrie Marquis

LEONAUR

A History of the French & Indian Wars, 1689-1766
The Conflicts between Britain and France for the Domination of North America
A History of the French War
by Rossiter Johnson
and
The Ohio Indian War
by Thomas Guthrie Marquis

ILLUSTRATED

FIRST EDITION

Leonaur is an imprint of Oakpast Ltd

Copyright in this form © 2021 Oakpast Ltd

ISBN: 978-1-915234-00-1 (hardcover)
ISBN: 978-1-915234-01-8 (softcover)

http://www.leonaur.com

Publisher's Notes

Contents

Thomas Guthrie Marquis

Preface

The history of the struggle between the Gaul and the Briton for possession of North America, though in form a straggling story, stretching over two centuries, offers one of the most interesting studies of national character and destiny. To treat it exhaustively in a volume like this was impossible, if not undesirable; but it is hoped that enough has been told to give the reader a clear idea of the character and sequence of all the significant events, and to suggest something of the philosophy of the long contest. A knowledge of this is absolutely necessary to any intelligent study of the subsequent history of our country.

The part played by the red man should not be overlooked. Bloody and terrible it was to the vanquished soldier, thrice bloody and hideous to the settler and his little family; but though it prolonged and embittered the struggle, it had no real effect upon the result. In the earlier wars on this continent, the tomahawk and scalping-knife were enlisted mainly in the service of the French against the British; but the Briton conquered the Frenchman nevertheless.

In later wars, the same savage weapons in savage hands were wielded for the English against the Americans; but the American conquered the Englishman. There is no more important lesson to teach the youth who must be our future soldiers and commanders than this, that in the warfare of nations the exercise of cruelty has never secured the ultimate victory. The power that only tortures and murders cannot become even a balance of power when two races are in conflict for precedence, or two opposite ideas for survival. Civilization must fight out its own battles.

An account of Pontiac's conspiracy, the final grand effort of the Indian to drive off the encroaching Saxon from American soil, would have formed an interesting sequel to the narrative of the French war;

but the limits of space forbade. I am indebted to my sister, Mrs. Joseph O'Connor, for valuable assistance in the preparation of this volume.

R. J.

New York, September 13, 1882.

CHAPTER 1

Early Voyages

For more than a hundred years after the discovery of the continent of America, at the close of the fifteenth century, no permanent settlement was made by Europeans in its northern portion. The New World was looked upon mainly as a land of adventure and discovery, a land holding the possibility of unimagined wonders and undreamed-of riches, waiting only for the hand brave enough and adventurous enough to seize them and carry them back in triumph to the Old World. The sailor and the merchant looked to it for the realisation of their brightest visions, and crowned heads confidently expected its wealth to replenish their exhausted treasuries; but not till the latter part of the sixteenth century was it sought as a refuge and a home by the persecuted adherents of the new religion, and as a missionary field by the reawakened zeal of the older Christian Church.

The claims of European nations to American territory were vast and vague. When an adventurer touched a strip of sandy shore, he at once planted upon it the flag of his nation, and took possession of the whole continent in the name of his sovereign. These indefinite claims—in some instances strengthened by colonization or confirmed by Indian grants—were afterward used as a pretext whenever individual interests or religious hatred or European wars excited any of the feeble American colonies to make themselves and their neighbours still feebler by intercolonial hostilities.

The most successful explorers were Italians; but they were all in the service of countries other than their own—in that of Spain, England, or France. The Spaniards made no attempt to establish colonies, or seriously to assert their claims, north of Florida; and there they came somewhat into collision with the English and French. To those two nations was left the great struggle for the possession of the northern coast and the interior.

The worst feature of their contests was the participation of the red men, with their savage and indiscriminate modes of warfare. That most of their peculiar atrocities were committed in the interest of France was not wholly due to greater depravity on the part of the French; for in later wars the English showed themselves quite willing to employ the same barbarous and irresponsible allies, knowing that their outrages would be perpetrated, not upon the hereditary foes of England, but upon Englishmen themselves.

Many of the leaders on both sides would have been glad to have their savage friends conform to the usages of civilized warfare; but when the Indian's zeal was once awakened and his thirst for blood aroused, it was impossible to hold him to a code which he did not recognise, and which to him seemed weak and cowardly. His own laws of war knew no mercy for the conquered. When he failed, he expected none; and when he was victorious, he deemed himself defrauded if he were forced to let prisoners go untortured and unharmed. Hence the horrible massacres that followed some of the French victories.

That the Indians fought more frequently and zealously on the side of the French, was due to the superior tact and skill of the French in dealing with them, and to the fact that they earlier saw the advantage of gaining and holding the friendship of the natives. The British at first adopted the policy of avoiding them as much as possible, of driving them back into the interior; they regarded them as incapable of civilization, and scarcely looked upon them as subjects for the influences of Christianity.

The French, on the other hand, tried from the first to Christianise, if not to civilize them. They drew them when they could into missionary villages near their own settlements, and sought to bind them to themselves by the bonds of a common religion. The wild life of the savages attracted many adventurous spirits from the French colonies, who lived among them as *coureurs de bois*, or wood-rangers, adopting their mode of life and gaining an influence which told largely for France in times of war.

Almost the only Indians who stood by the English were the Iroquois, or Five Nations, whose home was in New York. Even their friendship often wavered; and it might be said that their adhesion to the English was not because they loved them more, but because they loved the French less. Their enmity may have been caused by the fact that the French, in the early days of their settlement in the country, joined against the Iroquois with their enemies, the Algonquins of the St. Lawrence.

When the English woke to the importance of taking advantage of the distrust of the Iroquois toward the French, they were never successful in rousing them to the zeal in their cause which the Indians of Maine and New Brunswick displayed in the cause of the French. Yet, though the English colonies availed themselves, as far as they could, of the help of the savages, it must be admitted that the record of the French in America is stained with many more atrocities not justifiable by any rules of civilized warfare—descents on unarmed laborers in the fields, and midnight attacks on peaceful settlements, with all the horrors of indiscriminate massacre, which were incited and often led by Frenchmen, and even in some cases by the ministers of religion, and in periods of nominal peace.

The contests between the English and the French for the possession of American territory were not ended until the close of the Seven Years' War in 1763. It is a curious fact that while the colonies which England had settled with her own sons, and which helped her to conquer New France, had revolted and become an independent nation in twenty years, those then wrested from France, French in their origin and devotedly loyal to the French Crown, have contentedly remained under British rule for more than a century.

The English claims were based on the discoveries of John and Sebastian Cabot, Venetians living in England, who, in 1497-8, examined the coast from Labrador to Virginia. The Portuguese, in 1500, sent out Gaspar Cortereal, who explored the coast northward, and stole some of the natives, whom he took home for slaves. The Portuguese merchants therefore called the place *Terra de Labrador*, "land of laborers."

The best known explorers sent out by Spain, after Columbus, are Juan Ponce de Leon, who discovered and named Florida in 1512; Hernan Cortes, the conqueror of Mexico; Pamphilo de Narvaez, who discovered the land of the Appalaches; and Hernando De Soto, who found the Mississippi in 1541, and was buried in its waters the following year. Under the name of Florida, Spain claimed a vast country extending from the Atlantic to the Rocky Mountains, and from the Gulf of Mexico to the Arctic Ocean. This claim, based on the right of discovery, was further confirmed to Spain by a Bull of Pope Alexander VI., making the Spaniards exclusive masters of all America. The decree of the Pope, however, was not powerful enough to prevent Francis I. of France from attempting to gain some share in the glory and profits of discovery.

The first explorer sent out by the French Government was John Verrazzano, an Italian; though French sailors, in common with those of other nations, had resorted to the coasts of Newfoundland for years to fish for cod, some as early, at least, as 1504. Newfoundland and Labrador, or parts of them, were indefinitely called Baccalaos, a word said to mean codfish in the dialect of the Basque provinces. The sailors had a tradition that two islands north of Newfoundland were haunted by demons, whose clamour filled the air with confused sounds which were heard by ships venturing near the unholy coast. They were called the Isles of Demons, and were represented on maps of the time with their infernal inhabitants dancing about in wings, horns, and tails.

Verrazzano set out in 1523, with four ships, but encountered a storm, and finally crossed the ocean with only one, the *Dauphine*, carrying fifty men and provisions for eight months.

★★★★★★

The authenticity of this story, which rests upon a letter attributed to Verrazzano and published by Ramusio in 1556, has recently been called in question and, if not disproved, at least shown to be doubtful. I have thought best, however, to let the reader see it, with this warning as to its character. It was first disputed by T. Buckingham Smith, in 1864. J. Carson Brevoort defends the story, in his *Verrazzano the Navigator* (New York, 1874), and Henry C. Murphy rejects it, in his *Voyage of Verrazzano* (New York, 1875).

★★★★★★

He first saw the continent near where Wilmington, North Carolina, now stands; but, as the shores were thickly lined with savages, he did not dare to land. The Indians made signs urging the sailors to come on shore, and one, more daring than the rest, took some presents and swam for the beach; but, losing his courage when near the land, he threw all he had to them and started to return. A breaker, however, tossed him back upon the beach, and the Indians, running to his aid, took him ashore, and built a great fire. The terrified sailor, and his companions who were looking on from the boat, had no doubt that they were going to make a meal of him, or offer him in sacrifice to the sun. But he soon found that the fire was to warm him and dry his clothes. The Indians gathered about him, admired his white skin, caressed him, and took him down to the beach when he wanted to return to the boat, dismissing him with most affectionate embraces.

The *Dauphine* proceeded northward along the coast, carrying away an Indian child stolen from its mother in Virginia, explored New York Bay and Long Island Sound, and stopped in the harbour of Newport, where the white men were most cordially treated by the Indians. Having gone as far north as Newfoundland, Verrazzano returned to France, and wrote for the king the first known description of the Atlantic coast of the United States.

The most illustrious navigator sent out by France in the sixteenth century was Jacques Cartier, of the seaport town of St. Malo, in the north-western part of the kingdom. He was sent at the suggestion of Philip Chabot, Seigneur de Brion, Admiral of France, a favourite of the king, who induced his master to make another attempt to gain a footing in the country which had given so much wealth to the Spaniards. Cartier sailed on the 20th of April, 1534, with two ships of sixty tons, and one hundred and twenty-two men.

The voyage was so prosperous that Cartier reached Cape Bonavista in Newfoundland on the 10th of May. Finding the land still covered with snow and ice, he turned to the southeast, and landed at a port which he named St. Catharine. Then turning north again, he named some small islands Bird Islands. He was surprised, he says, to see a white bear as large as a cow on one of these islands, to which it had swum from the mainland, a distance of fourteen leagues. As soon as it saw the boats, it took to the water, and Cartier killed and took it the next day near Newfoundland. He sailed nearly around the island, which he described as the most wretched country to be found:—

> With nothing but frightful rocks and barren lands covered with scanty moss—but inhabited, notwithstanding, by men well-made, who wore their hair tied on the top of the head, like a bundle of hay, with birds' feathers irregularly inserted, which had a most curious effect.

Crossing to the mainland, he entered a deep bay, which he named the Bay of Chaleurs, on account of the heat. There is a tradition that it had before been entered by Spaniards, who, finding no signs of mineral wealth there, exclaimed, *Acá nada!* "Nothing there!"—an expression which the Indians caught up and repeated to the French, who supposed it to be the name of the country, whence the word Canada. It is more probable, however, that Canada is the Iroquois word *Kannata*, a village.

Having explored a large part of the bay, Cartier landed at Gaspé and took possession in the name of the King of France, raising a cross thirty feet high, on which was hung a shield with the arms of the country and the words, *Vive le Roy!* "Long live the King!" After discovering Anticosti, he returned to France, taking with him two Indians, who picked up a little French and served as interpreters the following year.

The reports of Cartier's voyage convinced the court of Francis I. that it was desirable to found a colony, both for the purpose of establishing a profitable trade and for saving the heathen, not only from their heathenism, but from the heresies that might be imported among them by the Protestant peoples of Europe. The Vice-Admiral Charles de Mouy obtained a fuller commission for Cartier, with three well-equipped vessels; and all the sailors assembled at the cathedral on Whitsunday, by Cartier's directions, and received the bishop's benediction.

They embarked on the 19th of May, in fine weather, but a furious storm arose the next day, and the scattered ships were tossed about for more than a month, but at last met in the gulf or Great Bay on the 26th of July. On the 10th of August, Cartier gave to a small bay in the mainland, north of Anticosti, the name of St. Lawrence, in honour of the saint whose day it was. This name was afterward extended to the whole gulf, and to the river also, which had before been known as the River of Canada, or River of the Great Bay, and by Cartier called the River of Hochelaga. Hochelaga was the chief Indian town on its banks, and stood on the site of Montreal.

They ascended the river, entered the Saguenay on September 1st, examined the mouth of that river, and then pursued their voyage up the great stream. The large island just below Quebec, now known as the Isle of Orleans, was so covered with grapevines that Cartier named it Bacchus Island. He stopped next in the St. Charles, just north of Quebec, near its mouth. On the site of the present city of Quebec— between Fabrique Street and the Coteau de Sainte Geneviève, it is thought—was an Indian town called Stadaconé. Here he received a visit from a chief, named Donnacona, who talked with Cartier by the aid of the two Indians who had been to France.

Cartier had heard of the much larger town farther up the river, called Hochelaga, and resolved to push on to it. The Indians of Stadaconé, who were of a different nation from those of Hochelaga, tried to dissuade him, representing that the way was long and beset with difficulties. When this failed to change his purpose, they pretended to have received a message from one of their gods threatening the French with storm and tempest, if they should ascend the river. Cartier sent back word to the god that he was a fool, and set out with one of the ships, the *Great Hermine*, and two long-boats. The anxiety of Donnacona and his people was probably caused by the fear that a rival nation might take from them the advantages of trade and alliance with this strange new people, from whose unknown abilities and resources they hoped not only gain, but an easy victory over their enemies.

The voyagers were obliged to leave their ships at Lake St. Peter, having missed the channel and run aground, and went on with only the two boats, reaching Hochelaga the 2nd of October. The town was round, and enclosed by three rows of trees. The middle row stood upright, and the other two were inclined and crossed above it. Then the sides of the pyramidal wall were covered with logs well fastened together. There was but one gate; and along the inside of the enclosing wall or palisade was a gallery reached by ladders, and stored with stones for the defence of the fortress. Inside of the town were fifty cabins, each over fifty paces long and fourteen or fifteen paces wide. These cabins were tunnel-shaped, made of saplings bent together, and covered with bark. Each was occupied by a large number of families.

The Hochelagans received the French with courtesy, feasted them, and gave them gifts. They looked with great admiration at the dress of the strangers, their armour and weapons, their trumpets, their fair skins and bearded faces. Cartier has left a description of a peculiar kind of service held among them. One day the warriors formed a circle, on the outside of which were the women and children, and in the centre the Frenchmen, all the savages gazing at them "as if they were going to play a mystery." Then the chief advanced, pointed at his decrepit limbs, and made signs that the French should heal him.

His example was followed by all the sick, the halt, and the lame, who came themselves, or were brought to the supposed healer. Cartier was perplexed, but seized the opportunity to make a religious impression on their minds. He recited the beginning of the Gospel of St. John, made the sign of the cross on the sick, and gave presents of knives to the men, beads to the women, and little tin lambs to the children. Then he prayed and recited aloud the passion of the Saviour, and the ceremony was concluded by a mighty blast from the trumpets, which set the savages nearly beside themselves with wonder and delight.

The same day Cartier climbed the mountain, and gave it the name which is now borne by the city and the island, Mount Royal—Montreal. Looking from its summit over the vast extent of wooded coun-

15

try, with the great river rolling by and the dark waters of the Ottawa descending to meet it from the unknown wilderness, he thought no better site for a city could be found, and hoped, no doubt, himself to lay there the foundations of a French Empire in the West.

On taking leave of the friendly savages, the French returned to the St. Charles, called by them the *St. Croix*, where they had left the greater part of the men. They found that barracks had been built during their absence and surrounded by a kind of entrenchment, sufficient to protect them from a surprise. The Indians, however, continued friendly. But the sailors were attacked by scurvy, and twenty-five of them died. Cartier himself fell sick, and all of them might have perished, had they not learned by accident of the Indian remedy for the disease—a decoction made from the leaves and bark of a tree called by the Indians *Anneda*, which is thought to have been the white pine. A week after they began using it, the sick were all restored.

In the spring Cartier set sail for France. Having got Donnacona and some of his principal men into his hands, he carried them with him; a piece of treachery which he excused by saying that the savages were making hostile preparations and attempting to get hold of Cartier himself. The Indians he took away were all baptized in France, and died there. Donnacona lived four or five years after his capture.

CHAPTER 2

Destruction of French Settlements

Either Cartier's report of his second voyage disappointed the hopes which had awaited the result of his enterprise, or the war in France drove the subject from the minds of those who had power to push on the undertaking; for nothing further was done till 1540, when a gentleman of Picardy, Francis de la Roque, Seigneur de Roberval, received a patent, declaring him Lord of Norumbega, the King's Viceroy and Lieutenant-General in Canada, Hochelaga, Saguenay, Newfoundland, Belleisle, Carpon, Labrador, Great Bay, and Baccalaos. This flourishing and pompous beginning had a most contemptible outcome.

The next year Roberval went to the St. Lawrence, sending Cartier, who was to be his pilot, in advance. The Indians at Stadaconé crowded about Cartier's ship, asking for Donnacona and their other countrymen who had been taken away, and Cartier told them Donnacona was dead, but the others were living in France in great state, and were not willing to return to their own country.

The Indians received the story with distrust, and when Cartier, after building a fort at the mouth of Cape Rouge River above Stadaconé, left most of his men there, and went up the river to Hochelaga, they killed two of those who were left. On Cartier's return, the men at the fort, which was called Charlesbourg Royal, discouraged both at the hostility of the Indians and the failure of Roberval to arrive from France, whither he had gone for supplies, clamoured to go home, and Cartier yielded. Near Newfoundland they met Roberval, who ordered them back; but Cartier stole away with his ship in the night. In 1543, he went out again, and brought back the remnant of Roberval's colony, much reduced by disease and executions for mutiny.

Roberval seems to have been stern and vindictive, uncompromising and impolitic in his management, and ill adapted to be the head of a colony where he had to rule a lawless band of adventurers and convicts within, and keep the peace with suspicious and crafty savages without. Under his rule, men were hanged for theft and insubordination, and the whipping-post was in frequent requisition. In one case several men were banished to an island and kept there for some time in fetters.

Cartier, after the inglorious ending of his career as a navigator, which had begun so brilliantly, settled down to a quiet life at his country-house in the suburbs of St. Malo, which was still, (1882), standing a few years ago.

More than half a century passed before the project of settling colonies in North America was revived. France had been torn by dissensions between the Catholics and Protestants; eight civil wars were waged during the reigns of Charles IX. and Henry III., a period of twenty-eight years. But the rule of the moderate and tolerant Henry IV. restored tranquillity to the kingdom; and the spirit of adventure and discovery revived. During the interval, the fisheries and the fur-trade had been carried on in the vicinity of Newfoundland by Frenchmen and sailors of other nations, and had grown to large proportions.

In 1598, the Marquis de la Roche received a grant from the king to colonise New France, with substantially the same title which had been conferred on Roberval. By the terms of this grant he was made an almost absolute monarch, having sole power to raise troops, make war, build towns, give laws, impose punishments, and grant pardons; but he was required to keep in view the establishment of the Roman Catholic faith. The gains and profits of the first voyage were to be divided into thirds, one for him, one to be distributed among his companions, and one applied to the expenses of war, fortification, and other common charges.

For the purpose of establishing this magnificent transatlantic feudal viceroyalty, the marquis gathered a company from the prisons, and under the guidance of a skilful pilot named Chedotel, landed at Sable Island, a desolate spot south of Cape Breton. Here De la Roche put ashore forty of his convicts, and went on to explore the coasts of Acadia, intending to call for the men on his way back; but contrary winds prevented a landing, and the wretched men were left alone on the sandy and barren island.

When they found themselves deserted, and the last hope of the vessel's return had died away, they built cabins of the wrecks of Spanish vessels. A few sheep and cattle were roaming about the island, sprung from some that had been on board the wrecked ships, or left there in a forgotten enterprise by the Baron de Lery; and these, with the fish they caught, furnished a living. When their clothes were gone, they dressed in sealskin. So, they lived for seven years. Various misfortunes had assailed De la Roche when he returned to France, and he had been unable to do anything toward their release; but at last the king heard of them, and sent Chedotel to bring them back.

The forty men were reduced to twelve, whom Chedotel took to France and presented before the king in the same dress in which he found them, "covered with sealskin, their hair and beards of a length that made them resemble the pretended river-gods, and so disfigured as to inspire horror. The king gave them fifty crowns apiece, and sent them home released from all process of law."

After the death of De la Roche, patents were granted to others, who used them mainly to enrich themselves by trade. But in 1603, the Sieur de Pontgravé, a merchant of St. Malo, having received permission from the king to continue discoveries in the region of the St. Lawrence and make settlements there, associated with himself Samuel de Champlain.

This great man was destined to become the real founder of New France. He was born at Brouage, in Saintonge, a department of Western France, in 1567. After serving in the army of Henry IV., he had gone to the West Indies as a captain in the Spanish service, and kept a journal, which he called *A Brief Discourse of the Most Remarkable Things Seen by Samuel Champlain of Brouage, in the West Indies*. He drew his own illustrations for it—maps of the coasts, pictures of strange animals, and Indians burned for rejecting the gospel or whipped for not going to mass. This manuscript is still preserved at Dieppe, and has been published in an English translation. The accounts which he afterward gave of his adventures in the French colonies, under the title, *Voyages in New France*, are an important source of information regarding the early history of those colonies.

Pontgravé and Champlain ascended the river to find Cartier's town of Hochelaga; but it was gone, probably destroyed in some Indian war. The rapids prevented them from going farther, and they returned to France, to find that a new commission had been given to Pierre du Guast, Sieur de Monts, of Saintonge. This gentleman was a Protestant, but agreed to establish the Roman Catholic religion among the Indians, while his own sect was to enjoy full freedom of worship. He went out with four ships, taking in his own some Catholic priests and some

Huguenot ministers, who edified the crew with their disputes, even "falling to with their fists on questions of faith." A Franciscan friar who wrote a history of Canada says the crew buried in one grave a priest and a minister, who happened to die at about the same time, to see if they would lie peaceably together.

De Monts went to Acadia, and landed his men on the southern shore of what is now Nova Scotia, and then sent out Champlain to explore the coast and find a place for a settlement. He entered and named the harbour of Port Royal, where Annapolis now stands, a place which holds an important position in the early history of America. Crossing the Baye Françoise, now, (1882), the Bay of Fundy, they entered the St. John's, naming it in honour of the saint whose feast fell on that day, and selected for the site of their colony an island in St. Croix River, called by them Isle St. Croix, and now known as Doucett's Island. The St. Croix they called River of the Etchemins, from the tribe of Indians living there.

During the winter Champlain explored the coast as far as Cape Malabar, taking possession of the country in the name of the King of France. Finding that the island selected had been chosen unwisely, De Monts moved his colony in the spring to Port Royal. A settlement had already been begun there by his lieutenant, De Poutrincourt, who had taken a fancy to the place, wished to bring his family and live there, and had therefore obtained a grant of Port Royal and the vicinity from De Monts.

The next year Poutrincourt brought from France with him Mark Lescarbot, an advocate from Paris, who proved a great acquisition to the colony, being quick and fertile in invention of schemes, and able to inspire the men with enthusiasm for carrying them out. He induced them to plant fields and construct roads, showed them how to make firebricks, and build a furnace for clarifying the gum of the fir and making pitch; and under his direction they built a watermill to take the place of the handmills they had been using. The priests had all died, and Lescarbot undertook to read and expound the Scriptures on Sundays. The supplies were abundant, and the winter passed with plenty of good cheer and fun, led by Lescarbot and Champlain. Lescarbot afterward wrote a history of New France.

To their feasts the Micmacs, or Souriquois Indians of Acadia, were made welcome. These Indians were firm and serviceable allies of the French during all the time of their occupation of the country; and their chief, an old man named Mambertou, became a great favourite with the settlers. Lescarbot wrote a poem commemorating a victory he gained over the tribe of the Armouchiquois.

De Monts, who had lost the privilege given him of carrying on the fur-trade to the exclusion of all others, succeeded in getting it restored, on condition that he plant a settlement on the St. Lawrence. He therefore removed his men and supplies, and Champlain went with him, leaving Port Royal to Poutrincourt, who had obtained a confirmation of his grant of the place from the king. At the same time the king notified him that something must now be done for the conversion of the Indians; and the king's confessor, Father Cotton, being directed to choose some Jesuit fathers to go over and begin the work, selected two, Pierre Biard and Enemond Masse.

But Poutrincourt was unwilling to take the fathers over. Some historians have supposed that both he and Lescarbot were secretly Protestants; but it is more probable that they merely shared the prejudice against the Jesuits as extremists in the Church and secret friends of Spain, which was not uncommon among good Catholics in France at the time. Poutrincourt gave Father Cotton to understand that he should soon embark at Bordeaux. Thither Father Biard repaired, and waited a whole year, but there were no signs of departure. The Jesuits complained to the king, and the king sharply rebuked Poutrincourt, who promised to go at once, and made his preparations; but at the last moment he begged Father Cotton to let the missionaries wait until another year, that the colony might be in a better condition to receive them.

Father Cotton let the matter go; and Poutrincourt sailed. When he arrived at Port Royal, wishing to show the king that America could be Christianised without the Jesuits, he began to gather in the Indians for religious instruction; he had with him a priest named La Fleche. Old Mambertou was the first convert, and others followed so rapidly that in a few weeks Poutrincourt was ready to send over to the king a list of twenty-five Indians who had been baptised into the Church. Mambertou received in baptism the name of the king, members of his household were called after the royal family, and the lesser Indians after other titled personages at the French Court.

The list was taken over by Poutrincourt's son, Biencourt. But Henry IV. had fallen by the knife of an assassin, and Biencourt gave it to the queen regent, supposing the matter of sending the Jesuits would not be pressed any farther. But they had succeeded in interesting in their favour the Marchioness de Guercheville, a woman of great energy, enthusiasm, and devotion to the Church, who assumed the role of patroness of the mission to the Indians, and collected money for building and furnishing a chapel. Two Huguenots who were associated with Biencourt refused to let the Jesuits go; but Madame de Guercheville raised money at court and bought them out. Then she purchased from De Monts all of his claim under the grant of Henry IV., which had now been revoked, intending to get it renewed; and she did afterward receive a royal patent for all of North America from the St. Lawrence to Florida, excepting Port Royal, which had been given to Poutrincourt. She made a contract with Biencourt by which the missionaries were to be supported from the proceeds of the fisheries and the fur-trade.

The missionaries at length reached Port Royal, in June, 1611; but there was never a very good understanding between them and Poutrincourt, who resented the Jesuits' interference with what he considered his own province. Lescarbot reports him as saying to Biard:—

I with my sword. Father, have hopes of Paradise, and you with your breviary. Show me my way to heaven, and I will show you yours on earth.

The missionaries were anxious to learn the Indian language; but those of the French who could have helped them would not. Old Mambertou, however, came to them for instruction in Christian doctrine, and helped them to some knowledge of his language, though he did not live long after their arrival. Biard, to show how the Indians had been taught by Father La Fleche, reported that when he was teaching him the Lord's Prayer, Mambertou objected to the petition for daily bread, saying, "If I only ask for bread, I shall get no fish nor moose-meat."

The story of Mambertou's death is interesting. Father Masse took him to his own house when he fell ill; but care and remedies were of no avail. Mambertou saw that he must die, called for the last sacraments, and exacted a promise from Biencourt that he should be buried with his own people. Father Biard said it could not be allowed; for to bury the chief in heathen ground would be a stumbling-block to the Indians. Biencourt urged his promise, and said the father had only to bless the spot where the chief should be laid. The missionary replied that this could not be done unless all the pagan bodies were first removed; and that, of course, was out of the question. But Mambertou was obstinate, and Biard declared he would have nothing to do with the funeral. The terrors of the world to come and the firmness of the Jesuit at last prevailed; Mambertou gave way, died with the consolations of the Church, and received Christian burial.

The Jesuits made some farther attempts to bring the savages into the fold of the Church. Biard went to visit the Kinibequi, or Kennebecs, and other Indians in what is now the State of Maine, in company with Biencourt; and Father Masse made an expedition with Louis, the son of Mambertou, from which he came back worn with sickness and hardship. But the *commandant* and his son treated their Jesuits grudgingly; the colony was growing feeble, depending on supplies from France and help from the Indians, and neglecting the care of the soil.

On the other hand, the Jesuits, in concert with Madame de Guercheville, made it uncomfortable for Poutrincourt in France. His funds were running low, and the colony was a constant drain upon them. He was forced to admit Madame de Guercheville as a partner, in order to get aid for Port Royal. She sent over another Jesuit, a laybrother, Gilbert Du Thet. But quarrels ensued at the colony; Du Thet was sent back; and Madame de Guercheville, who by this time had received her grant of the greater part of North America, determined to begin a new settlement.

She therefore sent out a vessel in the spring of 1613, under the command of the Sieur de la Saussaye, who, stopping at Port Royal, took on board the two Jesuits, and sailing on began a settlement on Mount Desert Island, which was named St. Saviour.

But the colony was destined to be short lived. Samuel Argall, a piratical adventurer of Virginia, set out for a fishing excursion off the coast of Maine. On his way, he heard of the new settlement from the Indians, and resolved to drive away the French, on the strength of patents from the English king giving to the London and Plymouth Company the control of North America up to latitude 45° N. After a short engagement, in which Brother Du Thet valiantly fired off a cannon which he forgot to aim, and soon after fell mortally wounded. La Saussaye surrendered.

Argall took possession, cut down the cross the Jesuits had raised, and, searching the baggage of La Saussaye, found and stole his commission. The next day he asked Saussaye to show his commission, saying that he should respect the authority of the French king, although the country belonged to the English. La Saussaye, of course, could not find the commission; whereupon Argall denounced him as a pirate, and gave up the French ship and the houses of St. Saviour to be plundered by his men.

After this he treated the colonists more mildly. He offered them a small bark to take them home to France; but it would not hold them all. Fifteen embarked in it, including the commandant and Father Enemond Masse, who went to look after their spiritual interests. At first, they had no pilot; but in a day or two, as they were coasting along, they found their pilot, who had fled from the English to the woods, and took him in. Near Port de la Hêve, on the southern shore of Acadia, they met two French ships, which took them safely to St. Malo.

The rest of the French prisoners were induced by Argall to go with him to Virginia. He promised that they should be treated well, allowed the free exercise of their religion, and be sent to France in a year if they cared to go. But when they reached Jamestown, where Sir Thomas Dale was acting as governor, Dale declared that they should all be hanged as pirates. Argall tried to protect them, pleading the terms of the surrender and the promises by which, he had induced them to come to Virginia; but Dale would not relent; he said they had been trespassing on English territory without authority, and they deserved the fate of pirates. Seeing no other way of saving them, Argall was obliged to produce the stolen commission of La Saussaye and confess his baseness. Sir Thomas was compelled to give up at sight of the commission from the French king, but he declared that the French should be driven out of Acadia.

This he at once made preparations to do, though that part of the continent was included in the grant made by the English king to the Plymouth Company, while Virginia was under the control of the London Company; so that the Virginians had no claim whatever to interfere with the French in Acadia. He fitted out three ships, and gave the command to Argall. Biard and Quentin, the Jesuits who had gone with Argall to Virginia, went with them, as did several others of the Frenchmen. They sailed first to St. Saviour, and destroyed all they had left at their previous visit. Next, they went to the island of St. Croix, where De Monts had had his colony, and razed the deserted buildings. Then they crossed the Bay of Fundy to Port Royal, guided, it is supposed, by Father Biard, who saw an opportunity to be revenged on Poutrincourt's colony.

Biencourt, who was in command, was absent among the Indians. But supplies had lately been sent from France, and these the invaders had the satisfaction of seizing or destroying by fire. Biard says, in his story of it:—

> And please God, that the sins committed there may have been also consumed.

They cut off the arms of France and the names of the founders of the colony, which had been cut in a large stone standing in the fort, and left the fort itself in ruins. Sailing up the river, they saw the fields and mills where the men were at work. Biard, it is said, tried to induce some of them to leave Biencourt and serve under Argall. But they rejected the treacherous suggestion with scorn, and one of them threatened to split the holy father's head open with a hatchet if he dared to make another of the kind.

Biencourt tried to make an agreement with Argall to divide the trade of the country; but Argall refused to consider him in any light but that of an intruder on the territory of King James. Biencourt also asked the surrender of Biard, to whoso treachery he attributed all the misfortunes of Port Royal; and the Jesuit, who was looked on with almost as much distrust by the English, was in a dangerous position. His own account says he was saved by his display of humanity and his forgiving spirit.

> He put himself on his knees before the captain at two different times and on two occasions, to pray for pity toward the French at Port Royal, to persuade him to leave them some provisions, their sloop, and some other means of passing the winter. And see what contrasting petitions were made to the captain; for at the same time when Father Biard was thus interceding for the French, a Frenchman was crying out from afar, with abuse and accusation, that the Father ought to be butchered. Now Argall, who has a noble heart, seeing the Jesuit's sincere affection, and the beastly inhumanity of that Frenchman, refused to listen to the accusations.

After the destruction of Port Royal, the French colonists were scattered. Some went to the settlements on the St. Lawrence; but most of them spent a miserable winter, roaming in the woods and getting what help they could from the savages. Poutrincourt gave up all hope of the colony; and in 1615, he was killed in a civil conflict in his own country. His son, with some few companions, among whom was Charles de la Tour, spent his life in Acadia and made efforts to rebuild Port Royal.

Argall sailed again for Virginia, taking back with him the Frenchmen of St. Saviour. But he encountered a storm at the very beginning of the voyage, and one of the three ships was lost; Argall's own reached Jamestown in safety, but the one having the Jesuits on board was driven northward and then to the Azores, where it put into port at Fayal. It was a fortunate storm for Father Biard; the ship carried a formal accusation from the Port Royal men to Sir Thomas Dale, against the Jesuit; and the governor, as Biard says:—

Was waiting to cut off his voyages by showing him the end of the world from the top of the gallows.

The ship, which was the one taken from La Saussaye in Argall's first expedition, and was now commanded by Turnell, the lieutenant of Argall, was in some danger from the Portuguese at Fayal, where it came to port; the officers were at the mercy of the Jesuits, who had only to accuse them as pirates. But Biard and Quentin promised the master of the ship that they would lie hidden while in port, a promise which Biard claims great credit for keeping.

When the ship arrived in England, Turnell was put into prison on suspicion of being a pirate. He had no papers to explain his position, and appearances were against him; he was in possession of a French ship; and he was only released on the testimony of the Jesuits. After spending some time in England, Fathers Biard and Quentin were claimed by the French ambassador and sent home. La Saussaye and his companions were at length shipped from Virginia to England, and in the end reached their own country. Madame de Guercheville sent La Saussaye to demand reparation in London; but she seems to have succeeded only in getting her ship restored. This was the end of the first serious attempt at French settlement in Canada.

CHAPTER 3

Quebec Founded, and Taken by the English

According to the terms of his grant, which required him to make a settlement on the St. Lawrence, De Monts sent Champlain to select a site and begin the work of building a town. Arriving at the spot where Cartier, more than seventy years before, had found Stadaconé, the capital of Donnacona, Champlain selected the same site for his settlement, and resolved to build a town on the promontory just where the Indian town had stood. All traces of Stadaconé had now disappeared. The Indians called this part of the river Quebec, signifying "a narrowing in," or a strait, the river here being only about three quarters of a mile in width.

The history of Quebec has justified the sagacity of Champlain's choice. Rising three hundred feet above the river, the steep wall of rock forms a natural stronghold and commands the stream below.

Here, in July, 1608, Champlain began preparations for the oldest permanent settlement in North America, except the one at Jamestown, Virginia, which dates from 1607. Having first put up some rude barracks for temporary shelter, the men made an embankment along the present line of Mountain Street. Then they built a wooden wall with openings for defence, and within the wall three houses. Outside the wall they dug a moat.

During the winter Champlain took care to gain the friendship of the neighbouring Indians. The supplies at the fort were abundant, and were freely divided with the famishing savages, who were accustomed to make very slight provision for winter. The Indians of the St. Lawrence belonged to the great family of the Algonquins, whose various tribes were scattered over Canada, New Brunswick, Nova Scotia, the

27

New England and Middle States, except New York, and parts of Virginia, Michigan, Wisconsin, Illinois, Indiana, and Kentucky.

Their deadly enemies were the Iroquois, or Five Nations, including the Mohawks, Oneidas, Onondagas, Cayugas, and Senecas, who lived in New York. In 1715, the league of the Iroquois was joined by the Tuscaroras of Carolina, and hence they are often mentioned in history as the Six Nations. The Hurons and Eries lay near the lakes which bear their names. At this time the Hurons were in league against their kindred, the Iroquois, with the Algonquins of the St. Lawrence.

These Indians had great hopes of the alliance of the French in their warfare against the powerful league of the Iroquois; and in the spring of 1609, they asked Champlain to join them in an expedition to the Mohawk country. Satisfied that his best policy lay in the alliance with the Algonquin tribes, and anxious to penetrate farther into the great unknown region at the west, in the hope of finding some clue to the passage to the East Indies, which was the dream of all the early voyagers, Champlain joined them with eleven other Frenchmen. This began an enmity between the French and those fierce and powerful tribes, which lasted for more than a century and a half.

The Indians assured Champlain that there was no obstruction along the water route they intended to take, and he therefore embarked in a shallop, while they took to their canoes. They ascended the St. Lawrence and the Sorel or Richelieu, which they called the River of the Iroquois. Hearing at length the noise of rushing water, Champlain left some of his men in charge of the shallop and, pushing on through the woods, came to the Chambly Rapid. Unwilling to abandon the undertaking, he told the Indians that, notwithstanding their deception, he would keep his promise and go on with them. He sent back the shallop with all his men but two, who refused to leave him; and the Indians shouldered their light canoes, walked through the woods past the rapid, and embarked on the stream above.

At night they made an encampment, protecting themselves on the land side by a strong abatis of trees, and arranging the canoes so that in case of a surprise they could embark with ease and celerity. Then they all went to sleep without sentinels, answering Champlain's remonstrances by saying that those who laboured all day needed rest at night.

Proceeding up the river, they entered the lake of which it is the outlet. To the east and southeast lay the rolling summits of the Green Mountains; to the west rose the Adirondacks, covered with silent woods, but suggestive of lurking and stealthy warriors of the dreaded nations. To the beautiful sheet of water, Champlain, first of white men to look upon it, gave his own name. The islands abounded in deer, and the beavers worked in peace, for hunters were afraid to pursue their game so near the haunts of the terrible Iroquois. The Algonquins dared no longer advance by day; they paddled their canoes at night, and rested hidden while the sun was up.

They had told Champlain of another rapid beyond the lake, and another lake beyond that rapid—Lake George now—and they intended to go to it. But one evening when they were paddling silently up the lake at about ten o'clock, another silent fleet of canoes suddenly appeared on the water in front of them. It was the Iroquois. Both parties took to the shore and began to fortify themselves. Then the Algonquins sent to ask the Iroquois whether they would fight immediately. The answer was that it was too dark; and they all danced and sang and shouted boasts and threats at each other through the night.

In the morning they prepared for battle. The Iroquois, about two hundred strong, marched through the forest under command of three chiefs, distinguished by the height of the birds' feathers they wore. Some had shields of wood or leather, and some had coats of mail made of woven twigs and cords. The Algonquins and Hurons issued from their defences and ran forward two hundred paces. When they were before the enemy they halted and separated into two divisions, leaving a space in the centre for the three Frenchmen. The Iroquois looked in wonder at the strange figure of Champlain, clad in glittering steel, surmounted by a plumed helmet. Then they moved to begin the attack. He aimed his arquebuse, into which he had loaded four balls, and fired; two of the chiefs fell dead, and the third was dangerously wounded. Then the allies raised a deafening cry and followed up the charge with a shower of arrows.

The Iroquois stood firm at first and returned the charge; but as Champlain was loading to fire again, his companions discharged their pieces, by which the frightened Iroquois were thrown into a panic, and fled in disorder. The allies pursued them a short distance, took some prisoners, and brought away the supplies of the enemy, of which they were sadly in need. On their way back they halted and brought out one of the prisoners for torture. Disgusted with their horrible ingenuity, Champlain remonstrated, for some time without effect; but at length he got leave to end the sufferings of the poor wretch by a shot from his arquebuse.

One of the Indians dreamed the following night that the Iroquois were in pursuit. Not doubting the omen, the allies took to flight, only halting when they reached the islands above Lake St. Peter, where they hid themselves for the night. At Quebec they separated, assuring Champlain that they should want his help in future wars.

When he returned from France the next spring, they were waiting for him. Another journey up the St. Lawrence to the Sorel, another wild engagement, in which Champlain was slightly wounded by an arrow, another defeat of the Iroquois, through their fright at the strange and deadly weapons of the white men, and Champlain was again a hero with the Algonquins. They gave him one of their prisoners, and the Hurons consented to take home with them a Frenchman that he might learn their language, on condition that Champlain should take with him to France a young Huron, who should bring back to them a trustworthy account of the country of their white allies, as seen through Huron eyes.

In 1611, Champlain attempted to establish a trading-post at Montreal, and had a site cleared; but the settlement did not thrive. In 1613, he went there, accompanied by a young man named Nicholas de Vignan, who had drawn considerable attention to himself in France, by stories of his adventures. He professed to have ascended the Ottawa River to a great lake from which it flowed; having crossed the lake, he said, he discovered another river leading to the North Sea; at the mouth of that river he saw the wreck of an English vessel, whose crew had been killed by the Indians. All this was told with so much detail and apparent honesty, that Champlain was deceived—the more easily as rumour said that Hendrick Hudson, during the voyage in which he discovered the bay that bears his name, had been put into a boat with eight others, and abandoned by his mutinous crew. Not doubting that the wreck was Hudson's vessel, Champlain resolved to ascend the Ottawa without delay, believing that he should find the long-sought northwest passage.

With Nicholas de Vignan, three other Frenchmen, and an Indian, he toiled up the river, in canoes, which had to be carried past the rapids and falls through the tangled forest, until they reached the Isle des Allumettes. Here was the home of the Ottawas, many of whom had been down to Montreal for trade and war, and were known to Champlain. They received him with kindness; but when he asked for help to continue his journey to Lake Nipissing, they told dreadful stories of the meanness, treachery, and sorceries of the tribe of the Nipissings.

Champlain said his companion, De Vignan, had been there, and had come back in safety. The Indians were greatly astonished at this, and plumply called Nicholas a liar.

"Nicholas," said the chief, "is it true that you said you had been to the Nipissings?"

Nicholas was silent for a time, then said in their language, of which he had some knowledge, "Yes, I have been there."

"You are an impudent liar," said the chief. "You know very well that you went to bed here every night with my children and got up every morning; if you went to those people, it must have been in your sleep."

Champlain took Nicholas aside, and conjured him to tell the truth. Nicholas swore that all he had said was true. Champlain then told the Indians De Vignan's whole story—of the lake, and the river to the North Sea, and the wrecked ship—all of which the Indians insisted were outright lies. In great perplexity Champlain took De Vignan aside again, and promised if he would now tell the truth to forgive what was past; but threatened that if he should be found out in a deception, he should be hanged without delay.

Nicholas thought it over, and then confessed. He had not expected that Champlain would have the perseverance to go so far as to discover the truth; and he was anxious to enjoy the glory of the discovery. Champlain was so enraged he could scarcely endure the sight of him; but he kept his word, protected De Vignan from the Indians, who officiously offered to despatch the liar for him, and let him return to Montreal and go on his way.

On his next visit to France, Champlain, who was a man of sincere piety, and is recorded to have frequently said that the salvation of one soul was of more value than the conquest of an empire, obtained four Recollect missionaries to return with him, for the spiritual welfare of the colony and the conversion of the Indians. One of them, Father le Caron, who was assigned to the mission among the Hurons, went to Montreal with Champlain. There they found the Indians assembled for the fur-trade, and anxious to get the help of the French in another expedition against the Iroquois. Champlain promised it, and went to Quebec to get ready. The Indians, impatient of the delay, set out for their homes to collect their warriors, and Le Caron and twelve other Frenchmen went with them.

Finding them gone, on his return to Montreal, Champlain set out to follow them. Passing up the Ottawa and the Mattawan, he crossed to Lake Nipissing, which he traversed, and entering the French River reached the Georgian Bay. He coasted along its eastern shore southward, and thence went overland to the Huron villages. In one of them he found the zealous Recollect, whose ardour had been kindled by the sight of so many heathen, and who wrote to a friend:—

> Alas, when one sees such a vast number of *infidels*, needing but a drop of water to make them children of God, what zeal he feels to work for their conversion and to sacrifice for it his repose and his life!

The Indians had built him a chapel of bark, and the priest had raised within it an altar with the sacred images and the candles; and after Champlain's arrival, the first mass was said in the little chapel, and the missionary work among the Hurons was begun.

When the war parties of the Indians were all gathered, they made their journey to the southeast, by way of Lake Simcoe, the Talbot River, Balsam Lake, and the rivers Otonabec and Trent, to Lake Ontario, and crossed to New York, landing somewhere near the site of Sackett's Harbor. Concealing their canoes, they struck southward, were soon among the Iroquois, and attacked some small parties whom they found in the woods and fields. The Iroquois took refuge in a fortified town, probably in the neighbourhood of Lake Onondaga.

The defences consisted of a kind of fort surrounded by an abatis of trees thirty feet high, which supported a gallery where great quantities of stones were kept, to be hurled down on assailants. The Hurons were repelled at their first attempt to take the fort. Then they set fire to the abatis; but the Iroquois had provided against fire by conducting water within the walls from a pond outside, and the flame was soon extinguished. Unable to control the Hurons, Champlain was obliged to let them carry on the attack in their own way; and after three hours of fighting they retired discomfited.

Champlain, although wounded, favoured renewing the attack; but the Indians insisted on waiting for some promised re-enforcements. As these did not arrive, the Hurons retreated after five days, and returned to their own country. Their confidence in Champlain was lost; they had supposed that his presence and the use of the fire-arms would always give them an easy victory. Sulky and disappointed, they refused to keep their agreement to send him back to Quebec; and he was obliged to spend the winter among the Hurons.

In 1622, the Iroquois attempted to exterminate the French, in retaliation for the help given to the Algonquins. One party attacked some

Frenchmen who were at the passage of the St. Louis Sault, or Rapid, and were repelled with loss. Another party went down to Quebec and besieged the convent which had been built for the Recollect Fathers on the St. Charles. But the fathers had a little fort; and, by means of prayers within and balls without, they succeeded in driving off their assailants. The Iroquois were forced to content themselves with some Hurons whom they found not far away, and made prisoners.

After various changes in the management of the affairs of the colony, which were not prosperous, they had been placed under the control of two Huguenots, William de Caen and his nephew Emeric. The colony had been carefully kept free from Protestants, who would have settled in New France in great numbers if they could have been allowed to do so and to enjoy the free exercise of their religion. De Caen was ordered to take over some Jesuits; but when they arrived, he would not permit them to stay at the fort or Château St. Louis, a building which Champlain had begun in 1620, for the citadel.

The jealousies between the Jesuits and the authorities, and between the Jesuits and the other orders, proved a fruitful source of trouble in Quebec for years afterward. On account of the complaints of the Jesuits that Emeric de Caen obliged Catholic sailors to join in the prayers of his Huguenots, De Caen was ordered to stop all Protestants from praying or singing psalms on the St. Lawrence. But the sailors remonstrated, and a compromise was finally agreed upon, by which the prayers were allowed and the psalm-singing only forbidden.

In 1627, Cardinal Richelieu deposed the De Caens and put the control of New France into the hands of the "Company of One Hundred Associates."

After the devastation of Acadia by Argall, the country, though claimed by both England and France, was neglected by both. Biencourt inherited a claim to Port Royal from his father, Poutrincourt—who held it in right of a grant from the French king—and lived in the country with his friend, Charles St. Etienne de la Tour, who had come to Acadia in boyhood with his father, Claude de la Tour, a French Huguenot. In 1623, Biencourt died, having bequeathed his interest in Port Royal and the surrounding country to Charles de la Tour.

Meantime, the King of England, James I., had granted the whole tract of land now forming New Brunswick and Nova Scotia, together with the peninsula between the mouth of the St. Lawrence and the Bay of Chaleurs, to Sir William Alexander, afterward Earl of Stirling, a now forgotten poet and dramatist. The entire territory was called

Nova Scotia; and the limits of Nova Scotia and Acadia were long afterward a fruitful subject of dispute and bloodshed between the English and the French. In 1622, Alexander made an unsuccessful attempt to plant a colony, and three years later an order of Baronets of Nova Scotia was created. Each baronet was to receive a tract of land six miles by three, and in return was to help in the work of colonizing the country.

In 1626, war broke out in France between the Catholics and Protestants. Rochelle, the stronghold of the Huguenots, was held by the rebels, and Richelieu was besieging it, determined to put an end to the Protestant power in the kingdom. The city was making a desperate resistance, and Charles I. of England sent a fleet to the help of the rebels. Charles de la Tour, who had built a fort near Cape Sable, sent to France for arms and ammunition to prepare him for defence, in case the English should take advantage of the troubles in Europe to attack Acadia. The message was taken by his father, who came back bringing the supplies, in company with one De Roquemont, who had charge of cannon, ammunition, and stores for Quebec.

When hostilities opened between England and France, an expedition was fitted out under the auspices of Sir William Alexander to attack the French in America, and the command was given to Sir David Kirk, a Huguenot of Dieppe, who had fled from religious persecution in France.

Stopping at Tadoussac with his ships, Kirk sent a party to destroy the settlement at Cape Tourmente, and another to summon Quebec to surrender. Champlain answered that he should hold his position to the last, and, putting his poor defences in the best possible order, waited anxiously for the expected supplies from France. But Roquemont's ships were intercepted by Kirk, who took some of them and sank the rest in the river. Supposing, from Champlain's answer to his summons, that Quebec was strongly fortified and garrisoned, he made no further attempt at the time to take it. But the following year he sent his brother Louis to besiege it. The loss of Roquemont's supplies, and the wrecking of another vessel which had been sent over with food, had reduced the people of Quebec almost to starvation, and they took to the woods, where they dug roots and picked up acorns for food.

Many of them wandered off to the Indians, some made their way to the sea-coast in the hope of getting a passage to France in fishing-boats. Champlain had only sixteen men left to defend the fort, and as Kirk offered favourable terms, he surrendered without resistance. The soldiers were to march out with their arms and baggage and a beaver robe apiece; the friars with their clothing and books; everything else was to be left in the fort. The French were to be furnished with a vessel to take them to France. Louis Kirk took possession of Quebec, July 20th, 1629, and the banner of St. George waved on its heights for the first time, just one hundred and thirty years before the victory of Wolfe.

The elder La Tour, who was with Roquemont's fleet, was taken prisoner and carried to England. There he was presented at court and received with great favour. Moved, perhaps, by the treatment of Protestants in France, he renounced his allegiance to his own country, married one of the maids of honour of the Queen of England, was created a baronet of Nova Scotia, and received a grant of land there from Sir William Alexander. His son was invested with the same title and was to share the territory with him. In return, La Tour agreed to plant a Scotch colony and convey to the English his son's fort at Cape Sable.

In 1630, he went over with his colonists in two ships; but his son received the proposal to throw off allegiance to France with great indignation, much to the discomfiture of his father, who had had no doubts of success. After several attempts to persuade his son to a change of mind, he landed his men and assaulted the fort, but failed to capture it, and then took his Scotch colonists to Port Royal. When it became probable that Acadia would be given up to France by England, his son invited him to Cape Sable, and built a house for him outside the walls of the fort, stipulating that neither he nor his wife should ever set foot within them.

Champlain urged upon the French Government the policy of insisting on the restoration of New France when the treaty of peace should be made. The question was seriously debated whether it was worthwhile to keep and colonise Canada. All attempts so far had involved large outlays, with small returns. There was no mineral wealth, such as the Spaniards and Portuguese had brought from their colonies; and Spain and Portugal, with all the treasure from Mexico and Peru, had declined rather than grown stronger.

On the other hand, it was argued that the right means had not yet been taken; that the monopolies granted to individuals had interfered with colonisation; that New France might be peopled with the overflow of population at home; that mines might still be discovered there; that the fur-trade and fisheries, properly conducted, might be a great source of wealth; and, above all, that France owed a religious duty to the heathen of the western wilds.

The restoration of New France was finally made one of the conditions in the treaty between the two powers which was signed at St. Germain-en-Laye, March 29th, 1632, when Canada, Acadia, and Cape Breton came once more under the dominion of France.

Champlain died in the fort at Quebec, December 25th, 1635, and was buried in a sepulchre built by the colonists, the site of which is not very definitely indicated in the accounts of the time. About the year 1866, the Abbé Laverdière found traces of the tomb on the site of the Recollect Chapel in Champlain Street. The ground had been broken up the year before for the laying of water-pipes; but a vault was found containing a coffin and human bones, apparently those of some distinguished person, and nearby were the remains of three others. On a wall of the vault which was still standing was found a part of the name, 'Samvel de Champlain'.

Champlain's adventurous and courageous spirit, combined with his pure and disinterested motives, and his remarkably clear and far-sighted judgment, make him one of the most attractive and heroic characters in the early history of America. Though an enthusiast in the work to which he gave his life, he was forbearing toward the cowardice, the avarice, and the half-heartedness of colleagues, even when they retarded and almost ruined his work. Though faithful to his creed, narrow in the interpretation of it, as was the fashion of his age, and zealous in spreading it, he never appears as a persecutor.

CHAPTER 4

The French in the West

The history of Canada for many years after the death of Champlain is little more than the history of the Jesuit missions and the fierce battles of the Algonquins and Iroquois, in which the French suffered with their Indian allies. The Mohawks had not only recovered from their superstitious fear of firearms, but had supplied themselves with them from Dutch traders in the New Netherlands. Determined to exterminate the Hurons and Algonquins, they descended the St. Lawrence in war parties, and surprised their foes on the way down to the French settlements with their loads of bear and beaver skins for the summer trade.

The Governor of Quebec built a fort at the mouth of the Richelieu to intercept them; but they easily avoided its guns by shouldering their birchen canoes at a point above and carrying them north-eastward through the woods, to be launched on the St. Lawrence below, while the garrison would not discover that they had passed.

By 1650, the Hurons were almost annihilated. Their principal towns had been burned, and the inhabitants slaughtered, dispersed, or carried away. A remnant was taken to Quebec by the missionaries, and settled in several places successively in the vicinity of the city. Some of them are said to be still living at the last place to which they were removed, called New Lorette. Some settled among their conquerors in Central New York, where they clung to the religion taught them by the Jesuits, and many good Catholics were found among them by missionaries in 1668. That part called the Tobacco Nation wandered from place to place through the Northwest, driven by the Iroquois and the tribes among which they attempted to settle. They rested successively on the Island of Michilimackinac, the western shore of Lake Michigan, the banks of the Mississippi, the western shore of Lake Superior, the Strait of Mackinaw once more, and at last at the western end of Lake Erie, where they were known as Wyandots. Under this name they fought with the French against the English.

In 1660, when a large party of the Iroquois were on their way to attack Quebec, a company of seventeen men, all between twenty-one and thirty-one years of age, under Adam Dollard, Sieur des Ormeaux, asked leave of the commandant of Montreal, in whose garrison they were, to go out and attack them. It was almost certain death; but their enthusiasm would take no denial, and the commandant gave a reluctant consent.

They were joined by a party of forty Hurons and four Algonquins, and at the foot of the Long Sault took possession of an old palisaded fort, built long before by the Algonquins. The Iroquois came, and a desperate fight ensued. The assailants were repeatedly repelled, and the French party, though suffering for want of water, held out bravely; but after four or five days they were deserted by all the Hurons except their chief, Etienne Annahotaha, persuaded by some of their countrymen who had been adopted by the Iroquois, and who told them that a large re-enforcement was on the way.

The re-enforcement came, but the fort held out three days longer. All the Frenchmen fell but one, and he, badly wounded, was carried away by the victors. The Hurons who deserted were treated as prisoners. But the Iroquois, although victorious, were discouraged and demoralised by the bravery of the heroes of the Long Sault, and returned to their own country.

In 1665, the Marquis de Tracy was sent over with two hundred soldiers to subdue the Iroquois. A fort was built, under command of an officer named Chambly, at the rapids in the Richelieu which bear his name, and another was erected on the site of the old Fort Richelieu, which had been built at the mouth of the river in 1642. The new fort was in charge of an officer named Sorel, whose name is preserved in that of the town and river. Salières, the colonel, built a third fort above Chambly, called St. Theresa. The three western of the Five Nations were now at peace with the French, but the Mohawks and Oneidas continued hostile.

Courcelle, the Governor of Canada, and Tracy marched their men into the Mohawk country, and took their five important towns, the Indians flying at their approach without striking a blow. In 1667, the Mohawks asked for French mechanics and missionaries to be sent among them. The request was granted, and the French had almost unbroken peace with them for twenty years.

According to the authorities, the founding of Montreal was brought about in a wholly supernatural way. A gentleman of moderate fortune, named Dauversière, living at La Flèche in Anjou, was directed by a mysterious inward voice to establish a hospital-convent on the island of Montreal, in the St. Lawrence; and about the same time a priest named John James Olier de Verneuil was also directed by an inward voice to send priests to the island of Montreal, to bring the American Indians into the true church. It is said that neither knew anything of the place; particulars regarding New France were published every year by the Jesuits, but these men saw the island in visions.

At length they chanced to meet, knew each other at once, and understood their common design. They formed a plan for establishing religious communities on the island, and for raising a colony to accompany them, and were soon joined by others, obtained a title to the island, raised some money, and resolved to send out forty men to begin a settlement under Paul de Chomedey, Sieur de Maisonneuve, who took charge in the same spirit of pious zeal which actuated the founders.

More associates were soon added to the company, many of them women of wealth, and another miracle supplied a leader for the nuns. Mademoiselle Jeanne Mance felt herself called to labour in Canada, and her spiritual director assured her that the call was doubtless divine. Chancing to go into a church at Rochelle, after she had determined to go, she met Dauversière, when the two instantly knew each other and understood each other's secret intentions as had happened before with Dauversière and Olier. Mademoiselle Mance went with Maisonneuve and his colony, in 1641, and in 1642, they laid the foundations of Montreal, which they called Villemarie—the town of Mary.

During all these years the missionaries were performing wonders of courage and devotion among the ungrateful and treacherous savages. Father Nicholas Viel, a Recollect, on his way home from among the Hurons to spend a time in retirement at Quebec, was drowned by the treacherous Indians who were bringing him in a canoe down the rapid of the River of the Prairies, back of Montreal; and the rapid is still called the "*Sault au Recollect.*" Fathers Gameau and Mesnard were murdered by the Ottawas.

The Jesuits were ready to enter every dangerous field, and even to rush to martyrdom; they established missions among the Hurons, notably that of Sainte Marie on the River Wye; they even attempted the conversion of the Iroquois. Father Isaac Jogues, taken prisoner by them as he was returning from the Huron mission, might have escaped, but thought it his duty to remain with his captive converts and prepare them for death. With two lay associates of his order, Goupil and Couture, he was carried to the Mohawk country and made to suffer every torture that savage ingenuity could devise. Goupil was murdered on suspicion of having bewitched children with the sign of the cross.

Jogues suffered not only from his wounds, but from hunger; for he would not eat meat that had been offered to heathen gods. But he thought himself sufficiently rewarded by the opportunity of baptising a few children and dying Indians. The following summer, going with a fishing-party to a place near Fort Orange, now Albany, he was assisted to escape by a Dutch trader; and the Dutch afterward paid a ransom for him, of the value of three hundred *livres*. He and his companions were the first white men to look on Lake George. At his next visit, three years later, he named it Lake St. Sacrament.

He went to France from New York, but returned to Canada in 1644, and volunteered to establish a mission in the Iroquois country in 1645. Undeterred by the recollection of the horrors of his former visit, he went back; but a sickness that prevailed among them during the summer, and the destruction of their harvest by caterpillars, were laid to the evil spell of a box of papers which he had left among them during a short absence. Jogues was seized on his return, and after being beaten, hacked, and treated with the utmost cruelty and indignity, was killed by a blow from a hatchet. His companion. Father Lalande, shared his fate, and their heads were set up on the palisades of the town.

Father de Noué, a Huron missionary, was found kneeling and frozen in the snow, in a midwinter journey to Fort Richelieu. Father Daniel was in the Huron town of St. Joseph when it was assailed by the Iroquois, and busied himself among the panic-stricken inhabitants, baptising and absolving. When the assailants forced an entrance, he directed those near him where to fly, and went to meet the enemy to gain time for them. A shower of arrows was sent at him; but the undaunted priest threatened the assailants with the vengeance of God, at the same time assuring them that repentance would gain his favour. A shot pierced his heart, he fell dead, and was burned in his church, where his body was thrown by the victors.

Charles Gamier and Noel Chabanel fell, the first by the Iroquois at St. Jean, the other by a renegade Huron convert who fancied the

Christian religion had been the destruction of the Huron nation. Jacques Buteux was slain by the Iroquois on a toilsome winter journey to the nation of the White Fish, whose country was north of Three Rivers. Jean de Brébeuf and Gabriel Lalemant were taken at the Huron town of St. Louis when it was destroyed by the Iroquois, and slain after horrible tortures. The skull of Brébeuf—whose body, together with that of Lalemant, was found on the scene of his martyrdom—is still preserved at the Hôtel-Dieu in Quebec, together with a silver bust of him which his relatives sent over from France.

In the pursuit of their calling, the Jesuits penetrated far beyond the frontiers of the colonies, and discovered lands and waters never before seen by Europeans. It was due in part to their explorations that the French laid claim to the Mississippi Valley and the region of the Great Lakes, and that they gained the alliance of so many of the tribes that inhabited the West, by whose help they came so near establishing their claim. Father Claude Allouez, a missionary to the Ottawas, explored the southern shore of Lake Superior in 1667, and in 1670, with Father Dablon, he explored the regions about the Upper Wisconsin. In 1673, Father Marquette, with Louis Joliet, discovered the Mississippi, and descended as far as the mouth of the Arkansas. Father Hennepin accompanied La Salle down the Illinois and up the Mississippi, and wrote descriptions of his voyages.

One of the most renowned of French explorers of the interior of the continent was Robert Cavelier de la Salle. Hearing of the great rivers at the west, he collected a party to go in search of them in 1669. The party numbered twenty-two, and included a priest, Dollier de Casson, noted for his great size and strength. It was said of him that when in his full strength, he could stretch out his arms and hold a man on each hand. The party set out from La Salle's seigniory on the St. Lawrence, which he called St. Sulpice. It was near the La Chine rapids, eight or nine miles from Montreal. They gave out that they were going to find a western passage to China. In Western New York they met Joliet, and learned something of his discoveries.

For some reason, La Salle and others of the party returned to the St. Lawrence; and on this account, it is said, his place was called in derision, La Chine (China), a name which it still retains and which is now applied to the rapid. De Casson and some of his companions went on, and were the first to sail through Lakes Erie and St. Clair.

In 1678, La Salle, having received a monopoly of the trade in buffalo-skins for five years, and permission to establish forts and trading-posts at the West, set out again. He built Fort Miami at the mouth of the St. Joseph, and Fort Crevecoeur on the site of Peoria, Illinois. In 1682, he descended the Mississippi to its mouth, and took possession for France. In 1684, he brought a colony of two hundred and eighty persons to form a settlement on the Mississippi; but they missed the mouth of the river and, going on to the shores of Texas, landed at Matagorda Bay. One of their four ships, the storeship, was wrecked, and two were taken away by the naval officer in charge.

A fort called St. Louis was built; but the colony languished, and in 1687, not more than one seventh remained. La Salle started northward by land with several companions; but some of them formed a conspiracy and assassinated him near a branch of Trinity River, while the survivors of his colony were nearly all murdered by the Indians.

In 1699, D'Iberville and his brother De Bienville, planted a French Colony on the Bay of Biloxi, the first in the present state of Mississippi. French Protestants asked leave to settle on the lower Mississippi, but were told that the king had not driven Huguenots from France to form a republic of them in America. In 1702, a fort was built on the Mobile River by the colonists of Biloxi—the first settlement in Alabama—and another was placed at the mouth of the Mississippi.

The French had now a chain of forts and trading-posts from the St. Lawrence to the Gulf of Mexico. The oldest settlement in the Mississippi Valley is Kaskaskia, originally a Jesuit mission; and besides the stations at St. Joseph and Peoria, there were posts at Detroit, Chicago. Vincennes, and other places on the line of the great lakes and rivers.

CHAPTER 5

Acadia

After the restoration of Acadia to France by the treaty of 1632, grants were made to Frenchmen in the country, and some colonists were sent out. There was room for a variety of interpretations of the treaty in regard to the territory near the Penobscot and Kennebec Rivers, according to the understanding of the limits of Acadia. The English trading-stations at Penobscot and Machias were broken up by parties of Frenchmen and the traders were plundered of their goods. The Plymouth colony attempted to re-take Penobscot; but the French had strengthened the place and continued to hold it, warning the English to encroach no farther than Pemaquid.

The principal grants of territory in Acadia were made to Nicholas Denys, Isaac de Razillay, and Charles La Tour. De Razillay's rights passed into the possession of D'Aulnay de Charnisay; and the story of a strange feud between him and La Tour is the history of Acadia for years. La Tour's fort and trading-station was at the mouth of the St. John, Charnisay's at Port Royal. Disputes and jealousies arose between them as early as 1635; and Charnisay attempted to dislodge his enemy by means of his influence at court.

He laid before the king and the prime minister accusations of treason and other crimes against La Tour; and in 1641, an order was sent to the accused to appear and make answer to the charges. At the same time Charnisay was ordered to seize him and take control of his fort, if he should refuse to obey the order. La Tour refused, on the ground that the order was based on misrepresentations. The vessel sent to take him to France carried back letters from Charnisay giving accounts of La Tour's defiance, and before the end of the year he himself went to France for help against his rival.

La Tour put his defences in the best possible order, and sent a messenger to Boston, a Huguenot from Rochelle, to propose an alliance. Though La Tour himself had been a Protestant, he had professed the Catholic faith; but his wife was still a Protestant, and Charnisay used that fact to excite prejudice against them at the French court. The authorities at Boston readily accepted La Tour's proposal for free trade between his colony and theirs; but they were more wary when it came to the question of furnishing him aid against Charnisay, and promised nothing. The next year La Tour sent his lieutenant to Boston with fourteen men and letters to John Winthrop, again asking assistance.

The people of Boston treated La Tour's men with great consideration, and were edified at their respectful attendance at the Puritan meetings, though they were Catholics. The lieutenant accepted with thanks, from one of the elders, a Testament in French, with notes by a Protestant minister, and promised to read it. He induced some of the merchants to fit out a ship and send it at once to open the trade.

On its way back, this ship stopped at Pemaquid, where it happened to meet Charnisay. He showed the officers an order from France for the arrest of La Tour, and gave them notice that he would seize any vessel he should find trading with the rebel. By giving mortgages on his lands to one Le Borgne, he had raised a large amount of money, with which he bought five vessels and hired five hundred men to serve against La Tour.

Failing of support from New England, La Tour sent to Rochelle in France, and a large armed vessel, carrying one hundred and forty men, was sent to him from that city. When this ship, the *Clement*, reached St. John, she found the harbour blockaded by Charnisay, who had come with two ships, several small vessels, and five hundred men, to assault the fort. Failing to take it, he established a blockade, hoping to starve the garrison into surrender. La Tour and his wife now stole out of the fort one night, reached the *Clement* in a small boat, and sailed directly to Boston, where La Tour with some of his men landed at Winthrop's garden on Governor's Island.

The governor called a meeting of the magistrates for the next day, and the captain of the *Clement*, to authenticate his mission, laid before them letters from the Vice-Admiral of France and the agent of the Company of New France, authorising him to carry supplies to La Tour, who was called the King's Lieutenant-General in Acadia. The fact that these papers were issued when an order for La Tour's arrest was in the hands of Charnisay, is explained by the confusion in the administration of the government, caused by the recent death of

Richelieu, and the expected death of the King, Louis XIIL, who died in May, 1643, before the *Clement* reached the St. John.

On the evidence of these documents, the authorities of Boston gave him permission to hire men and vessels with which to relieve his fort. The merchants of Boston were anxious to see La Tour reinstated, not only from friendship toward him, but for the interests of trade; for Charnisay was unfriendly and would have no commerce with them. Two of them let to La Tour four vessels, with fifty-two men and thirty-eight pieces of ordnance; and he raised a force of ninety-two soldiers and armed them for service. The agreement was, that these vessels should accompany La Tour to St. John and aid the French ship in his defence in case Charnisay's forces should attempt to interfere with him.

The owners of the ships sent an agent authorised to determine how far La Tour should be allowed to use them in the operations against his enemy. The New England soldiers were commanded by Captain Hawkins. Not until the five ships appeared in sight of the harbour of St. John did Charnisay suspect that La Tour was not shut up with his men inside the fort. Not daring to cope with the force brought against him, he ordered his vessels to set sail at once for Port Royal. La Tour's fleet gave chase, and Charnisay ran his ships aground opposite the mill of Port Royal, and his men went to work to strengthen the defences. Captain Hawkins sent Charnisay a letter from Governor Winthrop, explaining the attitude of his government in the matter, and proposing a reconciliation between him and La Tour; but Charnisay would not open the letter, because the address did not give him his title of Lieutenant-General, and he sent the captain a copy of the order for La Tour's arrest.

As the messenger reported that Charnisay's men seemed confused and frightened, La Tour wanted to make an attack at once, and Hawkins gave his men permission to follow him if they chose to do so. About thirty of them joined in the attack, and Charnisay's men were driven from the mill, three being killed and one taken prisoner. The New Englanders escaped without loss. La Tour lost three men. On the way back to his fort the ships took a pinnace of Charnisay's, loaded with a great quantity of moose and beaver-skins, which were divided between La Tour and the crews and owners of the Boston ships. Much uneasiness was felt in Boston about the seizure of Charnisay's pinnace, from fear that it would involve them in a quarrel with that enterprising and dangerous rascal.

Charnisay built a new fort at Port Royal, and then sailed for France to get more help to crush La Tour; while soon after his arrival there.

La Tour's wife reached Rochelle, in search of aid for her husband, Charnisay, by his influence at court, obtained an order for her arrest on the same ground as that for the arrest of her husband—that she was a traitor and a rebel. Hearing of it in time, she fled to England and finding friends there, she set sail for Acadia, in a ship loaded with supplies and munitions of war. The ship carried as a passenger Roger Williams, famous in the history of New England.

The master of the vessel spent so much time in trading on the way, that it was six months before they reached Acadia, and on the coast, they fell in with a vessel sent out by Charnisay to watch for them. The master concealed Lady La Tour and her party, and gave out that he was on the way to Boston; by which means they escaped, but the ship was obliged to go on to its pretended destination. When they reached that port, Lady La Tour brought suit against the owners of the ship for the damage she had sustained by the delay, and was awarded two thousand pounds. In satisfaction of this judgment, she seized the cargo of the ship, valued at eleven hundred pounds, and hired some Boston vessels to take her home with her supplies.

Before she was ready to sail for St. John, a messenger from Charnisay, Monsieur Marie, accompanied by ten Frenchmen, arrived in Boston with orders for the arrest of La Tour and his wife, and asked that the people of New England should help Charnisay to carry out the King's commands, or at least should refrain from giving any further aid to the rebel.

The magistrates explained their neutral position and their desire to effect a reconciliation between the rivals. Marie said La Tour should be assured of life and liberty if he would voluntarily surrender, but if taken in his rebellion he would be sure to lose his head; and Charnisay was determined to capture his wife on her way home, believing her to be the cause of her husband's obstinate rebellion. At length the magistrates agreed to sign a treaty of peace with Charnisay; but they reserved for their people the right to trade with whomsoever they chose. Having obtained this agreement, Marie hurried away before Madame La Tour set sail, in the hope of giving information to Charnisay in time for him to take her prisoner on her way, but he was too late; and Madame La Tour reached St. John in safety.

Charnisay soon had an opportunity for retaliation. La Tour went to Boston and sent back a small vessel laden with stores. Charnisay captured it and turned the crew, all English, out on a desolate island covered with snow, and kept them there ten days without fire and with no shelter but a ruinous cabin. Then he sent them home in an old shallop, without a compass; but they managed to get safely to Boston.

As Charnisay's ship was sailing away, it was hailed by two monks on the coast of the mainland, who wished to be taken on board. They had been sent out from the fort by Madame La Tour, on the discovery that they were secretly plotting in favour of Charnisay. They told him the fort could be easily taken; La Tour was away, and the place was poorly supplied with men and munitions. Charnisay therefore pressed on for another attack. But Madame La Tour was not disposed to surrender; she directed a fire against the ship, which killed twenty men and wounded thirteen, and Charnisay then retired in disappointment and wrath.

Two months later he returned to the attack once more. He had kept La Tour from reaching his fort by the vessels watching in the Bay of Fundy. La Tour's wife, however, withstood the siege three days, compelling Charnisay at that time to draw off his forces; and had it not been for the treachery of a sentry, who betrayed the fort for a bribe, she might have been finally successful. The traitor allowed the enemy to scale the walls while the garrison were at prayers. Even then the lady put herself at the head of the men, and made a spirited resistance. Charnisay at length offered to grant life and liberty to the garrison if the fort were surrendered; and knowing that she must yield at last, and anxious to save the lives of her men, the lady accepted the terms.

No sooner was Charnisay in possession, than, disregarding his compact entirely, he hanged all the garrison but one man, saving him only on the condition that he should act as the hangman. He compelled the lady to witness the execution with a rope around her neck, to signify that she deserved the same fate. Broken by the horrible scene, and the dangers and excitements of the siege, Madame La Tour lived only three weeks after the surrender of the fort, while her husband remained in Boston, ruined in fortune and homeless.

The next year Charnisay concluded a treaty of peace with New England. He claimed eight thousand pounds damages for the attack on his mill by the men under Hawkins in 1643; but his commissioners finally agreed to accept a small present by way of acknowledgment that the New Englanders were in the wrong in that affair. Governor Winthrop had an elegant sedan chair which had been on its way from the Viceroy of Mexico to his sister in Spain in a Spanish ship, when the ship was seized by an English adventurer, who gave it to Winthrop. This chair was frugally devoted to the work of repairing the friendship with Charnisay; and his commissioners departed with it and the treaty of peace.

In the following year Charnisay received a commission making him Governor and Lieutenant-General for the King in Acadia, and giving him the exclusive right to the fur-trade and the products of the mines. It remained for him to drive out Nicholas Denys, who was established in the eastern part of the peninsula, but this was accomplished much more easily and speedily than the expulsion of La Tour. The forts of Denys were taken, his fishing stations broken up, and himself and his family sent into exile.

Charnisay was now supreme in Acadia, and high in royal favour. His commission gave him the credit of having upheld the royal authority against armed rebels, of having built a seminary, provided friars to bring the Indians to a knowledge of the true religion, and driven foreigners from the king's dominions at the mouth of the Penobscot. But he did not long enjoy his triumph. In 1650, he was drowned in the river of Port Royal.

After the capture of his fort and the death of his wife, La Tour went to Newfoundland to get help from the governor. Failing in this, he spent the following years in Boston and Quebec, until news reached him of the death of Charnisay. He then went at once to France, received an acquittal from all the charges against him, and a commission as Governor and Lieutenant-General for the King in Acadia, and returned to take possession of his old fort. Charnisay's widow and children were still living in Acadia.

Madame de Charnisay made an agreement with the Duke de Vendôme, by which he was to help her to recover the rights granted to her husband, and to share with her and her children in the possessions to be recovered. But before anything had been done toward dislodging La Tour and Denys, who had also returned to his forts, La Tour entered into a compact with Madame de Charnisay which superseded the agreement with the duke, consolidated the claims, and restored peace between the families. This was no less than a contract of marriage between La Tour and Madame de Charnisay, signed in February, 1653.

At this time a new claimant appeared in the person of Le Borgne, to whom Charnisay had mortgaged his possessions. He was proceeding to dispossess La Tour and Denys, when he was interrupted by an enemy from without. Four vessels had been sent from England for operations against the Dutch colonies, and men were enlisted in Massachusetts; but news arrived of peace between England and Holland,

and the force was turned against the French in Acadia. La Tour surrendered at the first summons, being without provisions or stores for defence, and Le Borgne gave up Port Royal after a slight resistance. Acadia was now once more in the hands of the English, and garrisons of New England men were placed in the forts; but the French settlers and missionaries were allowed to remain.

La Tour, with his usual activity and fertility in resources, sailed to England and appealed to Cromwell to confirm to him the grant made to him and his father jointly by Sir William Alexander in 1630. The success which seemed always to attend him when he pleaded his cause in person, attended him here. Cromwell granted to him, in connection with two of his own faithful followers—Thomas Temple and William Crowne—an immense tract of land, including the whole coast of the Bay of Fundy to a distance of one hundred leagues inland, all of the peninsula, and a large part of the present State of Maine. A small rent was to be paid in beaver-skins, and only Protestants were to be allowed to settle in the country, but the French Catholic settlers already there were not to be disturbed. La Tour soon sold out his rights to Temple, and retired from public affairs. Temple made great improvements, and began to receive large returns in trade for his outlay, when the subject of the restoration of Acadia to France was again brought forward.

In 1667, by the treaty of Breda, which closed the war that England had been waging for two years with Holland and France, France gave back to England half of the Island of St. Christopher, which she had taken, and received Acadia.

The disputed post of Penobscot, or Pentagoet, was now occupied by the Baron de St. Castin, who carried on a large trade there. He had lived a long time among the savages, married an Indian wife, and had great influence over all the tribes of that region, belonging to the family of the Abenaquis. In the spring of 1688, Edmund Andros, Governor of New England, attacked St. Castin, on the ground that the land was included in a grant made to the Duke of York, at this time James II., King of England. St. Castin and his family fled to the woods, and Andros plundered his dwelling. The result of this was, that the Indians became restless, incited, it was supposed, by St. Castin; but the Revolution in England by which James II. lost the throne brought on a war between France and England, and the colonies in America prepared for hostilities.

ABENAKI COUPLE

ABENAKI WARRIOR AND WOMAN

Chapter 6

King William's War

At the opening of this war, the French had the post at Fort Frontenac, where Kingston, Canada, now stands, and one at Niagara, besides those on the western lakes and in the Mississippi Valley. In July, 1689, a thousand Iroquois attacked Montreal, massacred men, women, and children, burned houses, laid waste the fields, and carried away prisoners and plunder. The garrison at Fort Frontenac, panic-stricken, destroyed the fort and fled down the river in canoes, many of them losing their lives in shooting the rapids. After this disaster, the governor, Denonville, was superseded by the former governor, Count de Frontenac, one of the most efficient officers and one of the most striking and picturesque characters in the whole history of Canada.

Frontenac was instructed to carry out a plan laid before the Government by Callières, commandant at Montreal Callières was to ascend Lake Champlain under pretence of marching against the Iroquois, then surprise and take Albany, descend the Hudson, and seize New York, thus giving the French the finest harbour on the coast, and cut off the Iroquois from receiving arms and ammunition from the English. Callières was then to be appointed Governor of Albany and New York. He was instructed to allow only French Catholics in the province; the French Huguenots already there were to be sent to France, and all other Protestants banished to other colonies.

A fleet was sent over to attack New York while Callières was engaged in land operations, and Frontenac came over in one of the vessels, as did also some Iroquois whom Denonville had treacherously seized two years before, and sent over to work in the galleys. The fierce revenge taken by their nation forced him to ask that they should be sent back. Frontenac had the tact to make a firm friend of their chief on the passage, and the friendship was afterward of service to him.

The first news he received on his arrival was that of the massacre at Montreal, the loss of Fort Frontenac, and the abandonment of Niagara. On the other hand, the English posts at Hudson Bay had been attacked by two brothers of the Le Moyne family, Sainte Hélène and Iberville, and all but one had been taken. At the same time, the Abenaquis in Maine had been making havoc among English settlements. Their first attack was on Dover, or Cocheco, in New Hampshire, in June, and was in satisfaction of revenge that had been nursed for thirteen years.

In 1676, near the close of King Philip's War, Major Waldron, of the Dover militia, had treacherously seized over two hundred Indians with whom he had just made peace, hanged several, and sold the rest into slavery. In retaliation, the Indians selected Dover for the first assault. They sent two squaws to Waldron's house, who begged for a night's lodging, and were allowed to sleep on the floor. In the night they opened the gates, and the warriors rushed in. Waldron, who was eighty years old, seized his sword, with the exclamation, "What now? what now?" and defended himself bravely, till he was felled by the blow of a hatchet. Then they placed him in a chair, and cried, "Judge Indians now! Judge Indians now!" Some who were in debt to him cut great gashes in his breast with their knives, exclaiming, "So I cross out my account!" The old man fainted under the tortures, and was killed with his own sword.

At Saco several men were killed in July by Indians, who in August attacked Fort Pemaquid, garrisoned by fifteen men under Captain Weems. The one hundred assailants were all converted Indians, and were accompanied by their priest, a Jesuit named Thury. The fort surrendered the second day on condition of life and liberty to the garrison, a promise which was kept to Weems and a few others, while the rest were killed as they were leaving the fort, or carried away prisoners. Father Thury said it was due to his exhortations that the Indians refrained from torturing the prisoners, and "immediately killed those whom they wished to kill." These and other similar attacks broke up the settlements in Maine east of Casco Bay.

Frontenac now planned three expeditions against the English colonies—one from Montreal to devastate New York, one from Three Rivers to destroy the New Hampshire towns, and one from Quebec to make a descent on Maine.

The Montreal party of two hundred and ten was about half Frenchmen, bush-rangers largely, and the other half-converted Iroquois who

KING WILLIAM'S WAR

had settled near Montreal. They were reluctant allies against their heathen kindred, but more than willing to fight the English. The party was led by Mantet and Sainte Hélène, and accompanied by Iberville.

They marched in the dead of winter through the forests and up the frozen streams, drawing their provisions on sledges. When they reached Lake Champlain, the Indians asked where they were going. "To Albany." The Indians laughed at the idea of attempting Albany with such a force, and advised a descent on Schenectady, or Corlaer, as the French called it, from Anthony Van Curler, its founder. The leaders assented, and after a slow and painful march, the party reached the Mohawk River near the village.

There were dissensions in New York at this time between the followers of Leisler and the opposing party, and Schenectady was divided by the feud. The chief magistrate, John Alexander Glen, often called Captain Sander, and Lieutenant Talmage, who was in command of a small party of Connecticut militia at the block-house, were opposed to Leisler, whom most of the citizens of Schenectady favoured. For this reason, they laughed at the magistrate and the lieutenant, who urged them to guard against surprise and be prepared for defence. They left the gates of the city open, and set up images of snow for sentinels.

The French and Indians entered the village about eleven o'clock on the night of Feb. 8th, 1690, and formed a line within the palisades and around the houses, completely enclosing them. Then they raised the war-whoop, the first intimation of their presence to the villagers. The doors of the houses were battered down, and the wretched inhabitants brained at once with the tomahawk, or reserved for a more horrible fate. Sixty were killed, of whom twelve were children. Some fled through the eastern gate toward Albany and found shelter, many of them with limbs frozen by exposure to the excessive cold.

The next day a party went to the house of the magistrate, Glen, across the river. He was prepared for defence; but they assured him they had orders not to harm him or any one belonging to him. He had several times saved French captives by his influence with the Iroquois, and the officers in return for this service allowed him to take all his relatives from among the prisoners. He naturally found a great many—so many as to make the surly savages grumble at the great extent of his family connection.

The village was fired, and not more than half a dozen of the eighty houses escaped the flames: Twenty-seven prisoners were carried away, as well as a large number of horses and other plunder; and not more than one sixth of the inhabitants of Schenectady remained unhurt. About thirty Mohawks in the town were carefully spared by the French, who were fully awake to the importance of appeasing the Five Nations and cultivating their friendship.

The party from Three Rivers, numbering about fifty, fell upon the town of Salmon Falls, on the Piscataqua, March 27th. It had two forts, but neither had placed sentinels. The scenes of the Schenectady massacre were re-enacted; thirty-four were killed, and over fifty taken, some of whom were tortured on the retreat. The French were pursued by a small party from Piscataqua, and after a skirmish at a bridge over Wooster River, in which the pursuers lost a few men, went on to join the war-party from Quebec.

This party, under an officer named Portneuf, numbered nearly five hundred, after being joined by some Indians under St. Castin and the men from Three Rivers. They were on their way to the settlement at Casco Bay, near the present city of Portland. The place was defended by a fort and four blockhouses, and had about one hundred defenders under the command of Sylvanus Davis. Thirty of his men went out against the enemy, contrary to his orders, and all but four lost their lives. After a siege of four days. Fort Loyal surrendered on condition of liberty to the garrison and a guard to the nearest English town—all of which, according to the account of Captain Davis, was solemnly promised and sworn by the French leader.

Nevertheless, they were given to the Indians as soon as they had laid down their arms and left the fort; and when they protested were told they deserved no quarter, because they were rebels against their rightful king, James II. The Indians murdered some, and carried away the rest. The fort and town were burned, and the dead left unburied.

These successes of the French carried courage and enthusiasm to Canada, and aroused the English colonies to action. It was resolved, at a congress held in New York in May, that a land force should march on Montreal, while a fleet should be sent from Boston to capture Quebec.

Massachusetts had just fitted out seven vessels and seven or eight hundred men, and placed them under the command of Sir William Phips, to attack Port Royal in Acadia. It was a harbour for French vessels which roamed the waters and preyed on New England commerce, and a place of stores whence the Indians drew their supplies of arms and ammunition to carry on the border warfare.

Sir William Phips, at this time about forty years old, had had an adventurous career. Belonging to a family of twenty-six children reared in poverty and ignorance in the woods of Maine, he learned to read and write after he became a man. His boyhood was spent in tending sheep; he then became apprentice to a ship-carpenter, in whose service he spent four years. When he was twenty-two he went to Boston and married a widow older than himself. She had some property, and set him up in business; but he was not prosperous, and soon lost all his wife's capital. He was not discouraged, but began to follow the sea, and often told his wife that she should yet live in a "fair brick house in the Green Lane of Boston." The Green Lane was in the northern part of the city, and was occupied by well-to-do citizens.

In 1683, Phips heard of a Spanish ship which had been wrecked near the Bahama Islands and was supposed to have carried down with it a great deal of gold and silver. He thought a swift and easy way to the possession of the "fair brick house" would be to bring up some of this treasure from the sea, and accordingly went there in a small vessel, but did not get enough to pay for his outlay.

But while he was on this voyage, he heard of another Spanish galleon which had been wrecked fifty years before somewhere on the coast of the West Indies. There was a tradition that this ship carried down a vast amount of treasure, but no attempt had been made to recover it. Undiscouraged by his first failure, he went to England, and succeeded in getting an audience of the king, James II., who was so much impressed by the scheme that he appointed Phips captain of a ship called the *Rose Algier*, with eighteen guns and ninety-five men. Two years were spent in the West Indies, searching for the wreck without success. The sailors were discouraged, organised a mutiny, and arming themselves with cutlasses, came to the captain and demanded that he should turn pirate.

Phips, as brave as he was persevering, fell upon the leaders and used his fists so vigorously that he knocked down several of them and awed the rest into submission. It was not long before they made another attempt; and though he succeeded in quelling the second mutiny also, it would have been dangerous to keep such a crew much longer on the sea; the ship was old and leaky, and the captain thought best to go back to England. But before he went, he was so fortunate as to find an old man who remembered the shipwreck, and told him it was very near Porto Plata, on the northern coast of Santo Domingo, or Hispaniola, as it was then called.

Phips returned to England to get a better vessel and crew. The king had lost all confidence in the scheme and would have nothing more to do with it; but the Duke of Albemarle and some other noblemen fitted out a ship for him, and he sailed for Porto Plata. Here he anchored, and built a large boat to go nearer the reef where the wreck was said to have taken place than the ship could venture. Taking some skilful Indian divers in the boat, a part of the crew went to the spot and examined the waters, but could see nothing. As they were about giving up the search, one of the sailors noticed through the clear water a beautiful feathery seaweed growing from a rock at the bottom.

He told one of the divers to bring it up to him; and when the diver came up with the plant, he said he saw some great cannon at the bottom. This was enough. The galleon was found. The divers were sent down, and the first one that rose brought a lump of silver worth nearly two hundred pounds. The sailors rowed to the ship, and showed their prize to the captain. The crew all went to work, and brought up gold and silver and precious stones, bullion, coin, cups, and sacramental plate—to the value of three hundred thousand pounds. It is said that a captain who was with Phips lost his reason at the sight of such an amount of treasure.

The share of Captain Phips amounted to only sixteen thousand pounds. But this was enough to enable him to live in style in Boston in those days. The Duke of Albemarle sent Mrs. Phips a gold cup valued at a thousand pounds, and the king conferred upon Phips the honour of knighthood.

To Sir William Phips, then, who had become a man of importance in the colony, was entrusted the command of the expedition against Acadia, and he appeared off Port Royal on the 19th of May. The fort was in command of Meneval, the French governor, who summoned the inhabitants by firing a cannon; but only three of them came.

The next day Phips entered the harbour and summoned the commandant to surrender. Meneval sent Petit, a priest, to negotiate; and it was agreed that the troops, consisting of seventy men, should be sent to Quebec or to France, that private property should be respected, that the inhabitants be left in peaceable possession of their lands and the free exercise of their religion, and that the church should not be injured.

While Meneval was on board the flag-ship arranging the terms, some of the soldiers and citizens of Port Royal broke into a storehouse and carried off a quantity of goods, which they hid in the woods; and

Phips made this a pretext for violating all, or nearly all, the terms of the capitulation. He allowed his soldiers to break into the church, cut down the cross, and shatter the ornaments of the altar. The houses of the priests were plundered; and they, together with Meneval and fifty-nine of the soldiers, were carried to Boston and imprisoned.

The inhabitants were called together and asked to take the oath of allegiance to William and Mary; most of them did so, and were left unmolested; but a few refused, and their houses were pillaged. Phips organised a temporary government, with a sergeant of the garrison at the head of it, and a council of six chosen from among the inhabitants. They were instructed to govern the place for the King of England, and to allow liberty in matters of religion.

Meneval gave his money and personal effects to Phips for safe keeping; but when he wanted them returned, Phips refused, and Meneval petitioned the governor and Council at Boston to order Phips to restore them. They did so, but Phips paid no attention to it. Then Governor Bradstreet wrote to him, commanding him to comply immediately with the order, and Phips reluctantly gave up some of the money and some of the poorest articles of clothing, but kept the greater part of the articles, which Meneval thus enumerated:—

> Six silver spoons, six silver forks, one silver cup in the shape of a *gondola*, a pair of pistols, three new wigs, a grey vest, four pair of silk garters, two dozen shirts, six vests of dimity, four night-caps with lace edging, all my table-service of fine tin, all my table linen, etc.

Before returning to Boston, Phips sent Captain Alden to take La Héve and Chedabucto. He carried to Boston twenty-one pieces of ordnance, and a sum of money belonging to the king, besides the plunder taken from private individuals. Alden, who had captured the two places without much trouble, brought a large quantity of goods belonging to the fishing company.

A few days after their departure, a French ship, the *Union*, arrived at Port Royal with goods, provisions, arms, ammunition, and presents for the Indians, to ensure their continued loyalty to France. On board were some recruits for the garrison, an officer of engineers named Saccardie, and Meneval's brother, Villebon, who had been in Acadia before, and now came to lead the Indians against the English. When he found what had befallen the settlements of Acadia, Villebon determined to go to the River St. John, and occupy the fort at Gemseg, and accordingly crossed over, leaving orders for the *Union* to follow.

No sooner had he gone than two pirate ships appeared. Finding the town undefended, the crews landed, seized all they could carry away, and burned sixteen houses. They hanged two men, and taking the *Union* and her cargo, sailed off with Perrot, a trader, and Saccardie the engineer, after having tortured Perrot to make him tell where he had hidden his money. When Villebon learned of the disaster, he returned to Fort Gemseg, and told the Indians that the English had stolen their presents, but that he was going to France to get them much nicer ones, and exhorted them to be faithful to the French, to keep up the war, and to be ready to go with him the following spring. He then went to Quebec to sail for France.

When Phips returned to Boston, preparations for an attack on Canada were already far advanced. Aid was sought from England; but everything there was concentrated on the struggle in Ireland with the adherents of James II., and the colonists were left to fight, it out alone. The plan was, to march a land force under General Winthrop against Montreal, while a fleet was to sail from Boston for the capture of Quebec. Thirty-four ships, the largest of which carried forty-four guns, were made ready and manned with two thousand two hundred sailors and militia, under the command of Major John Walley. The success of Phips in Acadia led to his appointment as commander of the expedition.

The force destined for Montreal set out from Albany much reduced by sickness and the withdrawal of the militia of the eastern colonies, made necessary by attacks on the border settlements. Bands of Indians from eastern New York gathered at Albany to join the expedition, and those of the west were to be in readiness on Lake Champlain. But before they were prepared, the season was far advanced; the work of making canoes was stopped by the want of birch-bark, and it was too late in the season for elm-bark to be made available. The adherents of the two factions in New York politics quarrelled with each other and with the Connecticut soldiers; the supplies were insufficient; and the Indians of the western tribes failed to keep their engagement.

Captain John Schuyler was in advance with less than two hundred men, pushing on down the lake; but Winthrop, finding it impossible to do anything with the disorderly forces of the main body, marched them back to Albany.

Frontenac had prepared for the expected attack by strengthening the stockade forts along the Upper St. Lawrence, and holding a great council with the Indians who came down from the Upper Lakes to trade. He was now seventy years old; but, brandishing a tomahawk about his head, he danced the war-dance and sang the war-song, arousing the Indians to the highest pitch of excitement and enthusiasm.

Schuyler arrived just after Frontenac had gone to protect the other settlements. The Indians, who formed the greater part of his band, refused to attack the fort; and so the extent of the operations was the destruction of houses, harvests, and cattle, and the killing or capture of twenty-five settlers. Thus, the land expedition of the English was worse than a failure. It accomplished nothing; it stained their record by the use of the Indian method of attack on peaceful settlers; and it tended to bring them into contempt with their savage allies.

After a long delay, the fleet under Sir William Phips was prepared to sail from Boston. The weather was unfavourable, the ocean voyage was long, and Phips had no pilots acquainted with the St. Lawrence. So slow was the progress of the fleet that the advantage of surprise was lost. Two small French vessels were captured on the way; and from information obtained from them in regard to the state of the defences of Quebec, Phips anticipated a victory as easy as that at Port Royal.

But Frontenac had been employed during the summer in building palisades on the undefended side of the city; and Major Prévost, who commanded in Quebec during his absence in Montreal, receiving timely warning of the departure of the fleet from Boston, sent word to Montreal, and hastened to improve the defences of the city; the gates were barricaded, cannon mounted, palisades and moats placed wherever they were needed, and batteries posted in the lower part of the town near the river. Frontenac went down the river in a canoe as soon as he heard of the danger to his capital, leaving orders for all the forces at Montreal and intervening points to gather at Quebec.

On the 5th of October the fleet arrived before Quebec, and Phips demanded a surrender. The messenger was blindfolded and led by two officers in a roundabout course, followed by a tumultuous and jeering mob. When the bandage was taken from his eyes, he found himself in the presence of the governor and his superior officers. He delivered his letter to the governor and an interpreter translated it into French. The letter said:

> The war between the crowns of England and France doth not only sufficiently warrant, but the destruction made by the

French and Indians, under your command and encourage-
ment, upon the persons and estates of Their Majesties' subjects
of New England, without provocation on their part, hath put
them under the necessity of this expedition for their own security and satisfaction. And although the cruelties and barbarities
used against them by the French and Indians might, upon the
present opportunity, prompt unto a severe revenge, yet, being
desirous to avoid all inhumane and unchristian-like actions, and
to prevent shedding of blood as much as may be.

I, the aforesaid William Phips, Knight, do hereby, in the name
and in the behalf of Their Most Excellent Majesties, William
and Mary, King and Queen of England, Scotland, France, and
Ireland, Defenders of the Faith, and by order of Their Said
Majesties' government of the Massachusetts-colony in New
England, demand a present surrender of your forts and castles,
undemolished, and the king's and other stores, unembezzled,
with a seasonable delivery of all captives, together with a surrender of all your persons and estates to my dispose: upon the
doing whereof you may expect mercy from me, as a Christian,
according to what shall be found for Their Majesties' service
and the subjects' security. Which if: you refuse forthwith to do,
I am come provided, and am resolved, by the help of God, in
whom I trust, by force of arms to revenge all wrongs and injuries offered, and bring you under subjection to the crown of
England, and when too late make you wish you had accepted
of the favour tendered.

Your answer positive in an hour, returned by your own trum-
pet, with the return of mine, is required upon the peril that
will ensue.

When the reading of the letter was, finished, the messenger reminded Frontenac that it was ten o'clock, and his answer must be
given by eleven. The French officers exclaimed at the impudence of
the demand, and some of them said Frontenac ought to hang the
messenger of such a pirate as Phips had shown himself to be. Frontenac told the messenger that he need not wait so long for his answer;
that he did not acknowledge William of Orange as King of England,
knowing no King of England but King James; that the King of France
was about to restore King James to his throne; and that his subjects
in Canada were prepared to make war on the English colonists, who

were rebels against their lawful sovereign. He alluded to the violation by Phips of his agreement at Port Royal, and said:—

> I will answer your master only by the mouths of my cannon, and he shall learn that I am not to be summoned in this way to surrender.

The officer was led back blindfolded, as he had come, and when Frontenac's answer was received, Phips held a council, at which it was decided to make a combined attack by land and sea. Major Walley, with a force of militia, was to be landed above the St. Charles at Beauport, to ford the river, and climb to the rear of the town by the heights of St. Geneviève. Several of the smaller vessels were to support the land soldiers by ascending the St. Charles with provisions and ammunition, and assist in the attack with their guns. Then the larger vessels were to assail the city from the St. Lawrence side, and land a part of the troops to storm the defences.

Two days passed before it seemed best to the English to begin carrying out the plan. While they were waiting, the forces which Frontenac had ordered from Montreal arrived, under the command of Callières, so that the number of troops reached about three thousand. The city was full, the inhabitants of the Lower Town having taken shelter in the convent, the hospital, and the seminary of the Upper Town. Provisions were low, and there was danger of famine if the siege should be long continued. Masses were constantly offered, a picture of the Holy Family was hung on the cathedral spire, and the nuns kept up an unbroken stream of prayer to the Virgin and all the saints for the deliverance of the city.

At length on the 8th, at noon, boats were sent out to Beauport, below the St. Charles, carrying Major Walley with about twelve hundred men. Having landed, they began their march, but had not gone far when they were assailed from the woods and thickets by a band of French and Indians under Sainte Hélène. Walley's men charged bravely or them, and they retreated, but kept up a continual fire from behind the rocks and trees as they went, sending confusion into the ranks of the English. Walley drew his forces together and encamped, in expectation of the ships which were to support him.

Without waiting till Walley was in full readiness to climb the heights in the rear and co-operate with the attack from the fleet, Phips rushed on with his larger ships and drew them up before the town. He was greeted by a shot from the Château St. Louis, and at once opened with all his cannon. A rapid firing ensued on both sides, which was kept up until nightfall. Comparatively little damage was done by the English; their guns were not charged heavily enough with powder to give the balls much effect, and their gunnery was poor. Many of the balls struck the wall of rock, and many of those that reached the town had spent their force and failed to pierce the walls. The fire from the town was more effective; but Phips only waited till morning to renew the attack.

The next day the troops in the town were reinforced by the detachment which had been sent out against Walley's party; and under the direction of Sainte Hélène the guns of the batteries in the Lower Town were aimed against the fleet with good effect. All the ships were before the town; for those that should have gone to the aid of Walley were afraid to expose themselves to the danger; and there was no central command strong enough to enforce obedience—if, indeed, anything was thought of at the head of the fleet except the business immediately in hand. A few pieces of cannon and a little powder and food were sent to the shore, but Walley received no other assistance.

The ships were at length disabled by the fire and were drawn off beyond the reach of the guns of the town. The attack by water had proved a miserable failure; and Walley was too poorly supported to effect anything by land. On the morning of the 10th, the day after the repulse of the fleet, he went to consult with Sir William Phips. During his absence his men advanced to cross the St. Charles and make an attack, but were met by a party under Sainte Hélène and driven back with loss. Walley returned with orders to take them to the fleet, and boats were sent in the night, in which they were to embark the following night.

During the 11th, another skirmish took place, with about the same result. Walley's troops fought courageously, but were too poorly disciplined to fight with advantage; while the French and Indians fired from behind rocks and trees and farmhouses. Walley withdrew, and as soon as darkness came on embarked his troops in the boats and joined the fleet. As the ships were disabled, and the stock of ammunition low, the undertaking was now abandoned, and the fleet dropped down below the island of Orleans, where it stopped for repairs. After an exchange of prisoners, the vessels made their way slowly homeward.

While Phips was on his way down the river, three ships arrived from France bringing money and stores to Quebec, and ran up the Saguenay. Phips attempted to capture them, but failed. He reached

Boston in five or six weeks; some of his vessels were more than three months on the way, and several—as many as nine, by some accounts— were wrecked. This miserable outcome of an expedition from which so much had been hoped, carried dismay and foreboding to the New England colonies. In Quebec there was great rejoicing when the fleet disappeared down the river, marred only by the fear that the ships from France might be surprised on the way and captured. When they arrived in safety, the general joy knew no bounds. If the siege had been prolonged, the city would have suffered from famine and perhaps been forced at last to surrender; for the warning had not been long enough to give time for providing food for the great number that were gathered in the capital, and the supplies from France had not arrived.

A procession was formed, which carried the image of the Virgin to every church and chapel in turn, with appropriate ceremonies; *Te Deum* was sung in the cathedral; and the banner bearing the cross of St. George, which had waved at the mast-head of Phips's vessel, and was shot away by one of Sainte Hélène's cannon, was picked up from the river where it had fallen, and carried to the cathedral, where it hung for years. Frontenac sent the news to France, urging the Government at the same time to provide troops for the complete conquest of New York and New England; and a medal in honour of the victory was struck in Paris.

CHAPTER 7

Close of King William's War

The English made no attempt to secure their conquest in Acadia, and Villebon was appointed Governor by the French Government and instructed to lavish presents on the Indians and keep them and the French constantly engaged in war. All supplies would be sent from France, so that none of the men need be kept at home for the cultivation of the soil. The vessel which took Villebon to Acadia captured Colonel Edward Tyng, who had been sent from Massachusetts as Governor of Port Royal, and John Nelson, who was going with him. Nelson inherited a claim to Acadia, from his uncle, Sir Thomas Temple, to whom Cromwell had made a large grant, and he was well acquainted with the country and the language of the Indians. He and Tyng were taken to Quebec.

Villebon took possession of Port Royal without opposition, and administered to the colonists the oath of allegiance to the sovereign of France. He established himself at Fort Gemseg on the St. John, and set about the work of inciting the Indians to war. A chief named Moxus had already attacked Wells with two hundred Indians, and had been repelled by the garrison under Captain Converse. Seconded by the priest Thury, Villebon persuaded the Indians to form a great war-party, though some who had signed a truce with the English were reluctant.

They set out in January, 1692, and marched a month over icy streams and through bare forests to southwestern Maine. On the night of Feb. 4th, they encamped at the foot of Mount Agamenticus, and in the morning moved cautiously to the village of York. They caught a boy cutting wood in a forest, forced information from him, murdered him, and pushed on. Dividing into two parties, they began their work at a signal. There were five fortified houses, having projecting upper stories with loop-holes for guns. One was taken at the first assault.

The unprotected dwellings were attacked, and all their inmates who did not escape to the fortified houses were slain or taken captive. The minister, Mr. Dummer, was shot at his own door as he was about to mount his horse to visit a parishioner. After unsuccessfully attacking the other four fortified houses, the party withdrew with eighty prisoners, having killed nearly a hundred.

In June of the same year, an attack on Wells, by about four hundred Indians, was a complete failure. The Indians attempted to fire some ships lying in the river, by means of a burning raft, but it ran aground. The French officers tried to induce them to make a regular assault on the fort; but they carried it on in their own fashion, with a tremendous amount of noise and desultory firing. The men in the fort held out bravely; the women loaded their guns, and some fired; Converse answered defiantly every summons to surrender; and the Indians were glad to draw off with one prisoner, after burning the church and the deserted houses. Villebon consoled some who lived near his fort with a prisoner to burn, an Indian ally of the English, taken near the St. John.

During the summer. Sir William Phips, now Governor of Massachusetts, having authority to rebuild the fort at Pemaquid, set out with Benjamin Church, noted for success in Indian wars, and one hundred workmen. On the way they buried the dead left at Casco in 1690, and carried the cannon of Fort Loyal with them. Phips laid the foundations for a strong fortress of stone, and left the men to finish it. When done, it was the best fort the English had in America; the front wall was twenty-two feet high, and the great round tower at the southwestern corner twenty-nine feet high. Eighteen guns were mounted, and sixty men placed in it as a garrison. Phips named it Fort William Henry.

Madockawando, the Indian father-in-law of the Baron de St. Castin, had gone to Quebec to carry to Frontenac the news of the building of this fort, and Frontenac resolved to drive the English away at once before it should be completed. He had two ships of war, and arranged that they should sail with about four hundred men, take in as many more as they could get at Villebon's fort and Pentagoet, and then capture Pemaquid and destroy the settlements along the coast of the present States of Maine and New Hampshire.

John Nelson was still a prisoner in Quebec when Madockawando came with his intelligence, but was treated as a guest by Frontenac, and had apartments at the Château St. Louis. He discovered that an expedition was on foot, and, through his knowledge of the Indian language spoken by the chief, and in other ways, he managed to get some information as to the details. He bribed two French soldiers to desert, and carry a letter to Boston. A ship of war was at once sent from Boston to the defence of Pemaquid, which was not yet finished, and when the French vessels arrived, and found the place thus defended, they gave up the enterprise without attempting to strike a blow. Iberville, who commanded the expedition, was censured severely by Frontenac, and the Indians were so indignant that they threatened to break their alliance with the French.

The colonists, harassed continually by the Indians, their border settlements broken up, their harvests and cattle destroyed by these sly and faithless hordes, whom no treaties could hold, made repeated applications to England for help; and at length a plan was formed. A fleet under Sir Francis Wheeler was to be sent to Martinique, and after service there was to go to Boston, take on as many troops as the colonies should have been able to raise, and proceed to Quebec; the troops to be under the command of Sir William Phips. But the attack on Martinique was a failure. Six hundred of the men: were killed, and three hundred taken prisoners. Half of the sailors and three fourths of the soldiers died of yellow fever before the fleet reached Boston, and the epidemic was carried into the city. The design of an attack on Quebec was then necessarily abandoned.

The English made a treaty with the eastern Indians, supposing that all the tribes were represented; but Villebon, who had built a fort on the St. John nearly opposite the site of Fredericton, Fort Naxouat, took measures to stir them up to break the treaty. Taxus, a chief friendly to the French, was honoured and feasted at the fort, and Villebon gave him his best coat. He sent presents and ammunition to be distributed among the various tribes; and, what was of vastly greater importance to the French cause, he set on the Jesuits—Vincent Bigot on the Kennebec and Pierre Thury on the Penobscot—to incite their converts to the work.

Their plans were nearly defeated by tidings that the English were going to exchange prisoners at Pemaquid, according to the treaty; for the French had told them the English were trying to entrap them. Had it not been for the cunning of Thury, the Indians, or a large part of them, would have gone to their homes from the Penobscot, where they had been gathered by St. Castin and Villieu who had been appointed to lead them. But Thury privately told those chiefs who had not been present at the conference with the English, that Madockawando and

67

the others had taken altogether too much on themselves, and assumed too much importance in making a treaty without their concurrence. This was enough; their jealousy was aroused, they were all for war, and Madockawando and some of his followers who still held out were at length persuaded, at a dog-feast given by Villieu, by means of the presents of the French and the jeers of their savage companions.

About two hundred and fifty of them set out in canoes for Piscataqua. At Pemaquid, Villieu, disguised as an Indian, landed with a few savages and went to the fort, carrying some furs to trade to the soldiers. Leaving the Indians to make the bargain, he walked away unobserved, studied the plan of the fort, and made a drawing of it.

At the village of Oyster River, now Durham, in New Hampshire, the Indians took five of the twelve fortified houses; three families escaped, but two were slaughtered. The seven other houses were resolutely defended. The owner of one of these, Thomas Bickford, placed his family in a boat and sent them down the stream; then he went back to his house, and by keeping up a constant firing, now from one point and now from another, shouting orders as if to his garrison, and giving the assailants glimpses of him in different clothing at different parts of the house, he defended the place successfully alone, and saved his house and his whole family. About one hundred persons were killed, and twenty-seven carried away.

After mass had been said by Thury, the Indians took to their canoes. Some of them wanted to go home; but Taxus with a large party remained to work what havoc they could on neighbouring settlements. They divided into small bands, and killed some of the inhabitants of Groton, York, Kittery, and other places. Villieu on his return set out for Quebec to warn the governor of a rumoured expedition against that city, taking with him some Indians, and a string of thirteen English scalps, which were presented to Frontenac. During these years the Iroquois, incited by the New York colonists, went down the St. Lawrence and fell upon the least protected settlements from time to time, killing, burning, and capturing.

A large party of them, encamped near the mouth of the Ottawa, sallied out in bands, and kept the frontier in terror. Over one hundred men were marched against them under Vaudreuil, and routed a band of about forty near Repentigny; and when men and supplies arrived from France, a large force was sent against them, and their camp was broken up. After this defeat, they refused to keep up hostilities unaided by the English, and an expedition was then organised under Major

Peter Schuyler.

About two hundred and fifty men were gathered at Albany, half of them Indians. They descended Lake Champlain and the Richelieu in canoes, and debarked a few miles above Fort Chambly, whence they marched to attack the French at La Prairie, opposite Montreal. Callières, who was now Governor of Montreal, had been warned, and had gone over to La Prairie with seven hundred men, but he was too ill to command during the attack, which took place early in the morning of the 11th of August. The camp was broken up, the soldiers driven into the fort, and great loss inflicted on the French, and then Schuyler drew off his men, destroying the growing crops as he went.

On the way back he was met by a force of French soldiers and Canadian Indians from Fort Chambly, under an officer named Valrenne, who, knowing of their attack on La Prairie, had come out to cut off their retreat. A fierce combat followed. Some of the Indians ran away; but the English and the French fought with desperation, and the Mohawks remained steadfast. The force at La Prairie did not come up till the fighting was over. Schuyler's men at length succeeded in breaking through the centre of the enemy's rank, and then faced about and drove the French before them, forcing them to retreat. This is according to Schuyler's own account. The French also claimed the victory, and Valrenne was highly commended for having repelled the English.

As the Iroquois continued their raids on the French, it was resolved to invade the Mohawk country. A force of nearly seven hundred French and Indians set out from Montreal in the middle of January, 1693. After a weary march on snow-shoes they passed Schenectady early in February, went on to the first Mohawk castle, or town, and took a few prisoners without resistance. The second was taken quite as easily; but at the third the Mohawks, who had gathered there for a feast and a war-dance, fought desperately, though they were at last overpowered. The invaders lost thirty men, and the Mohawks about the same number.

The Canadian Indians had promised to put their captives to death in accordance with the command of Frontenac that no quarter should be given; and as many of these Canadian Indians were converted Iroquois, it was hoped that such a proceeding on their part would preclude any reconciliation from ever taking place between them and the Iroquois of New York. But they refused to keep their promise, and the French turned homeward with about three hundred prisoners.

Warning had been given at Albany of the French invasion, by a young man who had been carried away from Schenectady at the burning of that town in 1690. He was taken with the invading expedition, and ran away when he reached the neighbourhood of his old home. Schuyler hastily gathered two hundred men and, joined by three or four hundred Indians, marched against the French. Some Mohawks caught up with the French, and told them Schuyler was coming to *parley* with them, as peace had been declared in Europe. The Canadian Indians said they would wait; the French were distrustful, and anxious to push on their retreat. The Indians prevailed, and a fort was built of felled trees.

When Schuyler came up, instead of seeking a *parley*, he began to build a similar fort, or rather his Indians did. The French attacked it, and were defeated in three attempts; then they quietly packed their baggage and moved off in the night during a heavy snowstorm.

The Acadians were anxious that the fort at Pemaquid should be reduced. Not only was it a standing assertion of the English claim to disputed territory, but it kept them in constant fear of English influence over their unstable allies. There was need also of protection for the fisheries and the fur-trade, which were seriously encroached upon by the English, who offered much better terms to the Indians, both in Acadia and New York, than the French would. A pestilence had weakened the Indians of the east, who were hungry and needy, and disposed to seek the best market for their furs, regardless of their friendships or preferences.

They were still anxious to exchange prisoners with the English; but when they were at last summoned to Pemaquid, they were told that nothing could be done till they should bring in all they had taken. As the English had not brought their men, they thought this was asking too much, and refused to treat further. In 1696, the Governor of Massachusetts sent them another summons. The Penobscot tribe, the only one that answered, took five prisoners to give for five of their tribe who had been taken by the English, and arrived at Pemaquid in February, 1696. The fort was commanded by Captain Pascho Chubb, who received the Indians cordially, took back the prisoners they brought, and promised to give them some presents, and to send at once to Boston for their men, whom they desired in exchange.

He then proposed a conference near the fort, where nine of his men were to meet nine of the Indians, all unarmed. The Indians accepted, but the liquor which was freely given them rendered them less wary than usual, and they did not notice a party of soldiers who had

A Mingo Indian

A Stockbridge Indian

come out from the fort and stood ready for action at a short distance from the scene of the conference. Chubb's men carried concealed weapons, and at a signal fell upon the Indians and killed several of them, of whom two were chiefs. The Indians fought savagely, and several of the soldiers also fell. According to French accounts, the Indians themselves were treacherously disposed, but none the less this treachery of Captain Chubb roused their hatred of the English to new fury, and did more service to the French cause than all the persuasions and presents which Villebon had lavished upon his reluctant allies.

That officer had long been urging upon the government at Quebec the necessity of another attack upon Pemaquid; and now that the folly of its commander had made the Indians eager to take revenge, preparations for the expedition were pushed on with vigour. In the summer of 1696, the Acadians and Indians assembled on the Penobscot and the St. John, and waited for two ships of war under Iberville and Bonaventure, which were to come from Quebec. While they were waiting, two British ships and a tender from Massachusetts were hanging about the coast, and the crews made several attempts to land.

When at length the French ships, which had taken on board thirty Micmac Indians at Cape Breton, arrived at the St. John, a sharp engagement took place. One of the English vessels, the *Newport*, was captured; but a fog enabled the *Sorling* and the tender to escape. The victorious vessels took on fifty more of the Micmacs and their priest. Father Simon, who were waiting at the mouth of the St. John, and proceeded to Pentagoet. Here were Villieu, and St. Castin, and the faithful Father Thury with twenty-five French soldiers and three hundred Abenaquis. Attended by a fleet of Abenaqui canoes, the ships set out for Pemaquid, arriving there August 14th, 1696.

The Abenaquis, under the lead of St. Castin, were put ashore for the land attack, while Iberville summoned Chubb to surrender. Chubb replied that he would not give up the fort, "if the sea were covered with French ships, and the land with Indians." The attack began; the French and Indian marksmen surrounded the fort, hiding in places where they were sheltered from its cannon, and kept up a constant fire. During the night the heavy guns were loaded, and the batteries made ready for use by the next afternoon. Before they were fired, St. Castin sent word to Chubb that if he and his soldiers held out until the fort should be carried by assault, they would get no quarter from the Indians, who remembered his former treachery. The letter was followed by five bomb-shells.

Chubb immediately sounded a *parley* and offered to surrender, on condition that he and all his men should be protected from the Indians, and sent to Boston to be exchanged for French and Indian prisoners. Iberville sent them to an island in the bay, and despatched Villieu to take possession of the fort. One of the Indians whom Chubb had taken in February was found in irons in the fort, nearly dead with hunger and long confinement, and his countrymen were so incensed that they would have made short work with the garrison if Iberville had not taken the precaution to send them away.

The cannon of the fort were carried to the ships, and then the walls were blown up and the ruins fired. Notwithstanding the money and labour expended on the fort, and its apparent strength, it was not well planned. There were no casemates, and a shower of bomb-shells would have made havoc with the garrison. When Chubb reached Boston, he was thrown into prison on a charge of cowardice. He was liberated after several months and returned to his home in Andover; but Indian vengeance was on his track, and the next year he and his wife were killed by a party of savages.

Massachusetts had a force ready to send against the French, under Benjamin Church, when news of the capture of Pemaquid reached Boston, and Church started immediately with about five hundred men, partly Indians, embarked in sloops and whaling vessels. After doing a small amount of damage at Penobscot, he went on to Chignecto at the head of the Bay of Fundy, where he landed and took possession of the place without meeting any resistance from the twenty or thirty men in the settlement. The inhabitants saved their lives by producing a certificate that they had taken the oath of allegiance to the British Crown; but the soldiers plundered without restraint, and then burned the town.

After this easy triumph, Church sailed for the St. John. An officer named Chevalier was stationed with a few soldiers at the mouth of the river, while Villebon's fort of Naxouat was situated farther up. These soldiers were taken by the Indians of Church's force, and Chevalier was killed. One of the captured Frenchmen told Church where to find the cannon of the old fort, which were buried in the sand, and the New Englanders dug them up and put them on board. On the way back to Boston they met three ships from Massachusetts, with two hundred men under Colonel Hathorn. Hathorn deprived Church of his command for having conducted the expedition in such a manner, and turned the force back to attack Fort Naxouat. But, warned by the arrival of Church, Villebon had been strengthening his fort and gathering into it a force of settlers and Indians.

The attack began on the 18th of October, and continued two days without success. During the night of the 19th the English quietly embarked and sailed away, having had eight men killed and seventeen wounded, while only three of the French suffered injury. This was the end of hostilities between the British and French colonists during what is known as King William's War. But the Indians kept up a petty warfare, ravaging the borders of settlements and butchering defenceless families.

In the spring of 1697, a band of Indians reached the village of Haverhill, raised the war-cry, and began their horrid work. A man named Dustin was at work in the field, having with him his seven children, while his wife with the baby, one week old, and Mary Neff, a neighbour, were in the house. As soon as he became aware of the presence of the Indians, Dustin started for the house; but, seeing he was too late to be of any use there, he escaped to the woods with the children that were in the field with him. The savages killed the infant, set fire to the house, and took Hannah Dustin and Mary Neff to the woods with the other prisoners they had taken. Some of these were killed, and the rest were divided among the Indians, who separated and returned to their homes.

The two women fell to the lot of two families, who, taking a leisurely march northward, were on their way to some Indian village. They encamped one night in the forest, on a small island in the Merrimack, near the present city of Concord, N. H. The Indians went to sleep about their camp-fire, after having counted on their beads the prayers taught them by some Jesuit enthusiast at their mission station. Hannah Dustin had planned an escape and inspired Mary Neff and Samuel Leonardson, a boy captured at Worcester, to take part in it. When all the Indians were still, the three rose quietly, took each a tomahawk, and at a signal all struck together on the heads of the sleeping savages.

They struck with such nerve and skill that the two men of the party, two of the three squaws, and six of the seven children were instantly killed. A little boy was spared; and he and a wounded squaw who ran with him into the woods were the only survivors. In the morning Hannah Dustin took the ten scalps, together with the gun and tomahawk of the Indian that killed her child, and a canoe carried her and her companions down the Merrimack to their home. They received a bounty of five pounds apiece for the scalps, and a present was sent to them by the Governor of Maryland.

In the same year, 1697, a squadron of fifteen ships was sent out from France, under the command of the Marquis de Nesmond. It was to go to Newfoundland, capture any English ships that might be there, then sail to the Penobscot and take on board as many Indians and French soldiers as could be collected. It was expected that Canada would send fifteen hundred. This force was destined to take possession of Boston. One part was to land at Dorchester and enter the town from the south by way of the Neck; another was to land at Noddle's Island, take boats to Charlestown, capture it, and enter Boston from the north; while still another portion of the forces was to land directly in the town near Long Wharf. Boston once taken, the forces were to march northward along the coast, and, with the assistance of the fleet, take all the settlements. The towns were to be burned after everything of value that could be removed had been taken out.

Frontenac prepared his forces, and made ready to command them in person. But the fleet was detained by contrary winds until it was too late for the plan to be carried out that season. In September a treaty of peace between France and England was signed at Ryswick, and thus the scheme for destroying the New England settlements came to nothing.

But before peace was declared, the French had met with unqualified success in the north. As soon as Iberville had destroyed Pemaquid, he took charge of an expedition for the conquest of Newfoundland. The island was claimed by the English, by virtue of the discoveries of the Cabots and Sir Humphrey Gilbert, and the fishing settlements planted by Englishmen on the coast. The French, however, asserted that fishermen from Brittany, Normandy, and the Basque Provinces had fished on the coast long before, and that through them France had a prior claim.

At this time the French had a town and a fort at Placentia Bay, which gave them control of the southern coast. The eastern coast was occupied by a long line of small English settlements, the principal of which was St. John. Expeditions had been planned by each nation during the hostilities, for driving the other out; but all of them had fallen through.

When Iberville arrived, the Governor of Placentia was already at St. John with a fleet of privateers, attempting to take the place. Iberville joined him, and St. John was soon reduced to ashes. Then the ships were withdrawn, and Iberville with his soldiers and Indians marched along the eastern coast, attacking and destroying every town in turn. It was in the depth of winter; the ground was covered with snow and ice; and the soldiers went stumbling along the unbroken paths, tripping against rocks and logs concealed under the snow, but merry with the excitement of the march, and elated with their success; for the villagers surrendered without the slightest resistance, and the soldiers plundered without restraint. Nothing was left to the English but Bonavista and Isle Carbonnière.

In the spring, Iberville and his brother Serigny were sent to re-take Fort Nelson on Hudson Bay, which, after being taken by them in 1694, had fallen again into the hands of the English in 1696. The French called it Fort Bourbon. It was of great importance, being in the midst of a vast region abounding in valuable furs. The brothers set out with four ships of war and a transport. Although it was July when they entered Hudson Bay, the water was filled with floating ice, and the supply-ship was crushed. Iberville's ship, the *Pelican*, was in great danger, and when at last she got free and sailed into the unobstructed waters of the open bay, nothing was to be seen of the other three; they were still struggling amid the ice.

Iberville and his men sailed on alone to begin the attack; but before they reached the fort, they were overtaken by three armed English ships. There was a close and desperate engagement. One of the English ships sank under the heavy broadsides of the *Pelican*, with all on board; another surrendered, and the third sailed away and escaped. The *Pelican* was badly injured; and a fierce storm arising, she was stranded and split amidships by the fury of the wind and waves. The crew escaped to the shore, but they were in danger of starvation, and were about to make an attack on the fort as the only hope of saving themselves, when the three ships appeared. Fort Nelson, which was occupied by the traders of the Hudson Bay Company, was incapable of resisting an attack by mortars, and it soon surrendered.

In the summer of 1695, Frontenac rebuilt the fort at the head of the St. Lawrence, on the site of the present city of Kingston, which was sometimes known as Fort Catarocouay, but named by him now, as before under the French, Fort Frontenac. He was determined either to conquer the Iroquois, or to bring them over to alliance with the French, or rather, perhaps, to bring them over by conquering them, if they should refuse to make a permanent treaty of peace.

In the summer of 1696, he commanded in person an expedition

against the Indians of New York, and with twenty-two hundred men crossed Lake Ontario to Oswego. The Onondagas, when they heard of the advance of the French, set fire to their principal village, and fled. One old man of the tribe was found hidden in a hollow tree, and was dragged out. The Indians who were with the French wanted to torture and burn him, while Frontenac was anxious to save him; but the Indians were so clamorous, that it was finally decided to be the better policy to give him up. During the horrible tortures inflicted on him he never quailed, but taunted his tormentors to the last. When at length a mortal thrust was made, he said:—

I thank you; but you should have finished me by fire. Learn, dogs of Frenchmen, how to suffer, and you Indians, their allies, who are dogs of dogs, remember what you should do when you stand where I stand now.

A party was sent out to destroy the corn in the fields of the Oneidas, most of whom had fled, though thirty-five had staid to defend their town and were taken prisoners.

It was proposed that the army should next march against the Cayugas. But as it was of no use to march an army through the wilderness to take possession of a cluster of deserted wigwams, Frontenac decided to return home. In his despatches to the king, he represented the expedition as a brilliant triumph, which, indeed, would have been still more brilliant if the savages had made a stand, and given the French Army a chance to overwhelm and defeat them completely, but which, nevertheless, would be of vast advantage to the French interest, in preventing an alliance between the Iroquois and the Indian allies of the French. He took care, also, to say that the triumph could not have been effected had it not been for the rebuilding of Fort Frontenac, a proceeding in which he had gone contrary to the wishes of the king, and eluded his express orders. For this exploit he was rewarded with the cross of the Military Order of St. Louis.

Early in 1698, tidings of the peace which had been proclaimed at Ryswick, September 20th, 1697, reached Montreal, and in July official notice was sent with a letter from the king ordering *Te Deum* to be sung in the cathedral of Quebec. An exchange of prisoners was proposed between the colonies of the two nations in America; but a dispute arose between Frontenac and the Earl of Bellomont, Governor of New York, as to the exchange of the French prisoners in the hands of the Iroquois for the Iroquois in the hands of the French. Bellomont proposed to negotiate the exchange. Frontenac refused to treat with the Iroquois through the English, which would have been an admission that the Iroquois were English subjects, whereas he chose to regard them as rebellious subjects of France.

The death of Frontenac interrupted the quarrel. That able and intrepid officer had exercised a powerful influence on the fortunes of the French in America. Much less pure and disinterested than Champlain, exacting and quarrelsome, he continually exasperated his associates in times of peace; but when danger threatened the colony, they instinctively felt that in his leadership was almost certain victory. He died in November, 1698, at the age of seventy-eight.

He was succeeded by Callières, upon whom devolved the settlement of the dispute about the Iroquois, who declined to allow the English to negotiate for them, asserting their independence of both the foreign powers. After many councils, and many *wampum* belts, and much eloquence, the exchange was effected; but the question of the sovereignty of the west, and even of New York, still remained undecided. In the following year, 1700, the French in Acadia lost their efficient leader Villebon.

CHAPTER 8

Queen Anne's War

But a few years of peace succeeded the treaty of Ryswick. First came the contest in Europe over the Spanish succession—that is, the succession to the Spanish crown, which was bestowed upon one of the Bourbons, the reigning family of France. This threatened to give a great preponderance of power and influence to France, and William III though he was old and sick, resolved to fight against a dangerous accession to the power of England's ancient enemy. But another cause of war soon arose. James II., the dethroned King of England, died at St. Germain in September, 1701; and before he died, he received a promise from Louis XIV.; King of France, that he would recognise as King of England his son, James Stuart, often called "the Pretender"—or, in later years, after his son, Charles Edward, had also made a claim to the throne of his fathers, "the Old Pretender."

This recognition was, of course, a challenge to England, and preparations were made for war. William III. died in March, 1702, and was succeeded by Anne, the sister of his wife, and daughter of James II. War was declared by England against France, May 15th, 1702. The contest that followed is known in European history as the War of the Spanish Succession; in American history, it is usually called Queen Anne's War; or the Second Intercolonial War. On the one side were France, Spain, and Bavaria; on the other, England, Holland, Savoy, Austria, Prussia, Portugal, and Denmark. It was in this war that the Duke of Marlborough won his fame.

To the people of New England, war between France and England meant the hideous midnight war-whoop, the tomahawk and scalping-knife, burning hamlets, and horrible captivity. To provide against it, a conference was called to meet at Falmouth, on Casco Bay, in June, 1703, when Governor Dudley, of Massachusetts, met many of the chiefs of the Abenaquis. The Indians, professing to have no thought of war, promised peace and friendship by their accustomed tokens, and it was believed in New England that they were sincere, and would be neutral during any hostilities that might arise between the English and French colonies.

But, as usual, only a part of the tribes had been brought into the alliance, those on and west of the Penobscot; and a party of lawless plunderers, by attacking and pillaging St. Castings place, roused the resentment of the tribe on that river and disposed them to listen to the insinuations of their ancient allies. French persuasions were successful, and by August five hundred French and Indians were assembled, ready for incursions into the New England settlements.

They divided into several bands and fell upon a number of places at the same time. Wells, Saco, and Casco were again among the doomed villages, but the fort at Casco was not taken, owing to the arrival of an armed vessel under Captain Southwick. About one hundred and fifty persons were killed or captured in these attacks. In a night of February, 1704, a large party under Hertel de Rouville reached the town of Deerfield, Massachusetts, and hid themselves in a pine forest until morning. The people had received information from Colonel Schuyler that they were in danger of attack, and twenty soldiers were sent to them as a guard.

On this night, however, the watch went to sleep two hours before daybreak. The town was surrounded with palisades; but huge drifts of snow were piled up against them, and they were no defence. The invaders entered undiscovered, and in a few hours forty-seven of the inhabitants were killed, the town was in flames, and one hundred and twelve prisoners were on their way to Canada. The journey to Quebec was long and painful, and two of the men starved on the way, for the party had to depend on hunting for support. Most of the prisoners were in time redeemed.

On the 30th of July, the town of Lancaster was assailed, and a few people were killed, seven buildings burned, and much property destroyed. These and other depredations of war-parties along the coasts filled New England with consternation. The governments of Massachusetts and New Hampshire offered a bounty of twenty pounds for every Indian prisoner under ten years, and forty for everyone above that age, or for the scalp of one. Yet but few were taken, even at that price. It was then resolved to fit out an expedition for retaliation, and as usual the people of Acadia were selected to expiate the sins of the

The Deerfield raid, 1704

Indians and Canadians.

Colonel Benjamin Church was put in command of five hundred and fifty men, fourteen transports, and thirty-six whale-boats, convoyed by three ships of war. Sailing from Boston in May, 1704, he stopped at Penobscot, and killed and took captive a few French and Indians, among them a daughter and several grandchildren of St. Castin. At Passamaquoddy he met with similar success, and then sailed on to the Bay of Fundy. The ships of war were sent to Port Royal, where they did nothing but wait for him to come back. Church himself went on with the other vessels to Minas, farther up the bay. This place was built on marsh lands, enclosed by dykes. The soldiers cut the dykes, plundered and burned the dwellings, and took some prisoners.

Returning to Port Royal, Church discreetly refrained from attacking a fortified place, and the officers signed a declaration that their force was insufficient for an assault. Chignecto was next visited, twenty houses were burned, large numbers of cattle killed, and the whole settlement ravaged. The only thing that can be said in excuse for this kind of warfare is, that it was less cruel than the barbarous attacks for which it was intended to retaliate.

In 1705, four hundred and fifty men under Subercase—soldiers, Canadian peasants, adventurers, and Indians, well-armed, and with rations for twenty days, blankets, and tents—set out to destroy the English settlements in Newfoundland, marching on snow-shoes. They took Petit Havre and St. John's, and devastated all the little settlements along the eastern coast, and the English trade was for the time completely broken up.

Subercase was made Governor of Acadia in 1706. The following spring New England sent Colonel March to Port Royal with two regiments, but he returned without assaulting the fort. Governor Dudley forbade the troops to land when they came back to Boston, and ordered them to go again. Colonel March was ill, and Colonel Wainwright took command; but after a pretence of besieging the fort for eleven days, he retired with small loss, the expedition having cost Massachusetts two thousand two hundred pounds.

In 1708, a council at Montreal decided to send a large number of Canadians and Indians to devastate New England. But after a long march through the almost impassable mountain region of northern New Hampshire, a murderous attack on Haverhill, in which thirty or forty were killed, was the only result. Thirty of the assailants were killed by a pursuing party from neighbouring settlements, under Samuel Ayer, and some of the prisoners were rescued. Ayer himself fell a victim to his brave effort in behalf of his neighbours.

In 1709, a plan was formed in England for the capture of New France by a fleet and five regiments of British soldiers aided by the colonists. But a defeat in Portugal called away the ships destined for America, and a force gathered at Lake Champlain under Colonel Nicholson for a land attack was so reduced by sickness—said to have resulted from the poisoning of a spring by Indians—that they burned their canoes and retreated.

The next year, Nicholson was furnished with six ships of war, thirty transports, and one British and four New England regiments, for the capture of Port Royal. Subercase had only two hundred and sixty men and an insufficient supply of provisions. His soldiers were disaffected, and as soon as the ships appeared, they began deserting, complaining that they had been neglected and abandoned by their own country. Subercase had to order the canoes removed to prevent a general desertion.

Nicholson sent a summons to surrender, after three days' waiting, landed his troops after three days more, and bombarded the fort after another week. The inhabitants of the town petitioned Subercase to surrender. Nothing else could be done, and on the 16th of October the starving and ragged garrison marched out to be sent to France. For the last time the French flag was hauled down from the fort, and Port Royal was henceforth an English fortress, which was re-named Annapolis Royal, in honour of Queen Anne.

Subercase sent St. Castin to Quebec to carry the news, and Nicholson despatched a letter to Vaudreuil, the Governor, by Major Livingstone, threatening reprisals on the people of Acadia, if the barbarities of French and Indians in New England were continued. Vaudreuil replied that the French were able to avenge anything he might do; that they were not responsible for the acts of the Indians; that they had not treated prisoners with inhumanity; and that a truce might long ago have put a stop to hostilities if the English had been willing. He appointed St. Castin his lieutenant in Acadia, and directed him and the missionaries to keep alive the loyalty of the French and preserve the friendship of the Indians.

They were so successful that the next year, when the garrison of Port Royal was weakened by disease, death, and even desertion, the inhabitants refused to obey the commandant's order to bring in timber for repairing the fort. Sixty men sent out to seize a band of Indians and Acadians fell into an ambuscade; half were killed, and the remainder taken prisoners. The people of the town then sent word to the commandant, that since he, as they thought, had violated the terms of the surrender, they deemed themselves absolved from their agreement not to bear arms, and one of the priests went to Placentia for arms, ammunition, and an officer to lead the insurgents. But by this time news of the uprising had reached Boston, and two hundred men from there soon reduced the insurgents, captured the supplies, and forced St. Castin to fly to Quebec.

Immediately after his victory, Nicholson went to England to secure a force for the conquest of Canada; and about the same time Colonel Schuyler of New York went there for the same purpose, taking with him five Iroquois *sachems* to awaken interest in the cause, and to insure the fidelity of the tribes to the English alliance. The chiefs caused a great sensation throughout the kingdom. The court was in mourning, and the *sachems* were therefore dressed in black suits, but over them they wore mantles of scarlet cloth bordered with gold. They were taken in coaches to an audience with the queen; and presented her with belts of *wampum*, while one of them made a speech, saying:—

> We were greatly rejoiced when we heard that our great queen had resolved to send an army against Canada. We hung up the kettle, and took down the hatchet. But while we were getting ready, we were told that our great queen could not send the army. We were very sorrowful. We cannot hunt in freedom if Canada is not taken. So that if our great queen does not remember us, we must take our families and forsake our country, or stand neutral while the French are fighting our friends.

The Secretary of State, St. John, afterward Viscount Bolingbroke, planned the expedition. Fifteen ships of war and forty transports, placed under the command of Sir Hovenden Walker, carried seven regiments of veterans from the Duke of Marlborough's army, and a battalion of marines under the command of Brigadier-General Hill. They arrived in Boston on the 25th of June, and encamped on Noddle's Island, now East Boston. A great crowd of people gathered to witness the review of the troops. The admiral wrote:—

> They made a very fine appearance, such as had never before been in these parts of the world.

New England and New York had raised two regiments to join the fleet; and on the 30th of July sixty-eight vessels, carrying six thousand five hundred soldiers, set sail for Quebec. New York, New Jersey, and Connecticut collected about four thousand men, including a thousand Indians, to march against Montreal, under Colonels Schuyler, Whiting, and Ingoldsby, while Nicholson had the general care of the expedition. It was expected, also, that the Indian tribe called Foxes, in Wisconsin, whose alliance had been secured through the Iroquois, would begin hostilities against the French in the stations on the lakes.

When Vaudreuil learned that a hostile fleet was on its way to Quebec and an army marching toward Montreal, he first gathered the Onondaga and Seneca deputies and persuaded them to remain neutral. Then he gave a great festival, at which the war-song was sung and the hatchet raised. There were the Christian Indians of the settlements near Montreal, called the Sault and the Mountain; there were the Indians of the various mission stations of the Jesuits; there were Algonquin chiefs from the banks of the St. Lawrence, Ottawas, and Hurons, and Chippewas from beyond the lakes. The raising of the hatchet by the Hurons decided these remoter tribes; and when the festival ended, they were all declared allies of the French. Quebec was strengthened, and the settlements along the banks below were guarded sufficiently to prevent the landing of the hostile troops. Three thousand men were placed at Chambly to meet the army from Albany on its way to Montreal.

But the fleet was destined never to see Quebec. Admiral Sir Hovenden Walker was busy with ingenious plans for taking care of his vessels at Quebec during the winter after he should have taken the place. He said:—

The ice in the river, freezing to the bottom, would bilge them as much as if they were to be squeezed between rocks, (and concluded that) the better way would be to secure them on the dry ground in frames and cradles, till the thaw.

Meantime he remained in complete ignorance of the real difficulties and dangers that lay in his path. He had with him a French seaman of experience named Paradis, and by following his advice might have navigated the river in safety. But, refusing all counsel, he gave orders according to his own notions, and the fleet approached during a fog very near a small island; a sudden wind from the southeast drove the ships toward it, eight of them were wrecked, and eight hundred and eighty-four men were drowned.

After this disaster, the admiral ordered his fleet about and bore off to the coast of Cape Breton, where he held a council of officers. All agreed that it was not advisable to go on; there was but ten weeks' provision for the men, and a supply could hardly arrive in time from New England. In reporting it, Walker philosophised thus:—

Had we arrived safe at Quebec, ten or twelve thousand men must have been left to perish of cold and hunger; thus, by the loss of a part. Providence saved all the rest!

The admiral's ships sailed for England and the provincial vessels carried home the New England troops. Nicholson, who had reached Lake George when he heard of the issue of the attack on Quebec, returned home and abandoned his undertaking also.

In the following year, the French were assailed by a new enemy, the Foxes, or Ottagamies, whom the Iroquois had drawn into an alliance against them. A party of their warriors set out to burn Detroit, which was defended by only twenty men under Du Buisson. But, having timely warning, Du Buisson sent swift messages to the Jesuit stations to have the Indian allies of the French sent to his relief. They poured in from every side and surrounded the Foxes, who soon found themselves the besieged instead of the besiegers. They held out with desperate bravery, but were at last compelled to surrender. The warriors of the party were slain at once, and the rest divided as slaves among the conquerors. But the French had gained an implacable foe; and for a long time, the Foxes and some more numerous tribes with which they were leagued continued to harass the French posts at the West.

Negotiations for peace began in Europe in 1712, but were not concluded till the following year. The power of France had been humbled; and not only did the policy of England prevail in the settlement of questions regarding European territory, but England also gained large tracts of land in America which had been claimed by her enemy. Although France was left in possession of Louisiana, England gained Newfoundland, Hudson Bay and Straits with the land adjoining, the Island of St. Christopher, and Nova Scotia or Acadia, according to its ancient boundaries. The Iroquois, or Five Nations, were recognised as being under the dominion of the English, and it was stipulated that France should never molest them. The treaty of peace was signed at Utrecht, April 11th, 1713.

But there was still abundant room for future misunderstandings and disputes. The limits of the territory of the Five Nations were indefinite, the French applied the name Louisiana to the entire valley of the Mississippi and the Ohio, and the boundaries of Acadia had long been a subject of dispute. The French claimed that only the southern portion of the peninsula of Nova Scotia was properly included in Acadia; while the English applied the name to a great territory bounded by the St. Lawrence, the ocean and gulf, and a line drawn from the mouth of the Kennebec to Quebec, and including the islands of Cape Breton and St. John, now Prince Edward Island.

Large numbers of the Acadians, restive under British rule, removed to the provinces still under the control of the French, many of them to Cape Breton Island. A large settlement was formed at Louisburg on the south-eastern shore of the island. Here was a fine harbour, half a mile broad, and here in time arose the strongest fortress in America, protecting the French fisheries and forming a refuge for privateers in time of war.

The Abenaquis, seeing with jealousy the growth of the English settlements in their territory, sent an embassy to the Governor of Canada, asking if the French had really given up their country to the English. Vaudreuil answered that nothing was said about their country in the treaty; and the Indians, resolved to undertake their own defence, attacked the English fishermen at Canso, killing several and robbing them of all they had, and committing other similar depredations.

The New England people had long been suspicious of the influence of a Jesuit missionary, Sebastian Rasles, at Norridgewock, on the Kennebec. He had been at the Jesuit mission on the Chaudière, had travelled through the west in pursuit of his calling, and was familiar with many of the Indian languages. For twenty-five years he had been on the Kennebec, where he had gathered a flourishing congregation of savages, and built a church which he had decorated with pictures painted by his own hand, and whose glittering altar was looked on with reverent awe by savage eyes. His altar-boys were little Indians, gorgeous in red and white; and their chanting processions were a favourite bid for the admiration of the natives.

The old man shared the journeys and the dangers of his flock, and his influence over them was unbounded. This influence, there was every reason to believe, was used to incite them to depredations on the English settlements; he was said to keep a flag on which was a cross surrounded by bows and arrows, which he used to raise on a pole in front of the church when he gave them absolution before they set out on their warlike enterprises.

Father Rasles was therefore marked for destruction. On occasion of the Abenaquis threatening reprisals if some of their chiefs who were held by the Massachusetts Government as hostages were not released, a party of men under Colonel Westbrook was sent in December, 1721, to capture the priest. The hunters were away on the chase, and there was no one to protect him; but, warned of Westbrook's approach, he fled to the woods in haste, leaving his papers behind. Among them was his correspondence with the Governor of Canada, which proved that the suspicions against him were not unfounded. There was also a dictionary in manuscript of the Abenaquis language, which has been preserved, and was printed by the American Academy of Arts and Sciences in 1833. At about the same time the young Baron de St. Castin was also seized, as dangerous to the peace of the settlements in the east, and taken to Boston.

Exasperated by these attempts on their leaders, the Indians determined on war. They invited all the tribes of their own nation not only, but those near Quebec, to unite with them. The first blow was struck at Merry Meeting Bay, near the junction of the Androscoggin with the Kennebec, where Brunswick now stands. A party of sixty Indians captured nine families, but they afterward released all but five men, whom they kept as security for their hostages in the hands of the English. Two attacks on the fort at the River St. George were unsuccessful, as were nearly all Indian attempts on fortified places; but many fishing and trading vessels fell into their hands, and with these they cruised about the coast, compelling the captured seamen to serve as their crews. Two armed vessels sent out by the Governor of Nova Scotia re-took all the vessels, numbering more than twenty, and put a stop to the piracies for the time.

Parties sent out the next year, under Captain Harmon and Colonel Westbrook, made some reprisals on the savages. Harmon pursued a party of thirty-four, and killed fifteen of them as they lay by their camp-fires. Westbrook took a large party of men to a village on the Penobscot, supposed to have been above Bangor at Old Town; it was deserted, and they set fire to it, and all the buildings in it, including a well-built stockade fort, a chapel, and the residence of the priests, were laid in ashes. During this year the Indians were comparatively quiet, but in 1724, they broke out afresh. Men working in the fields, or for any reason away from the settlements, were liable to death or capture at any moment. At Kennebunk a sloop was taken, and every man on it was put to death.

Captain Josiah Winslow and sixteen men who were with him were surprised on the St. George, and every one of them was killed. Annapolis was attacked, and a party sent out from the fort was defeated. The priest of Annapolis, who was at Minas when the Indians gathered there, and might have given warning of the intended attack, was expelled from the colony and sent to Louisburg; another priest, who did send a warning, although it arrived too late, was thanked and promoted by the English; but the church authorities afterward superseded him, placing in Minas, where the English had stationed him, one more faithful to the French interest.

The same year another expedition was planned to seize the hated Father Rasles. He had been urged to fly to Canada; but though he knew the danger, he would not leave his post. "God has given this flock into my care," he said, "and I shall not leave it." This time the assailants succeeded in taking Norridgewock by surprise. The Indians made little resistance; all who could get away fled to the river, crossed it, and escaped to the forest. Father Rasles, who was in his *wigwam*, went forward to help his flock to escape by drawing the attention of the assailants to himself, and was struck down at once, killed, scalped, and trodden under foot. After pillaging the church and the dwellings, the soldiers set them on fire and retired. The mourning Indians buried their priest beneath the ground where his altar had stood, and now a monument to his memory marks the spot where he fell.

In the following year Captain John Lovewell, of Dunstable, impelled by patriotism, or the desire of adventure, or the bounty on scalps, led out a party of men. Ten Indians asleep beside the Salmon Falls River were surprised and killed, and Lovewell received one thousand pounds for the ten scalps. The next expedition was not so fortunate; it fell into an ambuscade on the Saco; and Lovewell and half of his thirty-four men lost their lives. Lovewell's Pond, near Fryeburg, where he fell, is named for him, and the brook flowing into it is called Battle Brook.

In the summer of the same year, a conference with the Indians was held at the fort on the St. George. They seemed disposed for peace, and in November four of the chiefs were called to Boston to form a treaty. They acknowledged the title of the English to Nova Scotia and Acadia, and promised to maintain peace and deliver up their prisoners. The treaty was faithfully observed, and the eastern colonies had a season of rest from the horrors of Indian warfare.

In 1726, the French built a fort at Niagara, where they had long had a trading-post; and in the following year, Governor Burnet, of New York, built what he called a "stone house of strength" at Oswego. The Governor of Canada remonstrated, and threatened to destroy it, but did not venture on any violence. In 1731, the French built Fort Frederick at Crown Point, thus asserting their claim to north-eastern New York.

CHAPTER 9

King George's War

Peace reigned between France and England for thirty years after the Treaty of Utrecht. Queen Anne, the last of the Stuart line of sovereigns, died in 1714, and was succeeded by George I., first English king of the House of Hanover, who inherited through his mother, the Electress Sophia of Hanover, granddaughter of James I. of England. He died in 1727, and was succeeded by his son, George II. It was during the reign of this king that England became engaged in the next war which involved the colonies of North America.

In 1740, Charles VI., Emperor of Germany, died. Many years before, he had taken measures to secure to his daughter, Maria Theresa, the succession to his hereditary dominions; and he hoped that after his death her husband, the Duke of Tuscany, would be chosen by the electors to wear the imperial crown. To secure the inheritance to his daughter, he proclaimed a law called the "Pragmatic Sanction," regulating the succession. Many of the powers of Europe demurred; but by ceding away parts of his dominions to the other monarchies of the continent, the emperor at length gained their consent. After his death, however, claims were made to his dominions by several princes, on grounds having more or less colour of justice in themselves, but all were set aside by the Pragmatic Sanction to which they had pledged their support.

The young queen had been carefully educated with a view to the position her father designed her to occupy. She had shared his counsels, and learned something of the art of governing. She was twenty-three years of age when her father died, and being gifted with beauty, unusual mental ability, and a high spirit, she was well fitted to attract the loyalty of her father's subjects

The first to attack the rights of the young queen was the King of

Prussia, Frederick II., called the Great. Raising some pretence of a right to the possession of Silesia, which had been under Austria for more than a hundred years, he prepared an army of thirty thousand men, and sent them into the country, in December, 1740, without having made any declaration of war, or any demand for the province; indeed, he had until then professed to be friendly to the interests of Maria Theresa.

After filling Silesia with his forces, Frederick sent an ambassador to the queen, offering to aid her against her other enemies, if she would cede to him the duchy which he had invaded, which she indignantly refused to do. He then overran the whole of Lower Silesia with his troops, and Prussia was successful in the first battle with Austria, that of Mollwitz, in April, 1741, though Frederick himself ran away. Then all the other claimants rushed on to the dismemberment of the Austrian Empire. France took the part of the Elector of Bavaria, who claimed the throne. Prussia, France, Spain, and Poland were combined against the queen. Thus, began the War of the Austrian Succession.

Maria Theresa was obliged to yield Silesia to Frederick, in June, 1742, but succeeded in maintaining her claim to most of her other dominions, while the Elector of Bavaria was thoroughly humbled. The war now became a struggle on the part of Austria to wrest Alsace and Lorraine from France, and Naples from Spain, and to make Bavaria a part of the Austrian dominions. England had aided Austria by subsidies and troops, and her forces met the army of France in the Battle of Dettingen in June, 1743. But it was not until March, 1744, that war was formally declared between France and England.

When the news of the declaration of war was sent to Louisbourg, orders were also sent that no offensive measures should be taken until reinforcements should arrive. But it was thought that a sudden attack on the small garrisons at Annapolis and Canso, before help could arrive from New England, could not fail of success. Du Vivier, a great-grandson of Charles la Tour, so prominent in the early history of Acadia, taking command of five hundred men, of whom two hundred were Indians, and several vessels, attacked the block-house at Canso, in May, 1744. Having no chance of a successful defence, the garrison of eighty men surrendered at once, and were taken to Louisbourg, on condition that they should be sent, at the end of a year, to England or to Boston. The buildings were all destroyed by Du Vivier's men.

It remained only to take Annapolis. The fort was an earthwork in a ruinous condition, held by one hundred and fifty men under Paul

Mascarene. Du Vivier took his prisoners to Louisbourg, and remained there some time, making preparations for going to Annapolis. Meantime, a rumour reached that place that five hundred French and Indians, on the way to attack it, were already on the river above the town. A vessel soon arrived from Boston bringing news of the declaration of war, and the officers and soldiers of the garrison sent their families to Boston by the return of the galley, two other vessels being sent with it, thus greatly relieving the place of those unable to bear arms. The men then went to work repairing the fortifications.

The Indians who had been with Du Vivier at Canso grew impatient waiting for his return; and they were easily persuaded by Belleisle, a scion of the St. Castin family, to march against Annapolis under his leadership without waiting for Du Vivier. They were accompanied by their priest, La Loutre, who, like most of the priests in Acadia, had been faithfully labouring to keep his flock loyal to French interests. If the Indians had been supported by Du Vivier's soldiers, Annapolis would probably have fallen; for it was not in a condition to withstand a determined assault. But the Indians pursued their usual methods, picking off stragglers and firing from under cover. The English sent out a party of workmen and soldiers, who drove them back and tore down all buildings that could protect them from the guns of the fort, and they were glad to escape with a few stolen cattle.

Re-enforcements were sent from Boston to the number of one hundred men or more. Du Vivier returned with two hundred soldiers, expecting a general rising among the inhabitants; but there was only a feeble response to his summons to them to enlist under the banner of France and bring in supplies for the expedition; and the Indians were disheartened by their failure. Many of the savages, however, joined him, and late in August he began his attack. After several days of ineffectual firing, he sent in a flag of truce, saying that three ships of war were on their way to his assistance, together with a large body of soldiers, and supplies of cannon and mortars, and offering to accept a capitulation conditioned on their arrival; but Mascarene refused to have any negotiations with him. The attacks were resumed and kept up night after night, until late in September, when another reinforcement arrived from Boston.

Having learned from a prisoner that Mascarene talked of attacking his camp, Du Vivier hastily drew off to Minas, and finally returned to Louisbourg. It was not long after Du Vivier abandoned the siege, that a part of his ships arrived; but finding him gone, they withdrew, while

Mascarene kept his men at work strengthening the defences during the autumn and winter, in expectation of another attack La Loutre gathered a force of Indians again, who were joined by some Canadian troops, and in the spring they made a feeble attack on Annapolis, and prowled about the country, but with no greater success than the capture of two trading-vessels.

The soldiers taken at Canso, who had been sent to Boston on parole, gave information regarding the condition of the fortress, and in January, 1745, the question of an expedition for its capture began to be agitated. Governor Shirley of Massachusetts had written to England the preceding autumn, asking help for the protection of Nova Scotia and the capture of Louisbourg; but as yet no answer had been received. In January he laid the project before the State Legislature in a secret session. It was at first rejected, so improbable did it seem that a provincial force could effect the capture of the strongest post in North America. But afterward, on a complaint from the merchants of Boston, Salem, and Marblehead, of the injuries to their vessels from the privateers which found refuge at Louisbourg, the project was reconsidered, and resolved on by a majority of one.

The other provinces were asked to render aid. Connecticut sent five hundred and sixteen men, New Hampshire three hundred and four; and these, with the three thousand two hundred and fifty raised in Massachusetts, constituted the whole force.. Rhode Island sent three hundred, but they arrived too late. New York gave some artillery, and Pennsylvania some provisions. The New England colonies furnished thirteen armed vessels. Commodore Warren, who was at Antigua, was solicited to send some of his ships, but declined doing so without express orders from England,

It was a question who should command this expedition. With the exception of some little irregular fighting with the Indians, peace had reigned throughout the colonies for thirty years; and there were no officers to be had in the provinces with any knowledge of the science of regular warfare. The choice fell upon William Pepperell, of Kittery, a colonel of militia, who, as a merchant, a landholder in three of the provinces, and a man of clear judgment and weight of character, would be likely to have influence with those of his countrymen who were to be led on this great undertaking.

Immense enthusiasm attended the fitting out of the expedition. Pepperell sought advice from the celebrated preacher, George Whitefield, on the question of accepting the proffered command, and

Whitefield answered that if he should fail, the responsibility for the blood of the fallen would be laid to his charge, and that if he should succeed, he would become an object of malicious envy to his fellow-citizens. In spite of this dark augury, Pepperell accepted. To the New Hampshire troops who asked him for a motto, Whitefield gave. *Nil desperandum, Christo Duce*—"Nothing is to be despaired of, Christ being the leader."

In this spirit of religious enthusiasm, one of the volunteers carried an axe wherewith to hew down the crosses and images in the French churches. All sorts of advice and schemes for the protection of the volunteers and the speedy capture of the fort were laid before the officers. One inventive enthusiast brought a model of a flying bridge which would land the army within the walls at a single bound. A minister had a scheme for avoiding the explosion of mines, and taking Louisbourg without the loss of a life. Another had made a complete plan of the siege, the camp, the batteries, the entrenchments. Governor Shirley's instructions were, that the army should land in the night and march to surprise the fortress before daybreak.

Late in March, 1745, the fleet set sail, carrying the army of fishermen, farmers, mechanics, and lumbermen, under their citizen General, William Pepperell, Brigadier-General Waldo, and their subordinate officers, mostly chosen from among the church deacons, justices of the peace, and other citizens of respectability and consideration in their townships. Among them was the soldier, Colonel William Vaughan, who had first suggested the enterprise to Governor Shirley.

Arriving at Canso early in April, they found the coast of Cape Breton so dogged with ice that not a vessel could enter the harbours, which made it probable that no news of their intentions could have reached the fort. While they were waiting, Pepperell had a block-house built in place of the one that had been destroyed the previous year, and garrisoned it with eighty men. Their spirits were raised by the capture of a richly-loaded vessel on its way from Martinique to Louisbourg, and still more by the arrival of four ships of war under Commodore Warren, who had received instructions from England to go to the help of the colonies, just after his refusal to proceed without orders had been despatched to Boston. More ships of war soon after arrived, and in a few days Louisbourg was blockaded. Warren's ships guarded the entrance to the harbour, and the places in the vicinity from which supplies might be sent were surprised and held.

Louisbourg was fortified with a stone rampart thirty feet high and forty feet thick at the base, which swept around the town in a circuit of two miles, and was surrounded by a ditch eighty feet wide. Six bastions stood out from this great wall, and there were embrasures for a hundred and forty-eight cannon and six mortars. On an island at the entrance of the harbour was a battery of thirty pieces, and on the shore opposite the entrance was the grand or royal battery of twenty-eight forty-two pounders and two eighteen-pounders, with a moat and bastions. Near the drawbridge, giving entrance to the town on the land side, was a circular battery mounting sixteen twenty-four pounders. This fortress, which was twenty-five years in building, cost thirty millions of *livres*, and was called the "Dunkirk of America," is now a lonely ruin, the former military importance of the place having entirely passed away.

The appearance of the fleet in Chapeaurouge, or Gabarus Bay, southward from the city. May 30th, was the first intimation of danger the French had received. They fired cannon, rang bells, and ran about in confusion; and a hundred and fifty soldiers, under an officer named Boulardiere, were sent out to prevent the landing. But Pepperell quietly sent a detachment farther up the Bay while Boulardiere's attention was fixed on the spot where it was supposed the attempt would be made, and Boulardiere was obliged to retire into the city again. About two thousand men were landed that day, and by the next night all were on shore. Colonel Vaughan took a party of New Hampshire men and marched past the city to the northeast harbour, where they burned a number of warehouses containing naval stores and large quantities of wine and brandy. The smoke was carried into the royal battery, a panic seized the men in charge of it, and they spiked their guns and fled.

In the morning Vaughan's men took possession of the deserted battery. Boat-loads of men from the city came to dislodge them, but Vaughan stood on the shore with thirteen men and prevented them from landing till reinforcements came. The spiked cannon were drilled out and turned on the city and the island battery, throwing a deadly fire within the walls and reaching the roof of the citadel. To a summons to surrender, on the 7th of May, Du Chambon, the commandant, returned a refusal; but his men had been so mutinous before the siege that he did not dare trust them to make a sortie, for fear of desertion.

In order to place batteries for more effective work, it was necessary to carry the guns over a morass. Sledges were made, and the men drew them by straps passed over their shoulders, sinking to their knees in the bog. This task consumed fourteen nights.

Several attempts were made by the besiegers to take the island battery, but all without success; one, a night attack, was a disastrous failure. The assailants, discovered before they could land, and met by a sharp fire, were glad to escape after nearly an hour's hard fighting, having lost sixty men killed and a hundred and sixteen prisoners. Despairing of taking the island battery, the Americans then placed a battery on the high cape at the lighthouse on the eastern side of the harbour, which commanded the island battery, and nearly silenced it.

The siege had now lasted almost six weeks, and the city had neither been entered nor had a breach been made in the walls. Other ships of war had arrived, and it was agreed that the fleet should sail into the harbour and bombard while the land forces attempted an entrance by storm. At this time the *Vigilant*, a French ship, carrying sixty-four guns, arrived with military supplies for the garrison, and was taken by a Massachusetts frigate under the command of Captain Edward Tyng. Pepperell sent news of the capture to Du Chambon under a flag of truce, and this so discouraged the commandant that he determined to capitulate, and on the 17th of June Louisbourg was surrendered, after a siege of forty-nine days. The garrison, the crew of the *Vigilant*, and some of the inhabitants of the town were sent to France.

When the American troops entered the fortress, they for the first time realised the strength of the place and the magnitude of the enterprise, the undertaking of which now seemed presumptuous, and its success little short of a miracle. With the feeling that Providence had manifestly interfered to give them the victory, they listened to the chaplain who proclaimed the gospel according to Calvin from the altar whence they had cast down the images and the tapers.

There was great rejoicing in Boston when a swift-sailing schooner brought news of the victory of which the anxious communities at home were beginning to despair. Commodore Warren had sent home two prisoners some weeks before, one the commander of a battery without the walls of Louisbourg, the other, captain of a captured ship; and these men had given descriptions of the strength of the fortress, which made New England tremble for its little army. But now bells were rung, cannon fired, and tumultuous crowds added their voices in a general shout of rejoicing.

In England the report that such a stronghold had been taken by an untrained army of provincials could hardly be believed. Sir Peter Warren, the naval commander, acknowledged the services of the colonists but grudgingly; and though it was the most brilliant success the English achieved during the war, English historians scarcely mention it. Voltaire, however, calls the capture of Louisbourg one of the most remarkable events of the reign of Louis XV.

General Pepperell was made a baronet for his share in the enterprise, while Governor Shirley received a commission in the regular army, and afterward held the chief military command in America. Colonel Vaughan went to England to present his claims, but failed to receive any reward for his services, and died in London in obscurity and neglect.

The capture of Louisbourg led to a project on the part of the English authorities to conquer Canada, and one by the French to recover Cape Breton and Acadia, and devastate the New England coast. Governor Shirley wrote to the British ministry, urging measures for the conquest of Canada, and in response the Secretary of State sent orders to the governors of the colonies, as far south as Virginia, to raise as many men as possible, and have them ready for action. A squadron of ships and some land forces were to be sent to Louisbourg, and there met by the New England troops, when the united force was to ascend the St. Lawrence to Quebec. At the same time the soldiers from New York and the southern colonies were to assemble at Albany for the capture of Crown Point and Montreal.

The colonial troops were readily raised, to the number of about eight thousand men, and waited for the fleet. But no fleet came. When the season was so far advanced that all hopes of its arrival were given up, it was thought best to employ the troops ordered to Albany in an attack on Crown Point; and the Iroquois as usual were found willing to join in the undertaking. The New England troops were ordered to Acadia, on the sudden intelligence that the inhabitants were on the eve of revolt, and that Annapolis was threatened by a body of French and Indians.

During the same season a large fleet had been gathered at Brest for the capture of Louisbourg, Annapolis, and Boston; and the Canadians and their Indian allies were to be ready to cooperate with the fleet by land. Six hundred Canadians, therefore, repaired to Acadia in June, and the Micmacs and Malicites rallied once more under the banners of France. This force was waiting at Chignecto in September for the arrival of the fleet, when the Governor of Canada, having heard that the New England forces were about to embark for Acadia, sent orders to Ramezay, their commander, to bring them back to Quebec. But as

Ramezay was about to go, he learned that the French fleet had arrived in the harbour of Chebucto, now Halifax.

This intelligence, which was received by Ramezay's men with great rejoicing, and had filled New England with consternation, was not so important as it seemed. The fleet which had started from France on the 22nd of June, under the command of the Duc d'Anville, comprised forty ships of war, with transports carrying more than three thousand soldiers and all kinds of military stores. It was the largest armament that had ever been sent to American shores. But a tempest had scattered the ships soon after they set sail, many of them were compelled to return, and when the Duc d'Anville reached Chebucto he had only three of his war-ships and a few transports left. An infectious fever was rapidly disabling the soldiers that remained, and on the 16th of September, a few days after the arrival, D'Anville himself suddenly died, not without suspicion of poison.

More ships having arrived, the officer next in command. Vice-Admiral d'Estournelle, proposed in a council of officers that the undertaking should be abandoned; for some ships which were to join them from Hispaniola had failed, their own ships were scattered, and twenty-four hundred of their men had died of the fever. Three ships from Hispaniola had been to Chebucto, but had returned to France on failing to find D'Anville's fleet. The abandonment of the expedition was violently opposed by the officers, headed by Jonquière, who had been lately appointed Governor of Canada and was next in command, and D'Estournelle, excited by the opposition, took the fever, and in a fit of delirium killed himself with his own sword.

Jonquière resolved to attack Annapolis with the forces that were left; but when they arrived off Cape Sable, another storm still further disabled the ships, and news was brought the commander that Louisbourg and Annapolis were both defended by English ships. So, the French vessels could do nothing but return to Brest.

Ramezay, with his Canadian and Indian followers, went into winter quarters at Chignecto, where his presence was a constant menace to Annapolis. Mascerene, commander of the garrison there, sent to Boston for troops, and five hundred men were accordingly despatched in December, and on their arrival were stationed at Grand Pré, near the River Gaspereaux in the district of Minas.

Ramezay determined to send a force against them, and in January, 1747, about four hundred Canadians and Indians set out, under an officer named De Villiers. For two weeks they travelled on snow-shoes and dragged their supplies on sledges along the wintry coast. The New England officers had some warning of the danger; but, supposing the enemy to be isolated by the season, they paid no attention to it.

On the 10th of February the French arrived in a dense storm of snow, which prevented them from being seen by the sentries. They had accurate information from the inhabitants of Grand Pré, and ten houses where the officers were lodged were selected for the first attack. There was a desperate resistance, but the New England soldiers were under too great disadvantage; sixty were killed, including the chief officer. Colonel Arthur Noble, and sixty-nine were made prisoners. The French lost but seven killed and fourteen wounded. Those of the English who remained could not escape, having no snow-shoes; a capitulation was at length agreed upon, and they returned to Annapolis under a promise not to bear arms in Minas and adjoining districts for six months.

After Jonquière returned to France, another fleet was prepared to carry troops to Canada and Nova Scotia, and placed under his command. He set sail in May, 1747, with six ships of war and some transports, accompanied by six merchant-ships and a frigate bound for the East Indies. An English fleet under Admirals Anson and Warren set out in pursuit, and a battle was fought off Cape Finisterre on the 3rd of May, which resulted in a complete victory for the English. They took six ships of war and all the merchantmen, with over four thousand prisoners. The captured treasure was afterward taken to the Bank of England in twenty wagons.

The people on the western frontier had been somewhat disturbed by French and Indian bands during the progress of the war. Rumford, now Concord, New Hampshire, was unsuccessfully attacked in 1746, and Fort Massachusetts, in Williamstown, was taken by a large party in the same year. Fort Number Four on the Connecticut was assailed by a large band in 1747, but was bravely and successfully defended by a garrison under Captain Phineas. The village of Saratoga was destroyed, and the inhabitants, thirty families in all, were slaughtered.

Nothing was done in America this year by the English, though the colonists believed that a reasonable amount of aid from England would enable them to bring all Canada under British sway. It was said that English statesmen thought the colonies, if their strength were revealed to them by such a conquest, and if the fear of French inroads from the north were removed, might be tempted to assert their independence; particularly as they were growing restive under some of the

Battle of Grand Pré

exactions and restrictions imposed upon them.

However, that may be—whether English statesman foresaw the events that were to occur within thirty years, or whether they had simply not awakened to the importance of their colonial possessions in America—not only was nothing done to reduce Canada, but Louisbourg was restored to France, much to the chagrin of the colonists who were so proud of its capture. The treaty of Aix-la-Chapelle, which put an end to the war, October 18, 1748, gave up Louisbourg for Madras, which the French had taken, and left the boundaries of French and English territory in America as undefined as they had been under former treaties.

Parliament agreed to pay to the colonists all the expenses they had incurred for the war, and in 1749 two hundred and fifteen chests of Spanish dollars and one hundred casks of copper coin were sent from England to Boston. This money, which amounted to about a million dollars, was carried to the treasury on twenty-seven carts and trucks.

CHAPTER 10

Acadia After the War

During the nominal peace which followed the Treaty of Aix-la-Chapelle, the representatives of the two governments were anxiously engaged in attempting to settle by actual occupation the question of boundaries, which was still left open by that treaty. It professed to restore the boundaries as they had been before the war; and before the war the entire basin of the Mississippi, as well as the tract between the St. Lawrence River and Gulf, the Bay of Fundy, and the Kennebec, was claimed by both nations, with some show of reason, as no convention between them had ever defined the rights of each.

Names had been given to vast tracts of land whose limits were but partly defined, or at one time defined in one way, at another time in another, and when these names were mentioned in treaties they were understood by each party according to its own interest. The treaty of 1748, therefore, not only left abundant cause for future war, but left occasion for the continuance of petty border hostilities in time of nominal peace. Commissioners were appointed, French and English, to settle the question of the disputed territory, but the differences were too wide to be adjusted by anything but conquest.

While the most important question was that of the great extent of territory at the west, and, as we shall hereafter see, both nations were devising means for establishing their claims to it, Acadia, or Nova Scotia, was the scene of a constant petty warfare. The French were determined to restrict the English province to the peninsula now known by that name. The Governor of Canada sent a few men under Boishebert to the mouth of the St. John's to hold that part of the territory. A little old fort built by the Indians had stood for fifty years on the St. John's at the mouth of the Nerepis, and there the men established themselves. A larger number was sent under La Corne to keep possession of Chignecto, on the isthmus which, according to French claims, formed the northern boundary of English territory.

In all the years that England had held nominal rule in Acadia, not a single English settlement had been formed, and apparently not a step of progress had been taken in gaining the loyalty of the inhabitants. A whole generation had grown up during the time; but they were no less devoted to France than their fathers had been. It was said that the King of England had not one truly loyal subject in the peninsula, outside of the fort at Annapolis. When the inhabitants did not choose to obey the orders of the English authorities, they represented themselves as being under fear of the Indians; and the Indians were constantly urged to their share in the proceedings by the persuasions and inducements of the priests and emissaries of the Canadian Government. No doubt, also, the bond of religion was the strongest influence that held the Acadians faithful to France.

Among the schemes suggested for remedying this state of affairs, was one by Governor Shirley, to place strong bands of English settlers in all the important towns, in order that the government might have friends and influence throughout the country. Nothing came of this; but in 1749, Parliament voted forty thousand pounds for the purpose of settling a colony. Inducements were offered to discharged soldiers and sailors, and to farmers and mechanics to join the colony. They were to be carried over free, to be furnished with farming and fishing implements, and to be maintained free of expense for one year.

Grants of land were offered also, privates from the army and navy were to receive fifty acres each, and officers more, according to their rank. No quit-rents were to be required for the first ten years. Twenty-five hundred persons being ready to go in less than two months from the time of the first advertisement, the colony was entrusted to Colonel Edward Cornwallis (uncle of the Cornwallis of the Revolutionary War), and he was made Governor of Nova Scotia. Chebucto was selected as the site of the colony, and the town was named Halifax in honour of the president of the Lords of Trade and Plantations. Within four months a clearing was made, and three hundred houses were built.

In July, a council was held at Halifax, when Governor Cornwallis gave the French deputies a paper declaring what the government would allow to the French subjects, and what would be required of them. They were to be left in peaceable possession of their property and the free exercise of their religion, provided they should take the oath of allegiance to the British Government, submit to its laws, and give all possible countenance and assistance to settlers who should be sent out under His Majesty's orders. To this the people replied by their deputies, asking that they might enjoy the privileges mentioned, under condition of taking a qualified oath, one that should exempt them from bearing arms in case of war, even in defence of their own province. Such an oath had been allowed in certain cases twenty years before; and the precedent was urged at this time. They wished to stand as neutrals, and, indeed, were often called so.

Cornwallis replied that nothing less than entire allegiance would be accepted. Then the deputies asked if they might sell their property and leave the peninsula, and were told that the Treaty of Utrecht gave them a year in which to withdraw from the province with their effects, if they preferred that to becoming subjects of Great Britain; but that now there was no alternative but confiscation or entire allegiance. About a month later the people sent in a declaration with a thousand signatures, stating that they had resolved not to take the oath, but were determined to leave the country. Cornwallis took no steps to coerce them, but wrote to England for instructions.

A treaty was made between the governor and the chiefs of the Indians in July; but on the occasion of the building of a block-house by the English at Minas, the Indians were instigated to violate the treaty, and attacks were made by them on Canso and Minas, and some vessels in the harbour of Chignecto. It was supposed that the missionary priest La Loutre was at the bottom of all the trouble with the Indians and much of the disloyalty of the Acadians; one means of coercion was always at his service, the refusal of the sacraments to the disobedient.

In the following year Cornwallis sent four hundred men, under Major Lawrence, to Chignecto to build a block-house. A little river called the Messagouche was claimed by the French as their southern boundary; and a force under La Corne had been keeping possession of the isthmus. On the southern bank was a prosperous village called Beaubassin, and La Corne had compelled its inhabitants to take the oath of allegiance to the King of France.

When Lawrence arrived, all the inhabitants of Beaubassin, about one thousand, having been persuaded by La Loutre, set fire to their houses, and leaving behind the fruits of years of industry, turned their backs on their fertile fields, and crossed the river, to put themselves under the protection of La Corne's troops. Many Acadians from other parts of the peninsula also left their homes, and lived in exile and poverty under the French dominion, hoping for a speedy change of masters in Nova Scotia.

Lawrence was obliged to abandon the work on which he had been sent, since La Corne had a very large force at his command; but later in the season he went again to Chignecto with a larger body of troops. Their landing was opposed by a band of Indians assisted by some of the Acadians, entrenched behind the dikes, and in the assault six Englishmen were killed and twelve wounded. This was the first blood shed since the peace of Aix-la-Chapelle. Lawrence's men proceeded to build a fort on the south bank of the Messagouche, which was called Fort Lawrence, and garrisoned by six hundred men.

In the same year a large French fort. Beau Séjour, was built on the northern side of the Messagouche, and a smaller one, Gaspereaux, at Baie Verte. Other stations were also planted, forming a line of fortified posts from the Gulf of St. Lawrence to the mouth of the St. John's. An instance of the treachery of La Loutre about this time is recorded. Captain Edward How, an officer well known to the country and the Indians, was sent to Fort Lawrence by the governor, that he might use his influence to keep the Indians peaceful. He sometimes met French officers on the Messagouche with flags of truce, and messages were in that way sent between the forts. La Loutre dressed an Indian like a French officer, and sent him down the river with a flag of truce, and Captain How came unsuspiciously to meet him, when some Indians who were concealed on the bank arose and shot him dead.

The Acadians made repeated attempts to induce Cornwallis to allow them to take the qualified oath, threatening to leave the province and to neglect sowing their fields. Cornwallis seems to have treated them with mildness and consideration, but was firm in his refusal to take less than an oath of full allegiance. Many of those who had exiled themselves asked permission to return, but through the influences brought to bear upon them by the French, declined to fulfil the conditions required. La Loutre told them that if they returned and yielded allegiance they should be allowed neither priests nor sacraments, and as he was Vicar-General for Acadia under the Bishop of Quebec, he probably had power to make good his threat.

In the following years, the Acadians refused to bring supplies to the English forts, even at their own prices, and in 1754, three hundred of them went to work at Fort Beau Séjour refusing the offer of employment on government works at Halifax. Their rebellious conduct was imitated by some Germans lately settled at Lunenburg, and the governor was obliged to send soldiers to subdue them.

The commission appointed to settle the question of boundaries had broken up without accomplishing any results; and it was resolved by the authorities in Nova Scotia and Massachusetts that an expedition should be sent against Fort Beau Séjour. The enterprise was planned by Governor Shirley and Colonel Lawrence, then in command in Nova Scotia. Great care was taken to keep the matter secret, that the garrison might be taken completely by surprise. Arms and boats had been taken from the Acadians; and during the summer, when it was rumoured that a French fleet had arrived in the Bay of Fundy, they offered memorials to the council, asking for the restoration of their arms, and exemption from the oath. This was refused; and the deputies, on again declining to take the oath, were ordered into confinement.

The governor then issued orders to all the French inhabitants to send in new deputies, who should express their final intentions with regard to the oath, warning them that any who now refused would not thereafter be allowed to take it, "but that effectual measures ought to be taken to remove all such recusants out of the province." Deputies were sent in representing over five hundred of the inhabitants; all refused to take the required oath, and were ordered into confinement. It had been determined to expel the people from the province in case they should refuse, the record of the council says:—

And, nothing now remained to be considered but what measures should be taken to send them away, and where they should be sent to.

Meantime, Massachusetts had raised about two thousand troops for the contemplated enterprise, who were under the command of Lieutenant-Colonel John Winslow. To this force were added about three hundred regulars, and the whole was placed under the command of Lieutenant-Colonel Monckton. They reached Chignecto on the 2nd of June, and the following day encamped about Fort Lawrence. De Vergor, commander at Beau Séjour, had neglected to take measures for strengthening his position, though some rumours of the intended attack had reached him. Now, however, having quite a large force at his disposal, consisting of a hundred and sixty-five soldiers, and several hundred Acadians who had obeyed the summons to come into the fort, he set to work to complete the defences.

On the 4th the English began by attacking the block-house at Pont-à-Buot, some miles east of Beau Séjour, and took it in an hour, the French running away in a panic and setting fire to the block-house and all the houses they passed on their flight to the fort. Several days were consumed by Monckton's men in making a bridge over the river and cutting a road by which to carry their cannon to an eminence north of the fort. Small parties had been sent from the fort to interrupt them, but without effecting anything. On the 13th their cannon were in place, and the attack began. The next day De Vergor received an answer from Louisbourg, whither he had sent for re-enforcements, that no men could be spared, owing to a threatened assault from an English squadron.

De Vergor and his officers tried to conceal this intelligence from the Acadians at the fort, who had been led to believe that certain help was to come from Louisbourg; but it was rumoured about among them, and many of them, on De Vergor's refusal to dismiss them, escaped from the fort in the night. On the 16th the mortars were in position, and the shells made such havoc in the fort that De Vergor resolved to surrender. The terms were soon arranged, and Monckton took possession the same evening. The garrison were allowed to leave with their arms, to be sent to Louisbourg, under promise not to bear arms in America for six months. The Acadians who had been forced to take up arms were granted a general amnesty. Many of them had asked De Vergor, when they were summoned to the fort, to threaten them with death unless they complied.

La Loutre, since none of the terms of the capitulation would apply to him, fearing the vengeance of the English, escaped in disguise, and made his way through the wilderness to Quebec. Here the bishop, who had not approved of his course in Acadia, reproached him with having neglected religion for politics. As he was without a home, friends, position, or influence in the New World, he embarked for France; but the vessel was captured by an English ship, and the Abbé La Loutre was imprisoned on the Island of Jersey till the close of the war. He came out, to find not only Acadia, but all of Canada and the Ohio basin, irretrievably lost to France.

After Beau Séjour, the smaller forts were quickly reduced. Some vessels sent to the mouth of the St. John's found the French fort deserted and burned. The name of Beau Séjour was changed to Cumberland.

The government had now determined to carry out the threat of expelling the Acadians from the peninsula. No doubt some justification for this act may be found in the long course of provocations given by them since they had beer under English rule. They had steadily refused to take the oath of allegiance to England, and had claimed the position of neutrals. Had they maintained this position, it's quite probable that the authorities would have allowed them to keep it undisturbed; but they had repeatedly abandoned it in favour of the French. On every occasion when the French seemed about to regain their supremacy, they gave them open aid; and at other times they looked on with indifference, if not with applause, at the barbarities of the Indians against the English.

And now, when the two countries were evidently on the eve of war, it was perhaps excusable in the dominant power that it should take measures to rid itself of an enemy within its own territory. Yet the exile of the Acadians remains one of the saddest incidents of history, and by almost universal consent is branded as a crime. The simple and pastoral character of the people is dwelt upon; and it is probable that the mass of them would have been innocent of hostile actions if they had been deprived of a few of the priests and leaders who were constantly inciting them against the English.

It was decided to distribute the Acadians among the various English colonies, in order that they might not go to strengthen the settlements of Canada. It was necessary to assemble them without letting them know the object for which they were called together, and then detain them until the transports were ready to take them away. They were to be allowed to carry with them their ready money and their household goods; all their other effects were to be declared forfeit to the Crown.

Arrangements were made for collecting the inhabitants at several places in different districts. At Chignecto and Annapolis the design was suspected, and most of the people escaped. Their houses were burned down, and as many of the fugitives as could be collected were put on board the transports. Winslow, who had charge of the business at Grand Pré in the district of Minas, was most successful. A proclamation was issued ordering all:—

Both old men and young men, as well as all the lads of ten years of age, to attend at the church of Grand Pré, on Friday, the 5th instant, at three of the clock in the afternoon, that we may impart to them what we are ordered to communicate to them.

No excuse would be accepted for failure to attend; but goods and chattels would be forfeited by disobedience, in default of real estate.

At three o'clock on Friday, the 5th of September, four hundred and eighteen men assembled in the church at Grand Pré, unsuspicious of the object for which they were summoned. The doors were closed and guarded, and the men were then addressed by Winslow, who told them:—

> You are called together to hear His Majesty's final resolution in regard to you. For almost half a century you have had more indulgence granted to you than any of his subjects in any other part of his dominions, though what use you have made of the indulgence you yourselves best know. The duty which is laid on me, though necessary, is very disagreeable to my natural make and temper, as I know it must be grievous to you. His Majesty's orders and instructions are, that your lands and tenements, cattle of all kinds, and livestock of all sorts, are forfeited to the Crown, with all your other effects, saving your money and household goods; and you yourselves are to be removed from the province. I am, through His Majesty's goodness, directed to allow you to carry away your money and household goods, so far as you can without discommoding the vessels you are to go in.

He promised that families should be kept together, and that he would make the removal as easy for them as possible.

The blow was sudden and terrible; they could not believe at first that it was anything but a threat. When they became convinced that it was really intended to tear them from their homes and scatter them among strange people, and that the guard made escape impossible, they begged to be allowed at least to go out and prepare for removal, offering to leave a number as hostages. Winslow thought it would not be safe to permit them to go out in a body; but he allowed ten to go at a time. Afterward, seeing some movements he thought suspicious among them, he was obliged to refuse even that privilege.

It was decided to remove the men to the vessels in the harbour, and keep the women and children on shore until the transports should arrive to carry them away. The men were so reluctant to obey the order to march to the ships that the soldiers had to drive them with their bayonets. The women and children crowded along the way, kneeling and praying, while the men marched past them singing hymns. Those left behind were kept near the shore, with insufficient food and clothing, for more than a month. Twenty-four young men escaped from the ships; but all but two of them returned, rather than stay behind and be separated from their families.

On the 10th of October the transports arrived; and care was taken to bring families together; but in the confusion they were separated in many cases. The number of those thus exiled has sometimes been placed at seven thousand. This is the estimate of the number that would have to be removed which was given by Colonel Lawrence when the scheme was first proposed, and probably includes nearly the whole population of the peninsula. More than three thousand escaped to the country about the Bay of Chaleurs, some went to Quebec, and some took refuge with the Indians; so that the whole number of those removed by the English did not exceed three thousand.

The houses and barns left by the exiles were burned to the ground. The cattle and horses were seized as spoils by the officers. The dikes which the people had raised against the ocean, enclosing some of the most fertile lands in the whole region, were left to to go to ruin, and the ocean broke over the deserted fields. The exiles were scattered through the British colonies, some as far south as Georgia. They became a charge upon the public, and even the support of paupers was grudgingly allotted them. A bill is on record which was sent in for the support of "three French pagans," and they were sent from town to town on one and another pretext, while their children were taken from them at the option of the town authorities. They clung with unfailing constancy to their own religion; and this, by keeping them a separate people among their captors, no doubt contributed much to the feeling against them. Yet instances are on record where their complaints were listened to and redress granted by the authorities, and where private generosity took pity on their sorrows.

Some of those who were sent to Georgia escaped to the ocean in boats and went coasting along the shore, in hopes to reach their native country; but they were stopped and detained on the coast of New England by orders from the authorities in Nova Scotia. One small colony went to Guiana. Some found their way to France; and two villages near Bordeaux are said to be inhabited by their descendants. Some planted settlements in Louisiana in the districts of Attakapas and Opelousas, where they and their descendants went for a long time under the name of "Cajeans."

Longfellow's poem *Evangeline* is founded on the removal of the inhabitants of Grand Pré.

CHAPTER 11

The Ohio Valley

The establishment of French forts and trading-posts at various points in the West has already been spoken of. Fort Frontenac at the head of the St. Lawrence, Fort Frederick at Crown Point on Lake Champlain, Fort Niagara at the mouth of the Niagara, and the posts at Erie, Sandusky, Detroit, Mackinaw, Chicago, and on the Maumee, the Wabash, and the Mississippi, formed a line of French stations, and supplied communication between the East and the Southwest. Missions and trading-houses were scattered through the regions of the lakes and the great rivers, at points favourable for trade and navigation; and one French adventurer, as early as 1731, had carried a line of trading-posts one hundred leagues beyond Lake Winnipeg, and built Fort de la Reine on the Assiniboin. After the treaty of Aix-la-Chapelle the attention of both governments was drawn to the necessity of vigorous measures west of the Alleghanies.

In 1749, the mission of La Presentation was established at Oswegatchie, on the present site of Ogdensburg, by a French priest, Father Francis Picquet. He hoped by means of it to effect what the French had laboured so long to accomplish by diplomacy and flattery, by the missions to the Mohawks and Onondagas, to break up the friendship of the Iroquois for the English, and win them over to the French interest. Father Picquet was with an expedition that destroyed Fort Edward during King George's War, an enterprise which he had been the first to suggest.

In 1748, he proposed to the Governor of Canada to found a settlement at Oswegatchie, a point which he thought most advantageously situated for intercepting the progress of the English and for influencing the Six Nations. He was directed to incite them to the destruction of Oswego, and thus secure to the French the uninterrupted control

A
General Map
OF THE RIVER OHIO
Plate the first

N. W. TERRITORY OF THE UNITED STATES

OHIO RIVER

PITTSBURGH

of the great highway along the lakes and their connecting waters.

After much opposition, he established himself at Oswegatchie with soldiers and workmen, built a saw-mill, and soon had a palisaded fort and several other buildings, and some lands cleared on which to settle a colony of Indians. During the peace, the settlement grew rapidly; in a few years there were three Indian villages gathered about the fort. At the visit of the Bishop of Quebec during the first year of the mission one hundred and thirty-two Indians were baptised. Picquet established a council from among the converts, and went with the most influential of them on a visit to Montreal, where they took the oath of allegiance to the King of France. He made a canoe voyage around Lake Ontario and up its tributaries, examined the forts, spoke to gatherings of savages, and noted the defects of the French management of the Indian trade. His success with the Iroquois was so great that the savages of that region were nearly lost to England, and perhaps would have been entirely so, had it not been for the influence of William Johnson.

This man came from Ireland and settled in the Mohawk Valley about 1738, taking charge of a large tract of land which had been granted to his uncle. Sir Peter Warren. He learned the language of the Mohawks, and became such a favourite with them that he was adopted into the tribe and chosen a *sachem*. They called him Warraghiyagey. He built two fortified houses, Johnson Hall and Johnson Castle. The Hall is still standing in the village of Johnstown. The Castle, farther up the river, was built of stone, with a parapet and four bastions.

The Indians were always made welcome, and were treated by Johnson with great tact, as well as confidence and liberality; sometimes, it is said, hundreds of them would lie down about him with their blankets after a feast, and go to sleep. A story is told which illustrates his sagacity. They had great respect for dreams; when they saw anything at Johnson's place which they particularly coveted, they were accustomed to tell him that they dreamed he gave it to them. Johnson humoured them until that kind of begging grew very troublesome, and then cunningly turned their faith in dreams to his own account.

"I dreamed too," he said to a chief who had just taken possession of some coveted article.

"What did you dream?"

Johnson told him he dreamed the tribe gave him a large tract of their hunting-ground.

The chief and his warriors were confounded. "You must have it," they said, "if you dreamed it; but don't dream anymore."

The Governor of New York made Johnson Colonel of the Six Nations, and in 1746, he was appointed Commissary of New York for Indian affairs, and in 1748, the command of all the soldiers of New York was given to him for the defence of the frontier.

Commissioners from the several English colonies met the chiefs of the Iroquois in a conference at Albany. They agreed that they would allow no Frenchmen to settle on their lands, and that the English should negotiate with the French for the restoration of Iroquois prisoners; and promised to use their influence to bring into the "covenant chain" the tribes dwelling west of the Alleghanies, Those about Lake Erie and the Upper Ohio had been friendly to the English during the last war.

The Governor of Canada, Count de la Galissonière, appointed in 1747, urged on the French ministry the policy of sending out competent engineers to build forts from Detroit to the Mississippi, and to colonize the country west of the Alleghanies with large bodies of French peasantry. No movement was made toward carrying out this policy; and all that Galissonière could do was to send out men in 1749, to take formal possession of the territory west of the Alleghanies, a movement which more effectually wakened the British colonies to the danger, without securing anything to the French which they had not held before. Celoron de Bienville was put in charge of three hundred men for the purpose, and was directed to take with him representatives of the western tribes friendly to the French, that they might seem to give their consent to the French claims, and also be influenced to drive English traders out of the country.

Bienville carried with him leaden plates which he was to bury at every important point along the Ohio and the lake shore, as far as Detroit. These plates were engraved with the arms of France and a Latin inscription. Following is a translation of the legend on one which fell into the hands of a Mohawk chief and was brought to Colonel Johnson's house by him for explanation:—

In the year 1749, during the reign of Louis XV., King of France, we, Celoron, commander of a detachment sent by Monsieur the Marquis de la Galissonière, commander-in-chief of New France, for the restoration of tranquillity in some villages of Indians of these districts, have buried this plate at the confluence of the Ohio and Tchadakoin, the 29th of July, near the River Ohio, otherwise Beautiful River, as a monument of the renewal of possession which we have taken of the said River Ohio, and of all those that therein fall, and of all the land on both sides, as far as the sources of said rivers, as enjoyed, or ought to be enjoyed, by the preceding kings of France, and as they therein have maintained themselves by arms and by treaties, especially by those of Ryswick, of Utrecht, and of Aix-la-Chapelle.

While the French were thus burying leaden plates, and decorating forest trees with the lilies of France, and sending armed men into the Ohio Valley to expel English traders from the disputed lands, the English colonies were anxiously considering the feasibility of forming settlements west of the Alleghanies. And while the colonists of the two nations were jealously watching each other, the Indians were jealously watching them all. The burial of the leaden plates roused their indignation against the French, who, they were sure, were trying to steal their country away from them. And they watched with equal distrust the steady progress of the settlements of Pennsylvania and Virginia.

The western slopes of the Alleghany Mountains were occupied by the Delawares and Shawnees, both of which nations had been conquered by the Iroquois and were subject to those fierce warriors, who exacted from them a tribute and would not allow them to bear arms. The Delawares, who had originally lived on the banks of the river which bears their name, sold parts of their land to William Penn, whose treatment of them was always humane and friendly; and they remained on the lands they still retained in amicable relations with the settlers. But as the colony grew, and more lands were needed, the Delawares were crowded back. Old title-deeds were brought forward by the proprietaries, and new interpretations put upon them, making them cover great tracts of land never intended by the savages who gave them.

One of these was called "the walking purchase." An old deed executed in the seventeenth century was brought forward in the eighteenth, and lands were claimed by right of it which the bewildered Delawares supposed they had reserved for themselves. The land conveyed was to be a triangle bounded on one side by the Delaware River, on another side by one of its branches to the distance from its mouth that a man could walk in a day and a half, and on the third by a straight line drawn from the point reached by the walker back to the Delaware. Bringing forward this deed, the proprietaries had a path cut along the margin of the creek, that there might be no obstructions or rough places in the way; then they trained a man according to the most approved methods for pedestrians, and when he had walked his day and a half after his training, they drew the line, not directly eastward to the nearest point on the Delaware, but in a long slope to the northeast, forming the broadest possible angle where it met the creek, and the narrowest possible where it met the river.

The Delawares refused to obey the notice to quit, as they had no knowledge of any title to the lands but their own, acquired by ages of possession. The Pennsylvanians sent for the Iroquois to enforce their demand. The Iroquois despatched some chiefs to settle the affair, who took the side of the English, browbeat the poor Delawares most unmercifully, and ordered them to go either to Shamokin or Wyoming. The Delawares, afraid to disobey their conquerors, moved to Shamokin and Wyoming on the Susquehanna, and as the encroachments of settlers continued, many of them with the Shawnees passed on still farther west, until now they were living about the headwaters of the Ohio. Remembering with regret their home on the Delaware, and with anger their wrongful dispossession, they were predisposed to join the French against their former friends.

In 1748, the Ohio Company was formed, for the purpose of planting settlements in the Ohio valley. It was composed of gentlemen of the provinces of Virginia and Maryland, and some in England. Among the stockholders were Lawrence and Augustine Washington, half-brothers of George. The king granted the company five hundred thousand acres of land west of the Alleghanies, south of the upper Ohio. It was designed to open a route from the settlements on the company's tract to the Atlantic coast, by connecting the headwaters of the Monongahela and the Youghiogheny with those of the Potomac, by short roads.

The Company sent out Christopher Gist to examine the country as far west as the Falls of the Ohio, to look out favourable sites for settlements and mark the passes of the mountains, the courses of the rivers, and the strength and disposition of the Indians. Gist found most of them disposed to be friendly to the English, but unwilling to commit themselves to an alliance until they could meet in a general council of all their nations. He and his men pushed on to the west, and were the first explorers of Southern Ohio. At Picqua, the chief city of the Miamis, they were invited to a council and promised the friendship of the nation. Some Ottawas came before the council broke up, with offers of amity from the French, but were sent away with the answer that the Miamis looked upon the English as their brothers and regarded as done to themselves all the hostile acts committed by the

48TH REGIMENT FOOT, 1751

GRENADIERS 44TH REGIMENT
FOOT, 1751

French against those brothers. Several English traders had been seized by order of the Governor of Canada and sent to the French fort at Otsanderket, or Sandusky.

Having gone as far as Louisville, Gist returned by a more southerly route, ascending the Kentucky. He had been instructed to invite the Indians to a conference at Logstown, about seventeen miles down the Ohio from the site of Pittsburg. In 1752 they came, and a treaty was made, the Indians agreeing not to molest settlements on the lands granted to the Ohio Company, but carefully avoiding any acknowledgment of the title of the English to the territory. The company built a station and made some roads, and a few settlers, among whom was Gist, went into the country and founded a colony between the Monongahela and the Youghiogheny, beyond Laurel Point.

In the summer of 1752, two Frenchmen led a party of over two hundred Indians against the Miamis, to force them to give up the six English traders among them and renounce the English alliance. Most of the warriors were away on a hunting-expedition; but the king refused to give up the traders, and in the assault that followed they were bravely defended by the few who had remained at home. The Miamis were defeated, however, their captured king was killed and eaten, and the French flag was raised over the deserted fort.

Most of the Indians of the West were ready to take up arms with the French; and the Miamis urged the English to carry out the plan of building a fort on the Ohio. But the colonies could not or would not bear the expense; and England did nothing, except to declare that the valley of the Ohio was a part of Virginia, and the encroachments of the French were to be regarded as acts of hostility. A few guns sent over from the ordnance stores were all the substantial aid received. It was intimated that the militia of Virginia ought to be able to maintain her rights.

The government of Canada was now under the Marquis Du Quesne, who determined to drive the English back from the Ohio, and for that purpose prepared a strong party of troops to establish posts on that river. Accompanied by a large force of Indians they ascended the St. Lawrence in the spring of 1753, and crossed the lakes to Presqu' Isle, on the site of Erie. A hunting-party of Iroquois on the banks of the St. Lawrence hastened to send the news to the grand council at Onondaga.

Messengers were sent out to warn the Miamis and the other friends of the Iroquois in Ohio, and runners carried the intelligence to Colonel William Johnson on the Mohawk in forty-eight hours. The Ohio tribes sent envoys to Niagara and Presqu' Isle, warning the French not to invade their country; but the French commander threw back the *wampum* belts before the faces of the envoys, and told them the land was his and he meant to have it. He established and fortified posts at Waterford, south of Erie, and at Venango, now Franklin, at the junction of French Creek with the Alleghany.

When the news of these proceedings reached Virginia, Robert Dinwiddie, the lieutenant-governor, determined to send a messenger to ask the French why they were invading the British dominions "while a solid peace subsisted," and for his envoy he selected George Washington, then twenty-one years of age and Adjutant-General of the State militia. As a surveyor he had grown familiar with forest life and learned something of the ways of the Indians He started on his mission late in October, with an interpreter, Christopher Gist as guide, and four other attendants. Passing the junction of the Alleghany and Monongahela, where he noted the military importance of the place, he pushed on to Logstown, and met some Delaware and Miami chiefs in council, who agreed to ally themselves with the English, if the French should still persist in their efforts to occupy the land.

A part of the chiefs went on with Washington to Venango. The boasts of the officers there intimidated some of the Delawares, but the Half-King, chief of the Miamis, gave up the belt that symbolised his peace with the French. Washington was directed to proceed to Fort Le Boeuf, at Waterford, where he would find the commanding officer. Toiling slowly up the river through the snow and mud, crossing swollen streams by bridges which they made themselves of felled trees, the messengers arrived at the newly-built fort, surrounded by the bark-roofed log cabins that served as barracks for the soldiers, who were busily employed in making bark canoes and pine boats for the descent of the river.

Legardeur de St. Pierre, the commander, received Washington with courtesy, but told him it was his business to take possession of the country, according to the orders of his superior, and that he purposed to do it to the best of his ability, and should seize every Englishman he found in the Ohio valley. As to the question of the rights of the two nations, it was not his place to discuss that; but he would forward the message of the Governor of Virginia to the Governor of Canada.

Having made the most of his opportunities for noting the numbers of the French and the strength and plans of their fortifications,

ROBERT DINWIDDIE

WILLIAM SHIRLEY

Washington set out with his men to return. The difficulties of the way were increased by the advancing winter. When they came to the place where the horses were left, they found them so weak that they continued their way on foot. Washington was so anxious to get back that he and Gist left the circuitous route by way of the streams, and with a compass to guide them took a straight course for the fork of the rivers. Washington was twice in danger of his life.

He was fired upon by a hidden Indian from a distance of not over fifteen steps and narrowly missed. The Indian was taken, and Gist would have killed him, but Washington forbade it, and released him. Again, after they had spent a day in making a raft, the raft was caught in the floating ice. Washington thrust out the setting-pole to stop it, and was thrown into the water, but saved himself by grasping one of the logs that formed the raft.

The answer of St. Pierre led to prompt action by the Virginia authorities. It was determined to build a fort at the head of the Ohio, and ten thousand pounds were voted for the purpose by the Assembly. Other provinces were called upon for aid, but most of the burden fell upon Virginia. A company of thirty-three workmen, sent out in haste to begin the fort and hold the place before the French should arrive, had scarcely begun, when they were surprised by an army of six hundred French and Indians under Contrecoeur, and summoned to surrender. Of course, there was no alternative; they gave up the place and were allowed to retire. The date of the surrender, April 17th, 1754, is usually taken as the beginning of the "Old French War."

Meanwhile a regiment of militia was hastily collected at Alexandria, and sent out under Colonel Joshua Fry, with Washington second in command. Washington went in advance with a part of the force early in April, and had reached Wills' Creek, near Cumberland, when he was met by the returning party from the head of the Ohio. He sent messengers to the governors of Maryland, Virginia, and Pennsylvania, asking for re-enforcements, and then went on without waiting for Colonel Fry with the remainder of the troops, intending to entrench himself on the Monongahela at the mouth of Red Stone Creek and there await the re-enforcements. He would then have been thirty-seven miles from the head of the Ohio.

The French commander, Contrecoeur, set his men at work to finish the fortifications the English had begun, and named the place Fort Du Quesne, in honour of the Governor-General of Canada. More men soon arrived, and St. Pierre sent out a scouting party under Jumonville to meet the advance of the English. Hearing by messengers from the Half-King that this party was lurking in the woods, Washington stopped at a place called the Great Meadows. During the night he advanced, surprised the Jumonville party, and completely defeated them, after an action of fifteen minutes. Ten of the French, including Jumonville, were killed, and twenty-one, more than half of them, taken prisoners. This action, which took place April 23rd, 1754, was the first fighting of the war in the Ohio valley.

Washington had thrown up a hasty entrenchment at Great Meadows, in a little hollow between two hills covered with trees, and after the fight with Jumonville he strengthened the fortifications, and named the place Fort Necessity. While waiting for re-enforcements, he employed his men in clearing a road toward Fort Du Quesne; but hearing that a large body of the French were on the way to meet him, he fell back to his fort, where he was attacked on the 3rd of July. The attacking party, consisting of six hundred French soldiers and a hundred Indians, was commanded by Villiers, who was resolved to avenge the death of his brother, Jumonville.

They took possession of one of the hills, and, sheltering themselves behind the trees, fired upon the English works below. Washington had but four hundred men, and a greatly inferior position; but he and his men made a stubborn resistance, fighting bravely for nine hours. Then the French sounded a parley and offered terms. The fort was surrendered, and the next day Washington's men, with their arms, and baggage, retired to the east of the Alleghanies, according to the terms of the capitulation. The Americans lost thirty men in the action, and the French three. By this defeat the English flag was banished from the Ohio valley. Washington began works on Wills' Creek, which were afterward completed and named Fort Cumberland.

These hostilities led to remonstrances and protests between the French and English Governments. Each declared a desire for peace and reconciliation, but war seemed inevitable, and both prepared for it. The English Government sent directions to the colonies to allow no encroachments by the French; and the Governor of New York was directed to call a council of Iroquois chiefs and bind them to the English interests by conciliation and presents.

A congress, therefore, assembled at Albany on June 19th, 1754, commissioners coming from all the colonies as far south as Maryland. Deputies from the Six Nations were also present. Gifts were scattered among them in great profusion, and they renewed their compact with

FRENCH ENCAMPMENT ATTACKED BY GEORGE WASHINGTON FROM FORT NECESSITY the English; but still there was widespread disaffection among them toward their old allies. The French establishment at Oswegatchie had drawn off half the Onondagas, and the Mohawks were indignant at what they considered trespass on their lands by English surveyors. The chiefs boldly reproached the English with their inaction and the slow progress of their preparations. A Mohawk chief said:—

> Look at the French, they are men; they are fortifying everywhere; it is but one step from Canada hither, and they may easily come and turn you out of doors.

The Iroquois claimed the lands occupied by the Delawares and Shawnoes, by right of their conquest of those nations. The Delawares and Shawnoes were still wavering, and might perhaps have been saved to the English, but the Pennsylvania agents took advantage of the assembling of Iroquois at the congress, and induced them to convey to themselves large tracts of land occupied by the conquered tribes. Those Indians heard of the transfer with great indignation, and were easily won over to the French. The council at Albany was memorable from the fact that it projected a confederacy of the American colonies.

Benjamin Franklin, a delegate from Pennsylvania, had made notes for a plan of union while on his journey to Albany, and when he arrived there, he found that some of the other commissioners had also thought out plans for the same purpose. Franklin's plan was substantially adopted, after much deliberation. Philadelphia was to be the seat of government. The President, or governor-general, was to be appointed by the king, and was to have a veto power on all measures of the Grand Council, The council was to be elected once in three years by the legislatures of the colonies, and to meet every year.

The number of delegates from each colony was to vary from two to seven. General matters of war, trade, and taxes were to be under the control of the council. The plan was favoured neither by the colonies, who thought it gave too much power to the President appointed by the Crown, nor by the Board of Trade in England, who rejected it on account of the power it gave to the people of the colonies; but it foreshadowed the union of the Americans, which resulted in their independence less than thirty years later.

CHAPTER 12

Braddock's Defeat

The English ministry now resolved upon a plan for attacking the French by four expeditions at about the same time, hoping to defeat them at every point where they had encroached on English claims, and drive them finally and forever from the disputed territory. The four expeditions were to move against the French in Acadia, at Fort Niagara, at Fort Du Quesne, and at Crown Point. The result of the operations in Acadia has already been detailed. The expedition assigned to the attack of Fort Niagara never reached its destination. That against Fort Du Quesne was most actively carried out, and most influential in its results. (See *Braddock's Campaign 1755: the Fort Duquesne Expedition During the French & Indian War* by Winthrop Sargent; Leonaur 2018.)

While these preparations were going on, England and France were nominally at peace. Both were sending troops to America, but both professed to be taking measures for defence only. In January, 1755, negotiations passed between the two countries on the subject of the boundaries. France proposed that the Ohio valley be left as it was before the last war; England proposed that it be left as it was at the Treaty of Utrecht in 1713. Then France proposed that the territory between the Ohio and the Alleghanies be left neutral, by which she would then have had all north of the Ohio and far on to the west, while the neutral country would have kept back the English settlers.

England then demanded that twenty leagues on each side of the Bay of Fundy should be added to the territory conceded by the French as belonging to Nova Scotia, and the country northward to the St. Lawrence be left neutral; that the French forts at Crown Point and Niagara, and all those between the Alleghanies and the Wabash, should be destroyed. Of course, the French would make no such concessions; but some show of negotiations was still kept up, while the warlike movements went on.

Six thousand men had been sent out from England for service in America. They were under General Edward Braddock, who was made commander-in-chief of all the forces in North America, Governor Shirley and Sir William Pepperell to be associated with him as next in command. Braddock had been in service on the Continent, and his military record was good. About three months after he sailed, a force of three thousand men was despatched from France to Canada, under Baron Dieskau.

Admiral Boscawen was sent to the Banks of Newfoundland to intercept the French squadron. Three of the French ships, the *Lys*, the *Alcide*, and the *Dauphin*, were separated from the rest and enveloped in the fogs of the Newfoundland coast, and when the fogs cleared away, on the morning of the 8th of June, they found the English fleet close upon them. "Are we at peace or war?" asked the commander of the *Alcide*. In reply Boscawen commanded his men to fire, and after a short engagement the *Lys* and the *Alcide* struck their colours. The *Dauphin* escaped to the harbour of Louisbourg. This affair naturally excited great indignation in France, and the French ambassador at the English court was withdrawn. In England it was not disapproved of, although it had been steadily asserted that only defensive measures for the protection of the English frontiers were to be taken.

Braddock arrived at Hampton Roads in February, 1755. In April he called a conference of the governors of the provinces to meet him for the purpose of raising a common fund for carrying on the war; but they were unable to pledge the support demanded of them. Virginia, whose frontiers were in the greatest danger, was most zealous in rendering assistance, and later Franklin used his influence in Pennsylvania to supply the pressing want of horses and wagons. Colonel William Johnson, at the suggestion of Braddock, was asked to treat with the Six Nations and take charge of the expedition against Crown Point. The governors agreed to raise eight hundred pounds for presents to the Iroquois, and Johnson consented to negotiate the treaty, though reluctantly, on account of the carelessness the English had previously shown in regard to the observance of their agreements with the Indians.

Braddock was full of confidence as to the result of his enterprise. He had great faith in himself, in "the king's regular troops," and in the tactics of war as he had learned them, great contempt for the provincials who were to serve in his army, and not the slightest suspicion that men who had spent their lives among the Indians could tell him any-

MAJOR ROBERT ROGERS,
Commander in Chief of the INDIANS in the Back Settlements of AMERICA.

RANGER IN WARM WEATHER UNIFORM

thing of value about savage methods of warfare. He sent despatches to the English ministry, promising speedy success. To Franklin he said:—

I shall hardly need to stop more than three or four days at Fort Du Quesne; then I shall march on to Niagara, and from there to Frontenac.

Franklin answered:—

To be sure, sir, if you arrive well before Du Quesne with those fine troops, so well provided with artillery, that place, not completely fortified, and, as we hear, with no very strong garrison, can probably make but a short resistance. The only danger I apprehend of obstruction to your march is from ambuscades of Indians, who, by constant practice, are dexterous in laying and executing them; and the slender line, near four miles long, which your army must make, may expose it to be attacked by surprise in its flanks, and to be cut like a thread into several pieces, which, from their distance cannot come up in time to support each other.

Franklin says Braddock smiled at his ignorance, and answered:—

These savages may, indeed, be a formidable enemy to your raw American militia; but upon the king's regular and disciplined troops, sir, it is impossible they should make any impression.

He paid no attention to Washington's advice that he should secure the aid of one hundred Indians under the interpreter Croghan, and treated them so scornfully that they withdrew in anger.

The troops were all gathered at Fort Cumberland, on Wills' Creek. Braddock spent some weeks there in preparations, disciplining the provincial troops to make them as much like regulars as possible, and disgusted with his slender success. He wrote in one of his letters:—

The American troops have little courage or goodwill. I expect almost no military service from them, though I have employed the best officers to drill them.

The wagons and horses procured by Franklin at last arrived, and on the 7th of June the army was ready to march. There were one thousand of Braddock's regular soldiers, twelve hundred of the provincial militia, a few sailors, and a few Indians. Washington was made an *aide-de-camp*. Two companies from New York were under the command

FORT CUMBERLAND AND WILLS' CREEK

of Horatio Gates, afterward famous as the American commander at Saratoga; one of the wagons was owned and driven by Daniel Morgan, destined to render important service in South Carolina during the Revolutionary War; and there was Hugh Mercer, who was to fall at Princeton. Side by side with these future leaders of the American rebels was Lieutenant-Colonel Thomas Gage, the future commander of the king's forces in their struggle with his rebellious subjects.

Many of the French troops had been sent away from Fort Du Quesne; but on the news of the English expedition re-enforcements were summoned, and the slowness of Braddock's march gave them ample time to reach the fort. The route through Pennsylvania would have been much shorter than that through Virginia. But the former expedition of Washington had taken the route by way of Wills' Creek, and the shorter route seems scarcely to have been considered. Five hundred men had been sent forward the last day of May to open the road, and carry stores to Little Meadows. The rest of the army moved slowly, making only five miles in three days. (See *Washington's Early Campaigns* by James Hadden; Leonaur, 2009.)

Washington looked on with impatience, while Braddock insisted on moving exactly in accordance with the methods practised in European warfare, he says:—

We halted to level every mole-hill and bridge every brook, by which means we were four days in getting twelve miles.

Even after the road had been widened by the advancing axe-men, it was almost impossible for the horses to drag the heavy wagons loaded with useless baggage through the miry ravines and over the rocks and stumps of trees, and they grew weak with the fatigue and the insufficient food afforded by the wild grass. After crossing the Great Savage Mountain, and toiling painfully through the thick gloom of the Shades of Death, the army reached Little Meadows, where some attempt at fortification had been made by the five hundred axe-men.

Here a council of war was held, and Washington's suggestion was adopted, that twelve hundred men should be selected to push on in advance with the artillery and the lighter baggage. Braddock went on with the twelve hundred, leaving the remainder, with the heavy wagons, in charge of Colonel Dunbar. Even then the progress of the advance party was very slow, and it was not until the 8th of July that they arrived at the fork of the Monongahela and Youghiogeny Rivers, twelve miles from Fort Du Quesne, where they encamped on a stream

BRADDOCK'S ARMY AT THE RIVER MONONGAHELA

known as Crooked Run. Braddock had at first refused to send forward any Indians as scouts; now it was with great difficulty that he could induce any of the few remaining with him to undertake the perilous task. Their march was haunted by the skulking allies of the French, who picked off stragglers and faithfully reported every movement of the British Army at Fort Du Quesne.

Braddock's men were now on the same side of the Monongahela as the fort—that is, on the eastern side; but a high rocky ridge very near the river on that side left such a narrow defile beside the stream, that the general thought best to cross at a ford near his camp, and, reaching a point above the narrow defile, to recross at a second ford at the mouth of Turtle Creek, eight miles below the fort. Early on the morning of the 9th of July, the army crossed the upper ford, and marched splendidly down the river in their scarlet uniform, with drums beating and colours flying, the finest spectacle, Washington said long years afterward, that he had ever witnessed.

At noon they recrossed the river, and entered a woody and hilly country cut through by three deep ravines, with seven miles yet to march. Gage led on a detachment through the narrow path, attended by the engineers with the workmen.

Indian scouts had carried swift intelligence of the English advance to Fort Du Quesne, and Contrecoeur, thinking it would be impossible to hold out against such an army, talked of retreat. But one of his captains, Beaujeu, advised sending out a party of soldiers and Indians to form an ambuscade, Contrecoeur consented, and the Indians were called together from their bark huts around the fort.

Not one was willing to follow Beaujeu in the dangerous undertaking, and he gave it up for the time. Another invitation met with an answer no more favourable; but the third time, when he said, "I am determined to go; and will you let your father go alone?" a sudden enthusiasm seized them, and they were ready to follow.

On the morning of the 9th, Beaujeu, Dumas, and Lignery led out more than eight hundred men, of whom six hundred were Indians. Among the Indians was the chief Pontiac, afterward well known in American history. The English Army was moving on without a single scout to give warning of the danger, when it was suddenly confronted by the fantastic figure of Beaujeu in a fringed hunting-dress and wearing on his neck a silver gorget, closely followed down the hill by a multitude of white men and savages. Beaujeu gave the word of command, and the Indians dropped into the ravines and joined the French

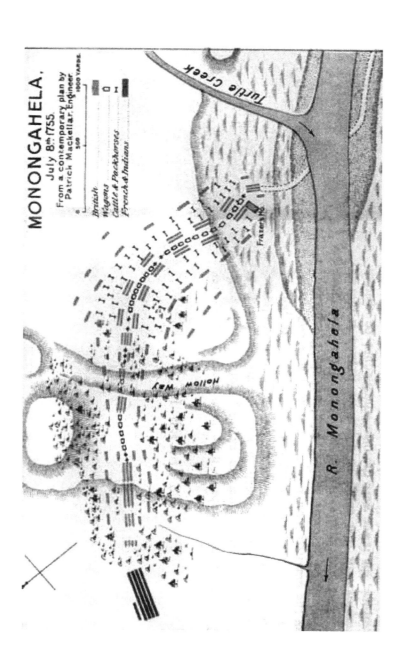

MONONGAHELA.
July 8th 1755.
From a contemporary plan by
Patrick Mackellar. Engineer.

0   500   1000 YARDS.

British
Wagons
Cattle & Packhorses
French & Indians

Turtle Creek

Fraser's Ho.

Hollow Way

R. Monongahela

on the hill in a murderous fire on the British regulars, who, though bewildered by the hideous yells and shrieks that arose from the ravines, returned the fire, and Beaujeu was one of the first to fall dead.

His loss dismayed the Indians, and they began to fly, but were rallied by Dumas, who sent them to attack the flanks of the English Army, while the French soldiers kept up the fire in front. Hiding behind the trees, the Indians picked off the Englishmen with unerring aim. A reinforcement was sent on by Braddock; but the advance party was driven back, leaving two of their pieces to the enemy, and meeting the reinforcements which were attempting to form, they became mingled and confused with them, and the entire force was thrown into disorder and unable to effect anything.

Braddock pushed bravely forward, and rode hither and thither, issuing commands, and trying to inspire his troops with his own courage. Four horses were shot under him, but again he mounted and again renewed his efforts. His officers were not outdone in bravery. Washington had two horses shot under him and his clothing torn by bullets; Gates was shot through the body; and only twenty-three of the eighty-six officers escaped unhurt. Twenty-six were killed and thirty-seven wounded. But the English troops were panic-stricken; they would not follow their officers; they loaded their muskets and fired upon their own comrades, or into the empty air. The provincials, understanding better the methods of the Indians, maintained their self-control, and, stationing themselves behind trees, returned the fire in the Indian method from the cover.

Washington urged Braddock to order all the men to fight in that way; but still the general could not see that there was any occasion for setting aside the rules of regular warfare. He drove the men out from their hiding-places, and insisted that they should form in platoons. At length he fell, mortally wounded, but continued to give orders as he lay bleeding on the ground.

After three hours of such fighting, during which half the men were killed or wounded, the soldiers, in an uncontrollable panic, rushed back from the field and fled in confusion across the river, throwing away their arms, Braddock was carried from the field by some provincials. The enemy did not follow across the river, but returned to the field to secure the plunder. Braddock's orders brought his men to a stand, but they were too frightened to maintain it, and broke once more into a straggling retreat, and on the 11th reached the reserves at the camp. The panic spread to Dunbar's men; all the stores at the camp

The shooting of General Braddock

were destroyed, and the whole army fled helpless through the woods, and past the settlements toward Philadelphia.

Braddock lay, in a lethargy, rousing himself at times to give commands, and once murmuring, "Who would have thought it? Who would have thought it?" Shortly before he died, on the night of the 13th, he turned to his lieutenant and said, "We shall better know how to deal with them another time."

The soldiers made his grave at Great Meadows, near Fort Necessity, where it still may be seen. The lower ford, where his army crossed to the fatal field, is known as Braddock's Ford.

The news of this defeat carried dismay through the provinces. It left the frontier settlements of Pennsylvania and Virginia open and unprotected from the Indians; and every unusual noise, even the maudlin howl of a drunken man in the streets, was thought by the terrified inhabitants to be the deadly yell that heralded the tomahawk and the scalping-knife. In August, Washington was appointed Commander-in-Chief of all the forces of the colony. His conduct during Braddock's expedition had brought him to the favourable notice of the country, and attracted attention in England. He had, it is said, been marked by an Indian chief, who persistently aimed at him, and told some of his warriors to do the same. Failing to bring him down, they concluded that some powerful *manitou* was watching over his life. A clergyman, Rev. Samuel Davis, said in a sermon:—

I point out that heroic youth. Colonel Washington, whom I cannot but hope Providence has preserved in so signal a manner for some important service to his country.

And Lord Halifax said:—

Who is Mr. Washington? I know nothing of him but that they say he behaved in Braddock's action as if he really loved the whistling of bullets.

One of the most disastrous results of the defeat was its effect upon the Indians. It inspired them with contempt for the English soldiers and respect for the military ability of the French. It decided the defection of the Delawares and Shawnoes, and incited them to petty ravages on the border. Scarooyadi, successor to the Half-King, refused to listen to French persuasions, and remained true to the English. He said:—

The defeat was due to the pride and ignorance of that great general that came from England. He is now dead; but he was a bad man when he was alive. He looked upon us as dogs, and would never hear anything that was said to him. We often endeavoured to advise him, and tell him of the danger he was in with his soldiers; but he never appeared pleased with us, and that was the reason that a great many of our warriors left him.

Washington was anxious to secure the aid of the Indians; and Scarooyadi was willing to go out at once, he said:—

Let us unite our strength. You are numerous, and the governors along the seashore can raise men enough; but don't let those from over the seas be concerned any more. They are unfit to fight in the woods. Let us go out ourselves, we that came out of this ground.

The Cherokees were also faithful to their friendship with the English colonies. Their chief proposed a conference with the Governor of South Carolina, notifying him of the attempts of the French and their allies to win over his nation. The governor met the principal Cherokee warriors in their own country, two hundred miles from Charleston; the alliance was renewed, and a large tract of land was ceded by the Cherokees to the colony. Fort Prince George, three hundred miles from Charleston, was built on the ceded lands.

CHAPTER 13

Battle of Lake George

The third expedition designed to establish the supremacy of England in the American territory which she claimed as her own, was to advance under Governor Shirley to attack Fort Niagara; and the fourth under Johnson to Fort Frederick at Crown Point. These two expeditions were to be composed of troops supplied by the northern colonies, and warriors of the Six Nations. In June nearly six thousand men were gathered at Albany. Among them were Israel Putnam, of Connecticut, who was to have so large a share in the deeds of the Revolutionary War; John Stark, of New Hampshire, destined to make himself famous at Bennington and Saratoga; and Ephraim Williams, of Massachusetts, who had just made a will at Albany by which he left a bequest to found the free school that is now Williams College.

After capturing Fort Du Quesne, Braddock was to march northward and meet Shirley at Niagara. The fort there was in poor condition; and Vaudreuil, Governor of Canada, was anxious for its safety, having heard from Indians of the preparations that were being made by the English. He wrote to the French minister:—

The preservation of Niagara, is what interests us the most; if our enemies should become masters of it and keep Chouaguen (Oswego), the Upper Countries would be lost to us, and besides we should have no more communication with the River Ohio.

But there was no immediate danger of the English becoming masters of Niagara; the news of Braddock's defeat was received before the last of Shirley's men had started up the Mohawk. They were to ascend the river in *bateaux*, and the *bateaux* were to be managed by forest-rangers who had been gathered for the expedition. The news of the

PART OF LAKE ONTARIO

THE RIVER

PLAN OF FORT NIAGARA,
with its ENVIRON.
Explanation.

A. *The Fort.*   E. *The Burying Place.*
B. *The Dock & Harbour.* F. *The Approaches.*
C. *Two Lime Kilns.*   G. *The First Battery.*
D. *The Brick Kiln.*   H. *The Second Battery.*
               I. *The Third Battery.*

Scale
40 Fathoms to an Inch

defeat so frightened them that many deserted; and when the army arrived at the carrying-place, at the head of the Mohawk, the men who were to transport the military stores by sledges also failed them.

The soldiers were disheartened, Shirley was slow and irresolute, and they did not reach Oswego till the 21st of August. A month was passed in building boats to take them across Lake Ontario; and just, as they were ready to embark, on the 18th of September, heavy rains and winds set in, and continued with little intermission for three weeks. Most of the Indians and some of the soldiers deserted, and sickness disabled many more. It was therefore decided that the attempt should be abandoned until the following year, that Colonel Mercer should be left at Oswego with seven hundred men, and Governor Shirley should return to Albany with the rest.

The French had designed to send their army under Baron Dieskau to take Oswego, expecting thereby to gain uninterrupted communication between their own forts, Frontenac and Niagara, at either end of Lake Ontario, and weaken the English influence over the Iroquois; and General Braddock's papers, which were captured, revealed the English plan of the campaign. Dieskau was about to start for Oswego with his army when information reached Montreal that Johnson's army was on its way toward Crown Point. Vaudreuil decided that it was of more importance to send the aid there than to attack Oswego; and Dieskau reluctantly consented to the change of plan. The French force assembled at Crown Point consisted of seven hundred regular troops, sixteen hundred Canadians, and seven hundred Indians, about half of the Indians being converted Iroquois from the mission villages of Canada.

The troops at Albany designed for Johnson's force were sent on early in July, under General Phinehas Lyman, and were occupied in building a fort on the eastern bank of the Hudson at the beginning of the portage to Lake George, which was named Fort Edward. On the 8th of August, Johnson set out from Albany with the artillery, *bateaux*, and provisions. He passed Fort Edward and encamped on the southern shore of Lake St. Sacrament, which he soon afterward named Lake George, in honour of George II. The camp was surrounded by woods and swamps on all sides except that which faced the lake.

It was Johnson's intention to build a fort at this point, and when his *bateaux* should arrive, to go up Lake Champlain to Ticonderoga, fortify that place, and then march against Fort Frederick. Ticonderoga is a point projecting into the lake, fifteen miles above Crown Point.

South View of Crown Point, 1760

But no fort was built, nor defences of any kind. The Indians came in slowly. The old Mohawk chief, Hendrick, told Johnson that Shirley had discouraged the warriors from enlisting under Johnson, between whom and himself there was a feeling of jealousy, and had tried to induce them to go with him to Oswego. But in time a large number of them regained their confidence in Johnson, and joined him in his camp. While the thirty-four hundred men were wasting their time in Johnson's camp, Dieskau's men were making active preparations at Crown Point for the expected attack.

After waiting some time, Dieskau resolved to advance toward the English Army, hoping to conquer it and leave the way open to Albany and Schenectady; he could then march on those places and cut off communication with Oswego, after which the capture of that place would be easy. Taking with him fifteen hundred men, six hundred of whom were Indians, and two hundred regulars, he went up the lake in boats, and landed at South Bay, on the present site of Whitehall. The army marched for three days, intending to attack Fort Edward. Halting on the road to Lake George, which had been taken by mistake instead of the one leading directly to Fort Edward, Dieskau sent a party of Indians to reconnoitre, who returned with the intelligence that their approach was known both at the fort and at the camp. The Indians, with their usual fear of cannon, were averse to attacking the fort, but were willing to advance against the camp. Dieskau assented, and marched toward Lake George.

When it was known in Johnson's camp that the French were approaching, warning was sent to Fort Edward. One of the messengers, a wagoner named Adams, was taken by the Indians and killed; the other returned with the intelligence that the enemy were about four miles north of the fort. A council of war was held the next morning, the 7th of September, and it was decided to send out a thousand troops and two hundred Indians to meet the enemy. Hendrick was the only one who saw the folly of the movement, he said. "If they are to be killed, they are too many; if they are to fight, they are too few." But Hendrick was overruled, and putting himself at the head of his Mohawks, he rode out to the fray at sunrise the next morning, the only mounted man of the party, unable, from his age and weight, to go on foot. The detachment was headed by Colonel Ephraim Williams.

As soon as Dieskau learned of their approach he prepared an ambuscade, arranging his men in a line which crossed the road and curved toward the advancing English on both sides of it. The French

AREA OF FORT EDWARD

troops were therefore disposed in the form of a horse-shoe, those at one end being hidden by a ridge covered with trees and bushes, and those at the other crouching in a swampy spot also concealed from the road by a thick undergrowth. When the English should have marched forward to where the French line crossed the road, Dieskau's men could close in on both sides and surround them.

As they entered the trap, Hendrick was riding in advance. He had gone some distance within the enclosing lines, but a part of the division was still without, when an Indian suddenly appeared close to him and said, "Whence came you?"

"From the Mohawks," answered Hendrick. "Whence came you?"

"From Montreal," was the reply, and immediately a shot was fired, contrary to the orders of Dieskau, who had directed his men to be quiet until the English were completely within the French line. The shot was the signal for a general assault, and the firing began on both sides and in front of the astonished troops. One moment they had been riding through a silent wilderness; the next they were surrounded by blazing muskets and whooping savages. Hendrick was one of the first who fell, Williams and many other officers shared his fate, and the command devolved upon Lieutenant Nathan Whiting.

The English gave way and retreated, fighting as they went, many of them spreading themselves out so as to oppose a wide front to the enemy, and darting from tree to tree where they could find shelter and fire upon their pursuers; the Canadians and Indians picking them off in the same way, and the French regulars advancing in a body and firing upon those who remained in a mass retreating along the road.

When the noise of the battle was heard at the camp, the soldiers there, who had at last begun the building of some hasty defences after Williams had gone out with his men in the morning, hurriedly dragged the cannon up from the lake shore and heaped up a breastwork of felled trees. A re-enforcement of three hundred men, under Lieutenant-Colonel Cole, was sent out to the help of the retreating division, and a stand was made at a little sheet of water, which received the name of Bloody Pond, and is pointed out as the grave of the unfortunate Frenchmen who fell upon its banks. Among them was the Chevalier Legardeur de St. Pierre, who was in command of the Indians. He was the officer to whom Washington delivered his letters from Governor Dinwiddie at Fort Le Boeuf.

When the fugitives reached the camp, they climbed over the breastwork of felled trees and wagons, and waited for the attack. Dies-

LAKE CHAMPLAIN

Crown Point

A MAP
of the
COUNTRY
between
CROWN POINT
and
FORT EDWARD.

N
E
W
Y
O
R
K

Ticonderoge

Snow

Wood Path from East & West

DROWN'D
LAND

Two Rocks

Sabath Day P.

Putnams Pond

N.W. Bay

LAKE GEORGE

Square I.
Round I.
Narrow

Long I.
Sloop

East Bay

South Bay

East Creek

Diskau's Path

Stone Creek

Fort Wm. Henry
Swamp

Hudsons River

Fort Edward

N
E
W
E
N
G
L
A
N
D

Miles

5   10   15

kau had intended to rush forward with the retreating division of the English and enter the camp at the same time. But the Indians halted as soon as they came in sight of the guns, and the Canadians followed their example. Dieskau advanced toward the centre of the camp with his regulars, and when the Indians and Canadians scattered themselves about the swamp and took shelter behind the trees instead of sustaining the regulars, he asked in disappointment, "Are these the boasted troops?"

The regulars, however, behaved well; they halted a hundred and fifty yards from the camp, and opened fire by platoons. It was about half-past eleven when the battle began. The three guns in the centre returned the fire of the French, and Johnson's men, sheltered behind the trees, picked off Dieskau's regulars with deadly precision. Johnson was slightly wounded in the beginning of the fight, and the command devolved upon Lyman, who conducted the defence with the greatest spirit and bravery. Unable to stand the fire, the French regulars went to each side of the camp in succession, and fired into it, but without much effect.

Excited and emboldened by their success, and re-enforced by the Mohawks, who had fled when the French appeared in sight of the camp, the Americans leaped over their defences and fought hand-to-hand. They had no bayonets, but they struck with their muskets, and clubbed and beat so furiously that nearly all the regulars who had survived their fire were knocked down and killed. Dieskau, wounded three times during the action, would not be carried away, but seated himself on the stump of a tree exposed to the fire, and tried to direct the movements of his men. When they were driven into a disorderly retreat, he was left on the field. As they were flying, he put his hand into his pocket, intending to take out his watch and give it to one of the pursuers who was about to capture him; but the man supposed he was drawing his pistol, and hastily fired, inflicting an incurable wound.

Lyman would have followed up the retreat, and a close pursuit might have resulted in the capture of almost the entire army; for two hundred troops were on the way from Fort Edward under the command of Captain Macginnis, and the French soldiers would have been caught between the two parties. But Johnson gave orders to call back the men; and when the French found themselves secure from pursuit they halted beside Rocky Brook. Here the half-starved men were preparing supper when the detachment from the fort fell upon them and put them to flight, after a sharp engagement, in which Macginnis

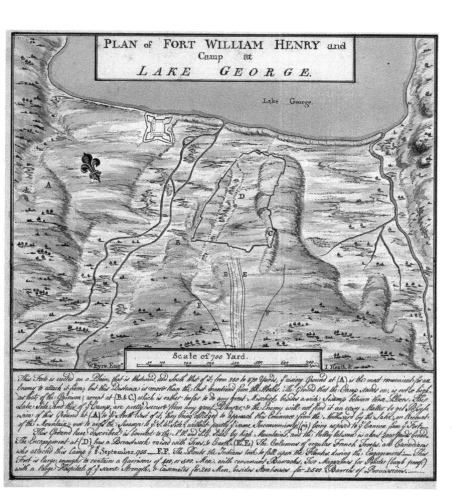

PLAN of FORT WILLIAM HENRY and
Camp at
LAKE GEORGE.

Lake George.

Scale of 700 Yard.

W. Eyre, Eng.   I. Heath, d.

This Forte is erected on a Plain, that is Washed, on South West of it, from 280 to 370 Yards, of rising Ground at (A) is the most convenient for an Enemy to attack it from; but this Distance is more than the least mentioned from the Works. The Ground that the Camp stands on, is not so high at that of the Garrison, except at (B & C.) which is rather too far to do any great Mischief, besides a wide Swamp between those Places. The Lake Side, and that of the Camp, are pretty secure from any great Danger; to the Enemy will not find it an easy Matter to get Posession of this Ground at (A) to the North West of it, they being obliged to approach that Eminence from the Northward by the Lable, on Accounts of the Mountains; nor to cross the Swamp to the S.E. Side, without purely of some Inconveniences (or) being exposed to the Cannon from the Fort.

This Ground here described, is bounded to the N.W. and S.E. Side by high Mountains, and the Valley between is about 400 Yards broad. The Encampment at (D) has a Breastwork raised with Trees, & Earth. (E, E.) The Columns of regular French Troops, and Canadians who attacked this Camp the 8 September 1755. F.F. The Route the Indians took to fall upon the Flanks during the Engagement. This Fort is large, enough to contain a Garrison of 400, or 500. Men, with convenient Barracks, Two Magazines for Powder (bomb proof) with a large Hospital of a scant Strength, & Casemates for 200 Men, besides Storehouses for 2500 Barrels of Provisions.

was mortally wounded. The French baggage and ammunition were captured.

The Battle of Lake George, resulting in a victory so complete, revived the spirit of the English colonists from the depressing effects of Braddock's defeat. Although the victory was not followed up by the occupation of Ticonderoga and the capture of Crown Point, the original object of the expedition, the country looked upon it as a great success. Johnson received a baronetcy and five thousand pounds from England, to reward him for the victory, which was largely due to Lyman. Dieskau was sent to England a prisoner, but returned to France at the peace of 1763, and not long afterward died from the effect of his wound.

During the autumn Johnson kept his men at work strengthening their position, and built a stockade fort at the south end of Lake George, which was called Fort William Henry. At the approach of winter, he garrisoned that and Fort Edward, and allowed the rest of the provincial soldiers to return to their homes. The French took possession of the important post of Ticonderoga, and busied themselves in fortifying it; two thousand soldiers were said to be assembled there in the autumn, with a large body of Indians.

But war had not even yet been declared between the two countries whose colonists were thus meeting on battlefields in the new world, aided by regular troops from over the seas. These hostilities were carried on under the name of measures of defence, by which each side professed to resist the aggressions of the other on territory of which it claimed the rightful ownership. The French, however, deeply resented the capture of their two ships by Admiral Boscawen, an act which could not be defended on any such ground; and they soon had still more cause for resentment. Sir Edward Hawke was sent out with a fleet under orders to take all French ships he met with, whether men-of-war or merchantmen; and letters of marque were issued to cruisers.

Great numbers of French vessels were on the return from Martinique with the products of the Jesuit plantations, and the fishing-boats were on their way from Newfoundland and the Labrador coast, laden with the results of the summer's work. Before the end of the year three hundred French vessels and seven or eight thousand French sailors had been carried into English ports. The king's share of the spoils amounted to seven hundred thousand pounds.

This alone was enough to bring on a war. But the French were not ready; and they returned an English man-of-war which had been

Battle of Lake George

taken by some French ships, protesting against the acts of England on the seas and stigmatising them as piracy. Preparations for the inevitable war went on, both nations seeking alliances among the other powers of Europe, appealing to the resentments, the prejudices, and the cupidity of their sovereigns. Prussia joined with England; Austria, Russia, and Saxony were on the side of France. In the general European struggle which followed, known as the Seven Years' War, the events of the colonial war in America were but lightly considered, though they determined the fortunes of a continent.

Governor Shirley was still continued at the head of affairs, though it began to be evident that his military capacity was by no means brilliant. He called a council of governors in the city of New York in December, 1755, and laid out a plan for the campaign of the ensuing year, substantially the same as that which had been arranged for that year, nothing having been effected but the conquest of Acadia. Forts Du Quesne, Frederick, and Niagara still remained to be taken; and expeditions for their capture were determined on for the coming summer, while a force was to move up the Kennebec to the settlements on the Chaudière.

CHAPTER 14

French Successes

War was at length declared by England, May 17th, 1756. Governor Shirley was removed from the command of the forces in America, and a still more incapable officer was appointed to the place, the Earl of Loudoun. Lord Loudoun's chief recommendation for the post was his zeal for the assertion of the rights of the mother-country over her colonies. He was also appointed Governor of the Dominion of Virginia, and his power as military chief was supreme over all the colonial governments. The provincial soldiers were to be put under officers of the regular army whom Loudoun might appoint; and he was given authority to quarter his soldiers on the inhabitants of the colonies at will.

General James Abercrombie was to be second in command. One hundred and fifteen thousand pounds was voted to the northern provinces to reimburse them for the campaign of 1755; at the same time they were forbidden to negotiate with the Indians, all dealings with whom were to be left to Sir William Johnson, who was responsible alone to Lord Loudoun.

Loudoun's slowness and indecision, combined with a great affectation of business habits, are exhibited by a story of Franklin, who went to New York in the beginning of April to sail for Europe in a packet which was to set out immediately, but was kept waiting till the end of June for his lordship's letters, which were always to be ready tomorrow; Franklin says:—

And yet, whoever waited on him found him always at his desk, pen in hand, and concluded he must needs write abundantly.

One morning while he was waiting for the ship's departure Franklin met in the earl's antechamber a messenger from Philadelphia named Innis, with a packet of letters from the governor to the earl.

Franklin wished to send back some letters by him to Philadelphia; and Innis told him he was to call the next morning at nine for Lord Loudoun's answer to the governor, and should then set out at once. Franklin prepared his letters and gave them to Innis the same day. Franklin continues:—

> A fortnight after, I met him again in the same place. 'So, you are soon returned, Innis,'—'Returned! no, I am not gone yet.'— 'How so?'—'I have called here this and every morning these two weeks past for his lordship's letters, and they are not yet ready.'—'Is it possible, when he is so great a writer? for I see him constantly at his *escritoire*.'—'Yes,' said Innis, 'but he is like St. George on the signs—always on horseback, but never rides on.'

The same characteristic was manifested in all of the earl's proceedings. Abercrombie was to go in advance with two battalions, but it was the middle of June before he reached New York. On the 25th he was in Albany. Oswego was threatened by the French, and he was urged to relieve it at once. Men, stores, and boats were ready, but Abercrombie was not. He was busy with preparations to quarter his soldiers on the town, and when that was done, he began to talk of fortifying Albany with a ditch and stockade, and ordered a survey for that purpose.

Colonel Bradstreet, who had been sent to Oswego with provisions and military stores, was surprised on his way back by a body of Canadians and Indians about ten miles from that place. A fight ensued, in which Bradstreet put the enemy to flight, but he had not men enough to venture on a pursuit. One of the prisoners revealed the designs of the French and their movements preparatory to an attack on Oswego, which Bradstreet reported to Abercrombie, who had ten thousand regulars and seven thousand provincials at his command. The roads were opened, and the two forts at Oswego were ready for occupation and well provided with stores of all kinds,

Abercrombie ordered a regiment of regulars to prepare to go to Oswego, but before they were ready Lord Loudoun arrived, on the 29th of July. More time was spent in debating the question of the status of the provincial officers and troops, and the regiment did not move until the 12th of August. The French under De Lery and De Villiers had been active during the spring in getting possession of the approaches to Oswego from Albany, and in the conciliation of the Indians of New York. De Lery came from Montreal with two hundred and sixty-five men, and on the 27th of March surprised the garrison of Fort Bull, at the Oneida portage, capturing them after a short resistance; and all but five were massacred, the fort was blown up, and the military stores destroyed.

A party of Indians descended upon some ship-carpenters who were working at Oswego, and returned to Niagara in triumph with three prisoners and twelve scalps. These small successes and the martial activity of the French inclined the wavering warriors of the Iroquois toward their alliance; and the Indians of the upper country about the lakes began to flock to Fort Niagara to form war parties.

During the summer the French forces were placed under the command of one of the ablest soldiers of his time, Louis Joseph, Marquis de Montcalm de Saint Veron. Small, quick, and active, Montcalm saw at a glance what ought to be done, and wasted no time in talking about it. Remaining only a few days at Quebec, he sent a force of men to Fort Carillon at Ticonderoga, and another, under De Villiers, to the Bay of Niaouré, to a spot now known as Six Town Point, in Jefferson County, to observe the movements of the enemy and keep him in check. Another regiment was sent by Montcalm to Niagara, accompanied by a skilful engineer, Pouchot, to strengthen the fortifications there.

On the 5th of August, Montcalm, taking two regiments of regular troops with him, left Fort Frontenac, and, encamping at the Bay of Niaouré, sent De Villiers and Rigaud de Vaudreuil to take a position not far from Oswego. Montcalm followed, and by the 12th of August the forces were gathered before the forts at Oswego and ready for operations.

Fort Oswego, or Pepperell, called Chouaguen by the French, stood near the site of the "stone house of strength," built by Governor Burnet in 1726, and was a large stone fort with four bastions. On an eminence across the river which commanded it Governor Shirley had placed Fort Ontario. The garrison consisted of sixteen hundred men under the command of Colonel Mercer, many of them raw recruits.

On the night of the 12th of August, the day when the regiments started from Albany to relieve the fort, the French opened trenches before Fort Ontario and felled trees for an abatis, finishing the work by daybreak. The batteries opened fire that day, and the garrison returned it with spirit as long as their ammunition lasted; for, in addition to the other blunders, Fort Ontario had been left with a very slender store. At three o'clock in the afternoon, they spiked their guns and crossed to Fort Oswego in boats sent over by Colonel Mercer.

MONTCALM'S VICTORY AT TICONDEROGA

The French took immediate possession of the deserted works, and the guns of Fort Oswego were turned upon them. Mercer had sent a party under Colonel Schuyler to a hill four and a half miles up the river, where they were entrenched, and designed to harass the French. But Montcalm despatched Vaudreuil with a party of Canadians and Indians to cut off communication between the fort and the hill, while his men kept up a continuous fire on Fort Oswego with their batteries and such guns of Fort Ontario as they could use. Mercer was killed by a cannon-ball on the 13th, and on the 14th the garrison resolved to surrender, Montcalm promising that they should receive "all the regard which the most courteous of nations could show."

The English lost forty-five men killed, and all the rest prisoners, one hundred and twenty-one cannon, six vessels of war, two hundred boats, and three chests of money, together with stores of ammunition and provisions. After removing the stores, Montcalm destroyed the forts in the presence of the warriors of the Six Nations who had accompanied him. Those Indians had always looked upon the erection of the forts as an infraction of their rights, and this act on the part of Montcalm was an acknowledgment of the justice of their claim and a profession of the intention of the French to uphold them in it, and not continue the trespass by keeping the forts for themselves.

In Montcalm's account of the surrender he says:—

Their stores were provided with everything to maintain our army during the next campaign. The least superstitious attribute our success to Providence. We have lost, notwithstanding, eighty men, and our little army had been swamped if that valour so justly attributed to the troops of Old England had extended to her colonies. Ours is now more flourishing than ever; trade entirely re-established; Lake Ontario ours without any opposition. We can hardly recover from our astonishment. The bulwark of New England was originally but the house of an individual whom the Iroquois had permitted to build; of this the king took possession some years afterward for purposes of trade. He increased it with all the works which we demolished. Their loss is incredible. The Canadians and Indians have had a very considerable slice of the cake; the latter perpetrated there a multitude of horrors and assassinated more than one hundred persons included in the capitulation, without our being able to prevent them or having the right to remonstrate with them.

This species of animal I look upon as mad dogs; when they are intoxicated, they are uncontrollable.

It is said that Montcalm, notwithstanding his pledge of honourable treatment to the prisoners, delivered up about twenty men of the garrison to the Indians to recompense them for the same number of their men who had fallen during the siege. It is possible that this and the slaughter of sick and wounded prisoners mentioned above, was, as he says, beyond his power to prevent. The rest of the prisoners were taken to Montreal, and exchanged not long afterward. The British flags were sent to Montreal, Quebec, and Three Rivers, where they were hung in the churches as trophies of the victory.

The Abbé Picquet, founder of the mission of La Presentation, on the site of Ogdensburg, was with this expedition, and raised a cross on the scene of the French victory, to which was affixed the motto. *In hoc signo vincunt*, "In this sign they conquer." By its side he raised a column with the king's arms and the inscription, *Manibus date lilia plenis*, "Bring lilies, with full hands."

Webb, who had set out from Albany the day the French began their operations at Oswego, was slowly advancing when he received the news of Montcalm's victory. Waiting only to fell trees to obstruct the passage of Wood Creek, a stream whose headwaters were near those of the Mohawk, and formed a part of the water communication between Albany and Oswego, he fled back to Albany in haste and terror.

Montcalm, supposing the English forces at Albany would now be turned against the French forts on Lake Champlain, hurried to Ticonderoga. But Loudoun had no idea of advancing. The expedition against Forts Carillon and Frederick was given up; and the general turned his attention to quartering his troops for the winter, after strengthening the works at Forts Edward and William Henry. The cities of New York and Philadelphia protested against being forced to give free quarters to the soldiers in the houses of the citizens; but Loudoun threatened to bring all the troops in North America and billet them upon those cities if they resisted.

While these things were going on, or failing to go on, at the north, and soldiers were lying inactive in the safety of the large northern cities, the frontiers of Pennsylvania and Virginia were suffering from the constant inroads of hostile savages, and it was impossible to raise men in numbers sufficient to impose the least check upon them. Washington had command of all the forces raised, or to be raised, in the province; but it was almost impossible to get men to respond to the calls for gatherings of the provincial soldiers.

The valley of the Shenandoah was especially exposed to these attacks. No farmhouse was safe, and no man sure of his life for a moment, on the road or the farm, in his own house, or even in the little stockaded forts. Winchester was in a state of continual alarm. Washington was sent for, and decided that a force of militia must be raised, and, aided by some of the soldiers from Fort Cumberland, must scour the woods in search of the marauding parties, which in many instances were led by Frenchmen.

A messenger was therefore despatched to Fort Cumberland; and all captains of militia were ordered to gather their men and read to them an exhortation, setting forth the danger, and appealing to their patriotism and their interest, to assemble on the 15th of April to join the expedition. The officers at Fort Cumberland sent back word that no men could be spared; that detachments had been sent out in various directions, and the garrison was no more than sufficient for the defence of the fort. The messenger reported that the woods were filled with lurking savages; his own clothes were pierced with bullets, his horse shot under him, and he had barely escaped with his life. The plan for assembling the militia turned out no better; on the appointed day only fifteen men presented themselves.

The Indians grew bolder; houses were burned and families murdered all about Winchester, and the inhabitants, growing frantic, gathered about Washington, imploring him to do something to avert the calamity; but he was paralyzed by the impossibility of raising men. In a letter to Governor Dinwiddie he wrote:—

I am too little acquainted with pathetic language to attempt a description of these people's distresses. But what can I do? I know their danger, and participate in their sufferings, without having it in my power to give them further relief than uncertain promises. The supplicating tears of the women and moving petitions of the men melt me into such deadly sorrow, that I solemnly declare, if I know my own mind, that I could offer myself a willing sacrifice to the butchering enemy, provided that would contribute to the people's ease.

This letter called forth an order from the governor for a force of militia from the upper counties to go to the relief of the frontier; and the Assembly voted an appropriation of twenty thousand pounds and an increase of the provincial forces to fifteen thousand men. Governor Dinwiddie proposed to expend the money in building a chain of forts along the Alleghanies from the Potomac to the border of North Carolina, and to garrison the forts with the new militia to be raised. In vain Washington laid before the governor the difficulties of carrying out such a plan. To place the forts near enough together for the scouts to keep watch of the whole line, and to prevent the marauders from breaking through at any point, without assistance from distant forts, would have called for a much greater outlay of money and vastly more men than the province could possibly raise.

Washington's own plan was, to build not more than four or five strong forts, with large garrisons, the largest and strongest to be at Winchester, a point where many roads met, where news could be quickly received from all parts of the valley, and where the defenceless inhabitants could take refuge in case of alarm. But Dinwiddie persisted in his design of building twenty-three forts along the frontier, and of maintaining Fort Cumberland at great expense, though it was so far away from the routes taken by the Indians that everything was over before the garrison could be notified. The erection of a central fort at Winchester was, however, agreed upon.

But the preparations for these great defensive works went on very slowly, and meantime the savages kept up their incursions. The people of the Shenandoah valley, despairing of protection, left their homes in large numbers, and moved to the eastern settlements. It seemed that the province of Virginia would soon be practically bounded on the west by the Blue Ridge.

A bold and successful attempt at retribution was made this year in Pennsylvania. An Indian town called Kittanning, about forty miles from Fort Du Quesne, was the rendezvous for parties of marauding Indians; and about one thousand people on the frontier had fallen victims in their raids. They were led by the chief Shingis, and another known as Captain Jacobs, a bold and brave Indian, who boasted that he could "take any fort that would catch fire."

To put a stop to these raids, a party of two hundred and eighty Pennsylvanians placed themselves under the command of Colonel John Armstrong. One of the officers under him was Captain Hugh Mercer, afterward of Revolutionary fame, who had served as a surgeon in the army of the Young Pretender, and after his defeat at Culloden escaped to America. The men marched rapidly from Fort Shirley on the Juniata, and reached the Alleghany without a suspicion on the part of the savages that vengeance was on their track.

On the night of the 7th of October, Armstrong's men drew near enough to hear the rejoicings of the Indians over their victories—the whoops, and screams, and sound of drums. When the carouse was over, the Indians made fires in the fields and went to sleep beside them without sentinels, Armstrong's men hid themselves until the moon had set and all the warriors were asleep; then, dividing into two parties, they attacked the village and the sleeping warriors in the fields at the same time. The Indians fought with desperate bravery; Captain Jacobs defended himself to the last, fighting through the loop-holes of his log house.

The village had been set on fire, and as the flames drew near his dwelling, he was offered quarter, which he refused, saying he would kill a few before he died. He and the warriors with him were at length driven out by the fire, and some escaped to the woods. Captain Jacobs attempted to get away, but was shot; as was also his son, who was said to be a giant seven feet high. The whole town was destroyed by the fire; the repeated explosions of loaded guns and bags and kegs of powder showing how well the Indians were prepared for future raids.

Both Armstrong and Mercer were wounded. On the return march, which was made as rapidly as possible for fear the alarm might reach Fort Du Quesne and a party be sent out in pursuit, Mercer was separated from his companions, and only reached the fort after fourteen days of lonely wandering through the woods, finding his way by the water-courses, and living on two dried clams and a rattlesnake, with a few berries.

The Six Nations were now fast passing over from their neutral position to the side of the French; the younger braves would have taken up the hatchet at once to fight under Montcalm for the prospering cause. The English, losing these fickle allies by their failures, were still to meet more reverses, and bring their military pretensions into still greater contempt.

CHAPTER 15

Louisbourg and Fort William Henry

During the ensuing year, 1757, the British cause in America reached its lowest ebb. The French, under the brilliant leadership of Montcalm, achieved so many successes that it seemed as if the Bourbon lilies would soon float over every stronghold of the continent. Loudoun continued to give away advantages by his slowness and cowardice; and the few brave dashes made by parties of provincials were of little effect, because not followed by any movement of the main forces. During the winter, which was very long and cold, the frozen waters of Lake Champlain formed a highway for war-parties on their deadly errands. An Indian chief, Aouschik, who had killed one of Montcalm's engineers the summer before, mistaking him for an Englishman, demonstrated the sincerity of his regret by bringing in thirty-three English scalps during the year. In the course of a discussion of a treaty between his nation, the Nipissings, and the French, he exclaimed:—

What need of councils, deliberations, and proposals, when action is needed? I hate the Englishman. I thirst for his blood. I am going to bathe in it.

And he broke into a hideous war-song, and led out his braves.

In January, John Stark led seventy-four men from Fort William Henry, on snow-shoes and skates, to Lake Champlain. They attacked a party of Frenchmen who were travelling in sledges from Fort Carillon to Fort Frederick, and took three of the sledges, with their horses, and seven prisoners. But just as they reached the land, in retreating, they were attacked in turn by two hundred and fifty French and Indians. Stark's men took shelter behind hills and trees, and fought till evening, when they retreated, leaving fourteen killed and six missing. (See *John Stark of Rogers' Rangers*, containing *The Life of General John Stark of*

A FIGHT ON SNOW-SHOES

New Hampshire by Howard Parker Moore and With Biographies from *Memoir and Official Correspondence of General John Stark* by Caleb Stark; Leonaur 2020.)

In February, Montcalm formed a plan for capturing Fort William Henry. Fifteen hundred men, under the command of Rigaud de Vaudreuil, starting on the 23rd, crossed Lakes Champlain and George, marching sixty leagues on snow-shoes. Their provisions were drawn on sledges, by dogs; and at night they spread bear-skins on the snow, or raised tents in stormy weather. On the 18th of March they were in front of the fort, but found themselves disappointed in their hope of a surprise; they had been discovered, and the garrison was on the alert. Rigaud thought it useless to attempt to carry the fort by assault, but set his men at work to destroy everything outside the works. For four nights they worked under fire, burning up the boats, the mills, magazines, and palisaded houses, and the cabins of the rangers. Three hundred and fifty *bateaux* and four *brigantines* were consumed. The fire of the garrison inflicted some damage, but they made no attempts by sorties to drive off the French or stop their depredations.

A council of governors held at Boston in January had agreed to raise four thousand men in the northern colonies, and New York and New Jersey were to be called on for proportionate numbers to increase Lord Loudoun's army for the summer campaign. In March, another council was held at Philadelphia, and Washington obtained permission from Governor Dinwiddie to be present, wishing to represent to Lord Loudoun the interests of Virginia. He was anxious that another attack should be made on Fort Du Quesne, at the same time with the operations in the north, since a large part of the garrison would be drawn away to the Canadian frontier.

Loudoun did not approve of the plan, as he desired the southern colonies simply to stand on the defensive. He gave orders, however, in accordance with Washington's advice, to withdraw the garrison from Fort Cumberland, leaving Maryland to supply that point, and make Fort Loudoun, at Winchester, the headquarters of the Virginia militia. Stanwix was stationed on the frontier of Pennsylvania, Colonel Henry Bouquet had charge of the Carolina border, and Webb was furnished with nearly six thousand men to defend the important posts about Lake George.

Loudoun's own work for the summer was to be the reduction of Louisbourg. Abandoning for the time the idea of capturing the forts on the English borders, he resolved to take the greater part of his forces to Halifax, where he was to be joined by an English squadron, and proceed to Louisbourg. The New England provinces had been greatly disappointed at the surrender of that fortress by treaty after they had taken it in 1745, by their almost unaided prowess, an achievement which they justly regarded with pride; and, in addition to this, the fact that Louisbourg, when held by the French, was a harbour of refuge for the cruisers that preyed upon the colonial vessels, made the project for retaking it very popular in New England.

Admiral Holbourne arrived at Halifax early in July with a squadron and a reinforcement of five thousand troops under Lord George Howe. On the 6th of the same month, Loudoun sailed from New York with six thousand men, having first laid an embargo on all the ships in the ports of British North America—an assumption of power which aroused the indignation of the colonies, and was not approved by the English Government.

Arrived at Halifax, Loudoun set his men at work, levelling ground for a parade and planting a vegetable garden to furnish protection against the scurvy. Then he kept them exercising in drills, and sham fights, and mock sieges, until the impatience of some of the subordinate officers broke out into open criticism. At the beginning of August, the troops were embarked for Gabarus Bay; but on the 4th information was received from a captured sloop that the French had nineteen ships of war and three thousand regular troops, besides many Canadians and Indians. The English had but seventeen ships of war, and Admiral Holbourne dared not attack the French nineteen. Loudoun also prudently resolved to put off the capture of Louisbourg until another summer, and some of the soldiers were left at Halifax, while he returned with the greater part of them to New York.

Horace Walpole had written in February of this year:—

I do not augur very well of the ensuing summer; a detachment is going to America under a commander whom a child might outwit or terrify with a pop-gun.

After news of the fiasco at Louisbourg reached England, he wrote:—

Shortly after came letters from the Earl of Loudoun, stating that he found the French twenty-one thousand strong, and that, not having so many, he could not attack Louisbourg, but should return to Halifax. Admiral Holbourne, one of the sternest condemners of Byng, wrote at the same time that he, having

Scale to this Plan of the Fort.

Fort
William
Henry.

B

Section through A.B.

A Scale to the Profile

but seventeen ships and the French nineteen, dared not attack them. Here was another summer lost! Pitt expressed himself with great vehemence against the earl; and we naturally have too lofty ideas of our naval strength to suppose that seventeen of our ships are not a match for any nineteen others.

★★★★★★

The clerk of a church in Halifax, on the news of the abandonment of the enterprise against Cape Breton, gave out, for the expression of his own feelings and those of the people generally, some *stanzas* of the forty-fourth psalm:—

O God, we with our ears have heard,
Our fathers have us told.
What works thou in their days hadst done
Even in the days of old.

Thy hand did drive the heathen out.
And plant them in their place;
Thou didst afflict the nations.
But them thou didst increase.

But now we are cast off by thee.
And us thou putt'st to shame;
And when our armies do go forth.
Thou goest not with the same.

Thou mak'st us from the enemy.
Faint-hearted, to turn back;
And they who hate us, for themselves
Our spoils away do take.

Like sheep for meat thou gavest us;
'Mongst heathen cast we be.
Thou didst for nought thy people sell;
Their price enriched not thee.

Thou mak'st us a reproach to be
Unto our neighbours near.
Derision and a scorn to them
That round about us are.
Rise for our help and us redeem
Even for thy mercies' sake.

★★★★★★

Loudoun was only two days out on his way to New York, when

he was met by tidings of more misfortune to the British arms. As soon as it was known by the French that he had sailed for Louisbourg, Montcalm resolved to strike another blow in New York, for which he had been making preparations during the entire spring and summer. Nothing had been left undone to incite the Indians and unite them for a blow at the English fortifications at Lake George. A grand council was held at Niagara on the 1st of July, at which the Iroquois gave belts to the Hurons, Ottawas, and other allies of the French, as a token of their intention to join the enemies of the English; and a belt was given in reply, which was covered with vermilion, signifying an invitation to war. They desired the Iroquois to bring to their father—that is, the French governor some of the bad meat they loved so well. By the "bad meat" they meant the English.

Another congress was held at Montreal, at which thirty-three nations were represented, including chiefs from Acadia to Lake Superior. "We will try our father's hatchet on the English, to see if it cuts well," said a chief of the Senecas. Montcalm sang the war-song with them every day of the council, and they loved him as a leader whom they never had seen beaten, who could open the way for them to an unlimited quantity of plunder and scalps. The tribes were assembled at Fort St. John, on the River Sorel. Their missionaries came with them, and masses and hymns of the church alternated with the fantastic dance and the unearthly yells that heralded the strife. When all was ready, they ascended the river and Lake Champlain in a fleet of two hundred canoes, and landed at Ticonderoga.

Several minor engagements took place while Montcalm was preparing for the main attack. A party went out under Marin to the vicinity of Fort Edward, and returned in triumph. "They did not amuse themselves with making prisoners," said Montcalm, as the one captive and the forty-two scalps were taken from the boat, and exhibited before the admiring eyes of the Indians. A slight skirmish took place at Harbor Island near Sabbath-Day Point. A party of three hundred was sent out from Fort William Henry under an officer named Palmer, to make observations, when a band of Ottawas who had been hiding for twenty-four hours suddenly rushed upon the twenty-two boats of the English, and made such havoc that only twelve escaped.

One hundred and sixty were taken prisoners; the rest were drowned, or fell under the fury of the savages. After this victory, the Ottawas wanted to go home. They felt that they had glory enough, and ought not to tempt the fortunes of war any farther. But Montcalm held another council, and bound all the Indians, by the presentation of the great belt of six thousand shells, to stay until the end of the expedition.

Fort William Henry was close to the shore of the lake, on ground so low that it seemed from a little distance to be resting on the water. The walls were low, and bastions rose at the four corners. The land immediately about the fort had been cleared and planted as a garden by the garrison. On the east was a morass, and the other sides were protected by a ditch. On the southeast was an eminence, the summit of which commanded the fort, and would have been a better site for the works. On the top of this hill a camp was formed with entrenchments, which contained about seventeen hundred men, and the fort four or five hundred.

Montcalm's whole army, fifty-five hundred regulars and Canadians and sixteen hundred Indians, crossed from Ticonderoga to the foot of Lake George. Here, as there was a scarcity of boats, a division was made. The Chevalier De Levis, with twenty-two hundred soldiers and six hundred Indians, marched by land along the rugged trail on the western side of the lake, while the rest of the Indians set out in their bark canoes, and the following day Montcalm embarked with the remainder of the army and all the baggage in two hundred and fifty boats. After rowing that day and most of the night, they came in sight of three fires arranged in a triangle which marked the camp of De Levis,

Here they halted, held a council of war, and selected a place for landing which was hidden from the fort by a point of land extending into the lake. During the night, two of the canoes had attacked two English boats which were out on the lake, and after a struggle, in which the Nipissings lost a great chief, one of the English boats was captured, and all the men in it were slaughtered, save two who were held as prisoners.

The next morning, August 2nd, the Indians threw out a line of canoes across the lake, and raised the war-cry. The English, taken by surprise, withdrew in haste from their tents and outlying barracks, while the detachment of De Levis scoured the woods, burned the barracks, chased the cattle and horses, and slew a small foraging party whom they surprised in the woods. Montcalm landed about a mile and a half from the fort, at the northwest, and advanced in three columns. One detachment of Indians and Canadians, under La Corne, took a position on the road leading to Fort Edward; another, under De Levis, formed an encampment south of the fort; while Montcalm, with the main body of the army, was on the west shore of the lake, at the edge

FORT TICONDEROGA

Redoubt finish'd by the order of Monsr de Pontleroy

Place of Arms

Redoubt which covers the Lower Town

Sarre

Lower Town Stockaded

Houses a Loup

2nd Bat.ⁿ of Berry during the attack

Wooden Blockhouse

HOSPITAL

The Place where Battoes & Canoes are laid up

of the forest. The 3rd of August was employed in preparing for a siege.

On the 4th, Montcalm sent a summons to Colonel Monroe, commanding at the fort, to surrender, and intimated that in case the garrison should resist, and the fort be finally taken by siege, he could not answer for the behaviour of his Indians. Monroe had not more than twenty-two hundred men; but relying on assistance from General Webb, who was at Fort Edward, fifteen miles away, with four thousand men, he answered that he would not surrender. "I will defend my trust," he said, "to the last extremity." The French then pushed on their preparations with vigour; they dug trenches, brought fascines for the batteries, and gabions for shelter, and drew the artillery from the landing-place.

The first battery was at length prepared, and opened on the fort in the morning of the 6th, to the great delight of the Indians, who had seen but little artillery practice, and were nearly beside themselves at the noise of the big guns. The fire was returned, but with much less power, while the trenches were carried so close to the fort that the Indians could stand near enough to fire upon the works without danger from the guns. Another battery was erected, and the sharp-shooters drew closer around the fort, hiding not only in the zigzags, but behind every forest tree or cover of any kind.

The walls of the fort were fast giving way under the fire of the batteries, and the garrison were falling under the deadly bullets; but Monroe still held out, hoping for relief; for General Webb was well aware, from the first, of the approach of the French Army, and of Monroe's brave defence. When Montcalm was coming over the lake, Webb was in the neighbourhood of Fort William Henry; and Israel Putnam, who was on the lake with a party of rangers, discovered the movement of the French and hastened to Webb with the news, urging him to oppose the landing; but Webb—enjoining secrecy on Putnam, it is said—fell back to Fort Edward.

On the second day of the siege, Sir William Johnson arrived at Fort Edward with some Indians and militia, whom he had hastily gathered after hearing of the departure of Montcalm's army from Ticonderoga. Finding that Webb was determined to do nothing, he asked to be allowed to make up a body of reinforcements from those who would volunteer to go. Webb consented at first, but afterward withdrew his consent; and the whole four thousand at Fort Edward remained inactive. A letter was despatched by Webb to the fort, probably on the day of Johnson's arrival, advising Monroe to surrender, as it would be impossible for him to send any help unless he himself should be re-enforced from Albany, and giving an exaggerated account of the strength of the French. The messenger was taken by a party of French on the road between the two forts, who read the letter, and then sent it on to Monroe.

On the sixth day of the siege, August 9th, when half of the guns of the fort had burst, and the ammunition was nearly gone, Monroe, knowing that he had nothing to hope for from Webb, hung out a flag of truce. In arranging the terms of capitulation, Montcalm invited the Indian chiefs to the council, in order to make it binding on them. The garrison were to march out with the honours of war, carrying their private effects, and delivering up the fort, with the entrenched camp and all its dependencies, and all the artillery, provisions, and warlike stores, to his Most Christian Majesty the King of France. The garrison and other troops were not to serve against his Most Christian Majesty or his allies for the space of eighteen months.

All French prisoners taken by land since the beginning of the war were to be delivered at Fort Carillon within three months; and, according to receipts given by the French officers to whom they should be surrendered, an equal number of the troops at Fort William Henry should be released from their engagement not to serve in the English armies. An officer was to be left as a hostage until the return of the escort to be provided for the English troops. The sick and wounded were to remain with Montcalm, who promised to take proper care of them and return them as soon as they were recovered. As a mark of esteem to Colonel Monroe and the garrison, for their honourable defence, Montcalm gave them "one piece of cannon, a six-pounder."

The English retired to the entrenched camp, and the French took possession of the fort, while the Indians spent the night in a wild carouse in honour of the victory. When the English marched out in the morning, carrying their arms and baggage, and accompanied by an escort from the French Army, the rage and cupidity of the Indians were at once excited; they were never able to understand the consideration shown to prisoners by civilized nations, and they had been drawn to the fight by the hope of plunder, as well as the thirst for blood.

At a favourable spot a short distance from the camp, they fell upon the luckless soldiers, stripped them of everything they carried, and even of the clothes they wore, and hewed them down without mercy. Attacked in this unexpected way, the troops who had just shown so much bravery in the defence of the fort were thrown into a panic of

Montcalm trying to stop the massacre

uncontrollable terror, and fled in all directions, some to the woods, some to the French soldiers for protection. Twelve to fifteen hundred were taken captive by the Indians, and many were killed.

In regard to the conduct of the French officers and soldiers during this horrible scene, the accounts are conflicting. According to one English statement, the French officers neglected and even refused during the massacre to take any of the measures stipulated in the surrender, and neither officers nor troops gave any protection; according to French accounts, Montcalm besought them to kill him, but spare the English, who were under his protection, while De Levis rushed into the midst of them again and again, at the peril of his life, to arrest the slaughter, many of the French officers received wounds in attempting to protect those whom they had rescued from the fury of the savages, and Montcalm bade the English defend themselves.

The great number of the captives seems to make it improbable that any very determined effort was made to protect them; but there is no doubt that the French officers, with whom rested the responsibility of carrying out the terms of the capitulation, did all that could be done by commands and entreaties to stay the fury of the savages, yet would not give any order to their soldiers which would imperil the friendship of the Indians. But they had industriously excited the fury of the savages by appealing to their lowest passions, and could not control it when their own purposes were accomplished.

About six hundred of the troops reached Fort Edward after escaping to the woods. Montcalm released the prisoners still kept by the Indians near the French camp, sending them to the fort with a powerful escort, and Rigaud de Vaudreuil was sent to ransom those who had been carried away. Fort William Henry was then razed to the ground, the English vessels were destroyed, and nine hundred men were set at work to load the stores for transportation. Among them were provisions for six months for an army of five thousand men.

The news of the capture of the fort and the slaughter by the Indians aroused the colonies, and Webb called loudly for help, fearing an attack on Fort Edward. Militia were sent from Massachusetts and Connecticut, but the French had departed without attempting anything further, and the shores of Lake George were a solitude.

Late in November of this year, a force of three hundred French and Indians, under an officer named Bellêtre, made a descent upon a settlement on the Mohawk called German Flats, near Fort Herkimer. Sixty houses, with the mill and other buildings, were burned, forty of the settlers were killed, and a hundred and fifty were carried away prisoners. A large amount of plunder was taken, one Indian, it is said, having thirty thousand *livres* (about six thousand dollars) in money. The mayor of the village lost four hundred thousand *livres'* worth of property.

Bellêtre was entrusted with messages by some of the Iroquois to their "father," the Governor of Canada, professing faithfulness, and asking for aid to resist the English. Sir William Johnson sent an interpreter to some Oneida and Tuscarora Indians at the German Flats, to demand why they, having knowledge of the intended attack, had not warned the people of the settlement. An Oneida chief replied that they did give warning to the Germans at the settlement, telling them to prepare for an attack, and send word to Warraghiyagey (Sir William Johnson); that the warning was disregarded and the message not sent, the Germans declaring they did not fear the enemy; and that they sent a warning, accompanied by a belt of *wampum*, on the day preceding the attack, of which no more notice was taken. The Germans present acknowledged the truth of the Indian statements before the interpreter.

Lord Loudoun was in New York when Fort William Henry was taken. One of his plans was, to form an encampment on Long Island, which he imagined would in some way protect the country. As the winter approached, the troubles about quartering soldiers were repeated. Boston refused, and Loudoun yielded, after having written:—

> I have ordered the messenger to wait but forty-eight hours in Boston; and if, on his return, I find things not settled, I will instantly order into Boston the three regiments from New York, Long Island, and Connecticut; and if more are wanted, I have two in the Jerseys at hand, besides three in Pennsylvania.

Thus, closed a year of disasters to the British cause in America. The French were in actual possession of very nearly all they had claimed previous to the war. They had the valley of the Mississippi, except a fort on the Upper Tennessee; they had the basin of the St. Lawrence and its tributary waters in north-eastern New York; and they had made an open passage to the west by the capture of Oswego. They had won over many of the Iroquois tribes; and the Cherokees, who still remained faithful to the English, showed signs of alienation. Acadia was in constant danger from the strong force of men and ships at Louisbourg. If they were not checked, they would have nothing to do but carry war into the heart of the English colonies.

At the same time, the British had not been more successful in Europe. Imbecility seemed to control all the acts of the administration and the military authorities. The Duke of Newcastle was again the nominal head of the ministry—Newcastle, the ignorant and incompetent nobleman, who is reported, if not with truth, yet with a happy hit at his characteristics, to have said:—

> Oh, yes, yes, to be sure, Annapolis must be defended; troops must be sent to Annapolis—pray, where is Annapolis? Cape Breton an island? Wonderful! Show it to me on the map. So it is, sure enough. My dear sir, you always bring us good news. I must go and tell the king that Cape Breton is an island.

But William Pitt was made Secretary of State, and Newcastle was obliged to leave to him the entire management of the war.

The disgraceful defeats in America had roused a storm of indignation in England. Loudoun was severely censured. Pitt said:—

> Nothing has been done, nothing attempted. Every door is open to France.

Loudoun was recalled; the quarrels with the colonies about raising a common fund for war purposes and taxation by Parliament were abandoned; all provincial officers, from colonels downward, were made equal in rank to corresponding officers in the regular army; and the colonies were asked to raise as many men as possible, and to clothe and pay them, Pitt promising that the king would recommend Parliament to reimburse them, while all munitions of war were to be provided by England.

While vigorous measures were thus taken by the English Government, and the outlook for the coming year was more encouraging, the victorious French in Canada began to feel that they were on the eve of reverses. The men had left their fields untilled, to follow Montcalm; rain had destroyed the crops, so that in some parishes there was not enough left to furnish seed; and France sent no supplies. Not only the army, but the entire body of inhabitants, were put on a reduced allowance. Montcalm predicted that New France must fall sooner or later, such were the numbers of the English, and such the difficulty of obtaining supplies in Canada.

CHAPTER 16

Louisbourg and Ticonderoga

For the prosecution of the war in 1758, Abercrombie succeeded Lord Loudoun, with command of the forces that were to attack Ticonderoga and Crown Point. Lord Howe, a young nobleman of military ability and great personal popularity, was made second in command. Admiral Boscawen was given charge of the fleet destined for Louisbourg. Colonel Jeffrey Amherst, who had served with distinction in Germany, was made a major-general and sent to America to command the land forces to cooperate with Boscawen; and under him were Brigadier-Generals Whitmore, Lawrence, and James Wolfe. The reduction of Fort Du Quesne was intrusted to Brigadier-General Joseph Forbes, who was called, from his obstinacy, "the Head of Iron." A large number of men was raised in the colonies, and twelve thousand were sent from England with Amherst, so that the entire British force in America was not far from fifty thousand.

Amherst, delayed by storms, did not reach Halifax till the end of May, when he met Boscawen's fleet just coming out of the harbour. The admiral had given him up, and, leaving a strong force to guard the town, was about to sail without him. On the 2nd of June, the entire force arrived at Gabarus Bay. There were twenty-two ships of the line, and fifteen frigates, with one hundred and twenty smaller vessels; and the army amounted to over eleven thousand men. In the brigade under Wolfe were Isaac Barré, the eloquent advocate of the cause of America in the British Parliament a few years later, and Richard Montgomery, a young Irishman, twenty-one years of age, destined to die under the walls of Quebec in a later struggle.

Amherst, hoping to surprise the garrison at Louisbourg, ordered great care and silence to be observed in making the landing. But in the morning the shore was enveloped in a dense fog, and as it cleared away, a high wind drove the surf on the beach so heavily as to make landing impossible, and give the French time for preparation. Lawrence and Wolfe, however, went out in the evening and reconnoitred the shore, notwithstanding the dangerous roll of the surf. They found that the French had thrown a chain of posts across the country, and placed batteries in a position to command the shore where a landing would be most likely to be attempted.

For six days they waited for the waves to subside; on the 8th of June, though the sea was still rolling heavily, a landing was found to be possible, and under cover of a fire from seven of the frigates, the boats were rowed toward the shore at Cormoran Creek, while three sloops were sent past the harbour to draw off the attention of the enemy. Many of the boats were upset, and some of them broken, by the violence of the waves. The French reserved their fire till the boats were close to the shore, and then poured on them a sudden volley which struck down many of the men, and disabled some of the boats. Wolfe's flag-staff was shivered; but, forbidding his men to return the fire, he urged on the rowers, and leaping into the sea, led his men through the surf. In a few minutes the whole division was on shore. The French retreated in disorder from their entrenchments, and the British pursued, taking seventy prisoners, and only retreating when they came within range of the guns of Louisbourg.

It was not till the 11th that the artillery and other supplies could be landed. On the 12th the French abandoned their outposts and concentrated their whole force on the defence of the town. Wolfe pushed on his men around the northern and eastern shores of the bay to Lighthouse Point, a promontory on the northeast side of the entrance to the harbour. Between this and the town, which occupied another promontory on the western side of the harbour, was Goat Island, standing in the middle of the entrance to the bay. Here the French had a battery. Wolfe placed a battery on Lighthouse Point, from which he could command Goat Island and fire upon the ships; and by the 25th the Goat Island battery was silenced. Leaving a detachment in charge of the battery at the Point, Wolfe took possession of another position, near the town, where he erected a battery to play upon the fort and the ships.

The siege went on for weeks; but its progress, though slow, was steady and sure. The heavy surf and the continuous rains interfered with the landing of munitions from the fleet and the work of the engineers. On the 9th of July, six hundred Frenchmen made a sally from the fort, and surprised a detachment of the English, killing their commander, the Earl of Dundonald, and putting his men to flight; but another English detachment coming up, the French were driven back with the loss of twenty dead and eighty prisoners.

The commander of the fort, the Chevalier de Drucour, held out bravely; he had under him between five and six thousand men—soldiers, sailors, and Indians—with five ships of the line, and four frigates, three of which he had ordered to be sunk at the entrance of the harbour. On the 21st of July, his three largest ships of war took fire from a shell. On the 22nd the citadel was burned, and the town of Louisbourg was soon a pile of ruins; forty of the fifty-two cannon were disabled, and on the night of the 25th two young English captains took boats of the fleet and, boarding the two remaining vessels, set fire to one and carried off the other. The celebrated Captain James Cook participated in this enterprise.

With the town in ruins, the cannon silenced, the ships gone, and the English ready to sail into the harbour, Drucour proposed to capitulate; but thinking the terms offered too severe, he would have refused and submitted to a general assault. The clamour of the inhabitants, however, decided him to yield. The garrison, with the sailors and marine—five thousand six hundred and thirty-seven in all—were made prisoners of war and sent to England; and Cape Breton and Prince Edward's Island were taken possession of by the English troops.

The capture of Louisbourg, after so many reverses, aroused great enthusiasm throughout America. Captain Amherst, brother of the general, carried the news to England. Eleven stand of colours, the trophies of victory, were borne through the streets of London by a procession, to the sound of martial music, laid at the feet of the sovereign, and then hung up in St. Paul's Cathedral. Boscawen and Amherst were honoured with official acknowledgment of their services; but the daring and dash of Wolfe made him the popular hero of the enterprise.

In August, seven ships of the line and three frigates under Sir Charles Hardy were sent to carry a body of soldiers under Wolfe to destroy the French settlements along the coast, beginning with the villages of the unfortunate Acadians in the northeast, and passing along the shores of the Gulf of St. Lawrence to Gaspé, and thence as far up the river as the season would permit, while Monckton was sent to the settlements on the Bay of Fundy and the River St. John. The villages were laid in ruins, and the inhabitants were scattered or carried away. The *intendant* in charge of Mont Louis, on the St. Lawrence, offered a

LOUISBOURG, 1758

hundred and fifty thousand *livres* to save the stores which were gathered at that flourishing fishing-station; but there was no authority for anything but destruction, and the place was left in ruins.

Amherst had hoped to follow up the capture of Louisbourg with that of Quebec. But the length of the siege and the lateness of the season made it unadvisable to attempt it, and the news from Lake George decided him to move his troops in that direction.

At the beginning of July, 1758, the largest army that had ever been gathered on American soil by any European nation was encamped on the shore of Lake George, preparing for an attack on the French fortresses at Ticonderoga and Crown Point. There were six thousand three hundred and sixty-seven regulars, and nine thousand and twenty-four provincials. Abercrombie was commander-in-chief, and under him was the young and gallant Lord Howe, whose brother was afterward commander of the British Army in America, in the time of the Revolution. Among the provincials were Stark, Putnam, Bradstreet, and Robert Rogers with his famous company of rangers.

Rogers and his men had made a reconnoissance and brought back a plan of the works of Fort Carillon and the surrounding country. The fort was on a point of land extending into Lake Champlain where it is joined by the outlet of Lake George. In front of the fort and south of it was the little bay formed by the junction of the waters; on the east was Lake Champlain. Between the fort and the waters of the lake where they widen slightly at the north of the little peninsula, the ground was low and marshy; the only approach by land was on the northwest, and there Montcalm, who was in command with about three thousand men, had made an entrenchment, with an abatis of felled trees, whose parapet was covered with interwoven branches.

On the 5th of July, Abercrombie's army embarked on Lake George in one hundred and thirty-five whale-boats and nine hundred small boats. The artillery was placed on rafts, and the fleet moved down the lake with banners and music. The first night they landed at Sabbath-Day Point; but before midnight they re-embarked, and by nine in the morning had reached the little river which forms the outlet of the lake, where they landed and formed in columns.

This river, which is very winding, and interrupted by rapids and falls, is nearly four miles long. The direct road from Lake George to Ticonderoga crossed it by two bridges, and at the bridge nearest the fort the French had built saw-mills. Montcalm, when he learned of the presence of the English on the lake, sent out two regiments to oppose the landing, but afterward recalled them, only placing three pickets at the portage, and sending out three hundred men under De Trépézée for observation.

Instead of landing on the east side and taking the road, the English, seeing that the French had burned the bridges, landed on the west side and marched through the woods, following the windings of the river. Trépézée's men, thus left behind, and cut off from the fort, struck into the woods to march around the English, and get to their own army before the landing should be finished, but they lost their way; and having groped about in the woods for twelve hours, they unexpectedly came face to face with an advance party of the English under Lord Howe, near Trout Brook, or Bernes River.

In the skirmish that ensued, the Frenchmen fought bravely, hand-to-hand, or sheltering themselves behind the forest trees. Lord Howe was one of the first to fall, struck by a musket-ball in the breast, and died immediately. Maddened by the loss of their favourite leader, his men fought still more fiercely, and the French were soon overpowered. Not more than twenty escaped; Trépézée was mortally wounded; a hundred and fourteen were made prisoners; the rest fell on the battlefield or were drowned in the stream.

The death of Lord Howe was an irreparable loss to Abercrombie's army. All spirit and decision in the ordering of its movements seemed to die with him. Abercrombie had no generalship, no courage, and no confidence in the advice of provincial officers. With the soldiers, Howe had gained a wonderful popularity. A French writer who was at Ticonderoga says of him, calling him, with a Frenchman's difficulty in getting hold of English names, "Lord Ho, or Hau":—

Abercrombie had with him a young nobleman of great ambition, who was a decided favourite with the army, and had succeeded in imparting to it his own brave spirit. He had come in April to reconnoitre the position of Fort Carillon, and seemed to be intrusted with the direction of every plan of attack in the campaign. He had induced all the officers to dress like the common soldiers, warned by Braddock's defeat, where the officers were picked out as marks for the bullets. He persuaded the men to cut their hair short, and all were supplied with a kind of gaiters like those worn by Indians and Canadians, and called *mituzzes*. Their haversacks were rolled in a blanket. They had each thirty pounds of meal, a pound of powder, and four pounds of balls, besides their cartridge-boxes full; an army thus equipped would need no magazine for a month.

Their canteens were filled with rum. Both officers and men mixed their own meal with a little water, and baked it in cakes by putting it on a flat stone under the ashes, an arrangement which answered very well for a light expedition. The soldier thus found everything necessary for his use, and was no more loaded than ordinarily. The officers and men had only one shirt apiece, which was doubtless of cotton and well made. Lord Ho set the example by himself washing his own soiled shirt and drying it in the sun.

It was probably this hearty way of mingling with the soldiers, and making the details of camp life and equipment interesting, which, united to his brilliant courage and his recognition of every man's value, inspired the affection of the army. After his death. Stark remembered how closely Lord Howe had questioned him about the situation of Ticonderoga and the approaches to it, as he lay on a bear-skin in his tent, that night at Sabbath-Day Point. Massachusetts erected a monument to his memory in Westminster Abbey.

The next morning, the 7th, Abercrombie took his army back to the landing-place. Bradstreet went forward with a detachment, rebuilt the bridges, and took possession of the saw-mills near the second bridge, about two miles from the fort, which were in an advantageous military position. The army then followed, and encamped there for the night.

In the morning, Abercrombie sent out his chief engineer and other officers of the regulars, to reconnoitre. They saw the abatis of felled trees in front of the lines; but, owing to the thick woods and the morass, were unable to make very clear observations. The engineer and many of the officers judged the breastwork to be a very slight defence. Stark warned the general that it was stronger than it looked. But, with his usual contempt for provincials, he disregarded the warning, though a minority of the British observers agreed with Stark, and determined to march on the work at once, without waiting for the artillery.

He was farther persuaded to move quickly by the report that Montcalm already had six thousand men, and was daily expecting De Levis with three thousand more from the Mohawk. As a matter of fact, De Levis had already come in with his eight hundred men, and the whole force did not exceed three thousand. Montcalm was undecided all the morning whether to remain or retreat to Crown Point, but at length determined to wait for the attack, and his men were marched into the entrenchments during the forenoon.

Abercrombie's forces were arranged in three lines. In the first were Bradstreet's boatmen, with the rangers on one side and some companies of light infantry on the other. The second was composed of Massachusetts militia. Behind these were the regulars, openings being left in the two forward lines for their advance. The rear guard was composed of Connecticut and New Jersey militia. Abercrombie, who remained far in the rear, gave orders that not a shot should be fired until the breastwork should be surmounted.

At one o'clock on the 8th, the advance began. The regulars marched through the spaces between the companies of provincials, and led on the attack, the grenadier companies first, followed closely by Murray's Highlanders. Marching on through the underbrush and over the swampy ground, they made a dash at the abatis, and then they realised the fatal strength of the entrenchments. The abatis consisted of felled trees, with sharp branches pointing outward; and the top was made still more formidable by interwoven branches piled closely upon it. Stumps of trees and rubbish of all kinds added to the obstruction, which extended for a hundred yards in front of a breastwork of logs, and sloped gradually downward from it toward the assailants.

The French held back their fire till the hapless regulars were hopelessly entangled among the sharp branches and stumps, climbing over the bogs, and stumbling among the rubbish. Then came a sudden blaze from muskets and cannon, and hundreds of them were mowed down. But still they struggled on; many of the Highlanders, active and lightly equipped, forced their way to the breastwork, but only to die by the bayonet. Half of the regiment fell, and nearly all of the officers were either killed or wounded. Fresh troops rushed on, only to meet the same fate; their musket-balls fell harmless against the defences, while the merciless fire from behind the breastwork had full play upon them.

The whole afternoon passed; Montcalm saw every movement, and promptly sent reinforcements to such points as needed them. When the English attempted to turn the left, aid was sent to the left; when they concentrated between the centre and the right, Montcalm was speedily there with a reserve. De Levis and Bourlamaque were equally vigilant and active. (See *Montcalm at the Battle of Carillon (Ticonderoga) (July 8th, 1758)* by Maurice Sautai; Leonaur, 2011.)

During this terrible slaughter, Abercrombie was at the saw-mills,

HIGHLANDERS AT TICONDEROGA

and there was apparently no one to give general orders or withdraw the men from the useless sacrifice; but it was at length ended by an accident. Some of the English, advancing through the woods, saw firing directly in front of them, supposed it to come from the French lines, and returned it promptly; but when the smoke cleared away, they saw that they had fired upon an advance party of their own men. Confused and panic-stricken, they turned and fled; the panic spread, and the whole army was soon in bewildered flight.

Abercrombie had lost, in killed and wounded, nineteen hundred and forty-four, but his army still largely outnumbered Montcalm's, which had lost in all three hundred and ninety. It was in reality four times as large. According to the number he supposed Montcalm had, Abercrombie's was twice as great; and even had De Levis arrived with the three thousand men he was wildly reported to have, the English force would still have outnumbered the French by three thousand. Yet this discrepancy was largely offset by the carefully prepared entrenchments.

The English held Mount Defiance, which commanded the fort, and a battery there might have done good execution; but Abercrombie seems not to have had any idea of renewing the attack, but rather to have thought only of putting as many miles as possible between himself and the foe. Hardly had the soldiers reached the saw-mills, and begun to rally, after finding they were not pursued, when he gave orders for a retreat to the landing-place. Supposing he had intelligence of a pursuit by the enemy, the troops broke into another flight, while apparently the general did not try to arrest them, or restore order.

A French writer who was at Carillon says Montcalm's men found more than five hundred pairs of shoes with buckles in the mud on the road to the falls the next day. Arrived at the landing-place, they would have thrown themselves into the boats in the same confusion; but Bradstreet was there with a small force that had not yet lost their heads, and forming a guard in front of the landing-place, would not allow a man to embark. Order was restored to some extent, and the troops remained at the landing for the night. The next morning, they crossed the lake, to the site of Fort William Henry. Here the general employed them in preparing defences, while he sent his artillery and ammunition to Albany for safety, and even ordered them to be sent on to New York,

Thus, disgracefully ended the expedition for which such elaborate preparations had been made, and from which so much had been expected. The troops had fought with unflinching valour for four hours, and nothing but the blunders of the general was responsible for the failure. The regulars bore the brunt of the battle, and more than four fifths of the loss fell upon them. The Highlanders lost half their number. These men belonged to clans which had always been faithful to the cause of the Stuarts, and disaffected toward a government which they still regarded as an usurpation; but they had been formed into regiments by the keen-sighted policy of Pitt, and soon showed themselves to be among the most daring and effective soldiers that England could bring into the field. The Indians brought by Johnson took no part in the battle, remaining simply as spectators. ((See *The Black Watch at Ticonderoga* by Frederick B. Richards; Leonaur 2007.)

A letter from the Earl of Bute to Pitt, in regard to the battle, illustrates the value of the judgment passed at home upon the conduct of the generals:—

> I think this check, my dear Pitt, affects you too strongly. The general and the troops have done their duty, and appear, by the numbers lost, to have fought with the greatest intrepidity, to have tried all that men could do to force their way. The commander seems broken-hearted at being forced to a retreat.

CHAPTER 17

Frontenac and Du Quesne

Strengthening their entrenchments, and receiving re-enforcements of three thousand Canadians under Rigaud de Vaudreuil, and six hundred Indians, the French employed the time after the battle in organising and sending out detachments to surprise parties of the English, attack outlying settlements, and bring in prisoners, plunder, and scalps. The thousands of men lying at Lake George under Abercrombie seemed powerless to protect the country about them to the distance of twenty miles. On the 17th of July, a party of twenty men was cut off near Half-Way Brook. On the 27th, a detachment of five hundred Canadians and Indians made an attack near the same place on a convoy of fifty-four wagons. Sixteen prisoners, a hundred and ten scalps, and a large amount of plunder were the result.

Rogers was sent out with seven hundred men to intercept this party on the way back to the camp, but failed to find it, and was then directed to scour the country south and east of Lake Champlain. On the 8th of August, he was surprised by a force under a Canadian officer named Marin, and a sharp contest ensued. The French at first gained the advantage; but the bravery of Rogers and his rangers soon turned the fight in their favour.

Major Israel Putnam and twelve or fourteen others, being separated from the rest, were taken prisoners, and all but Putnam were murdered. He was tied to a tree after an Indian had struck him in the cheek with his tomahawk, and wood was piled about him and kindled; but just then he was seen by Marin, who hurried to his rescue, took him from the hands of the savages, and carried him away a prisoner. A few months afterward he was exchanged.

About this time Fort Stanwix, afterward a post of considerable importance, was built by Brigadier-General Stanwix, on the site of the present village of Rome. It stood on the portage between the Mohawk River and Wood Creek, the only spot where the water communication between Schenectady and Oswego was interrupted; being therefore on the highway between the Hudson and Lake Ontario, it was a post of military importance.

The only thing of consequence accomplished by any of the forces under Abercrombie was due to the bravery and sagacity of Bradstreet, who applied for permission to lead a detachment against Fort Frontenac. He had cherished for three years an ambition to take this fort, but had not succeeded in persuading his superiors that it was possible. A council of war now unwillingly gave him permission, and twenty-seven hundred provincials were placed under his command. They were met at Fort Stanwix by one hundred and fifty Iroquois, of whom forty-two, under the Onondaga chief, Red Head, joined the expedition.

In attempting to pass down Wood Creek, Bradstreet was seriously hindered by the obstructions that General Webb had placed in it when he turned back from his tardy march to Oswego, after its surrender. The removal of the logs from the river involved a great deal of labour. Having embarked the artillery and stores, the army marched to Oneida Lake, and thence went by water to Oswego, where the large wooden cross was almost the only memorial they found of the struggle of two years before.

Embarking in open boats at Oswego, they crossed the lake and landed within a mile of Frontenac. This fort was a quadrangle, about one hundred yards square; it had sixty guns and sixteen small mortars, thirty of the guns being mounted, and contained a large quantity of stores, some of which were to be sent to Fort Du Quesne and other western posts, and merchandise intended for the Indian trade. It was garrisoned by one hundred and ten men under an officer named De Noyan.

The *commandant* was warned, of the threatened attack, and sent to the Governor of Canada for re-enforcements; but none came, before Bradstreet arrived. A French writer intimates that the governor neglected to send them on account of personal dislike to the *commandant* of the fort.

He (the *commandant*) was a philosopher and a poet, and sometimes meddled with physic. His aim was to be a little spicy, which had gained him some enemies. Vaudreuil, who was not learned, detested him, although under some obligations to him. He was sixty-eight years old, and infirm, but at this advanced age retained all his spirit, and would have done honour to the post that had been given him, if he had had a large enough force.

Bradstreet planted a battery behind an epaulement of some old entrenchments, and opened fire. A breach was soon made, and the next morning the garrison surrendered. Besides the stores in the fort, the shipping on the lake, consisting of nine vessels of from eight to eighteen guns each, fell into the hands of the victors. Some of the vessels were heavily laden with furs of great value.

Abercrombie had given strict orders that the fort and stores should be destroyed, although there was no apparent reason why it could not have been held, and accordingly Bradstreet destroyed all the artillery and stores, and all of the vessels but two, which he sent to Oswego with the most valuable part of the cargoes, and left the fort in ruins. It was afterward restored by the French.

After his success at Louisbourg, Amherst, hearing of Abercrombie's disaster, decided to go to New York with a portion of his army, and do something if possible, to retrieve the defeat. Landing at Boston in September, with five battalions, he went to Lake George, held a conference with Abercrombie, and, leaving the re-enforcements, returned to Halifax to await orders from England.

The third expedition planned for the year—that against Fort Du Quesne—was in command of General Forbes, whose force consisted of twelve hundred Highlanders, three hundred and fifty Royal Americans, and nearly five thousand provincials of Pennsylvania and Virginia, with some from South Carolina. The Virginia regiments were under the command of Washington, who was ordered to Fort Cumberland, arrived with his troops on the 2nd of July, and at once began cutting a road to Raystown (now Bedford) in Pennsylvania, where Colonel Bouquet was stationed, awaiting the arrival of General Forbes.

It was decided not to take the army to Fort Du Quesne over the road already made, which had been followed by Braddock's army, but to open a new one through Pennsylvania from Raystown. Washington strongly opposed the waste of time; but the Pennsylvanians were determined to have a route to the west through their own territory. Braddock's despatches had given the officers of the English Army an idea that the road passed over by his men was extremely rugged and difficult, abounding in mountains, ravines, and torrents, so that the Pennsylvania traders had little difficulty in persuading them that it would be far better to take the proposed new route, which was fifty miles shorter, and, as they represented, less obstructed.

General Forbes arrived at Raystown with his army in September, having been two months on the way from Philadelphia. He was very ill, and was carried in a litter. Colonel Bouquet was sent forward to Loyal Hanna (now Ligonier), about forty-five miles from Raystown, with a detachment of two thousand men, where he formed a military post.

In August, intelligence had been received that the French had only eight hundred men at Du Quesne, including Indians. But now four hundred more, under an officer named D'Aubry, had arrived from the west. This was unknown to the English, and Colonel Bouquet resolved to attempt a brilliant achievement—the capture of the fort with his own men before the arrival of the main force. Without the knowledge of General Forbes, he sent forward eight hundred men under Major Grant, some of whom were Highlanders, and some Virginia men from Washington's force, under Major Lewis. Washington had equipped them in light Indian hunting-dress, for greater expedition on the march.

Fort Du Quesne was fifty miles distant from Loyal Hanna. Grant was instructed to reconnoitre the country around the fort, and gain all the information he could about the force of the enemy; but he was anxious, like his superior, to seize the glory of victory before Bouquet's men should be sent out; and, moreover, he was ignorant, like most of the British officers, of Indian modes of warfare, and was confident of victory if he could bring the French to an open battle.

He placed his men on a hill that still bears his name, and sent out a party at night to reconnoitre the fort. They set fire to a log house near the wall, and in the morning, the 14th of September, had the drums beaten in several places. The French, through their scouts, had long before learned of his approach, but kept perfectly quiet, even after this display of bravado. Grant then arranged his regulars in battle order, leaving Major Lewis behind with the provincials to protect the baggage, and sent an engineer with a guard to take a plan of the works in sight of the fort. Still there was no sign from the French; but just as Grant began to think the garrison was overcome with fear, and would give up without striking a blow, there was a sudden sally of men under D'Aubry, who attacked his army in front, while countless Indians rose from ambush on both sides.

Grant and his Highlanders fought with great bravery; but, as had happened with Braddock's men, they were thrown into confusion by the fire of the concealed Indians. Lewis came up with the greater part of the Virginians, who fought courageously, but could not save the day. The Indians came out from their concealment when the English ranks were in hopeless confusion, and fought hand-to-hand with their tomahawks. Grant and Lewis were both taken prisoners, and the whole force was put to flight.

When Lewis went forward to the battle with the main body of Virginians, he left Captain Bullitt with fifty men to guard the baggage. Now, as the panic-stricken fugitives fell back, pursued by the triumphant savages, Bullitt, having sent the valuable baggage still farther back, hastily threw up a barricade with the rest of the wagons, and rallied a few of the flying soldiers behind it. When the Indians drew near, a destructive fire was opened from the barricade; many fell, and the rest were checked, but more arrived, and they advanced to storm the barricade, when Bullitt made a sign of surrender, and advanced with his men until they were within thirty feet of the enemy; then they suddenly lowered their guns and fired a volley, and rushed on with their bayonets. The Indians, in their turn, were panic-stricken, and retreated, giving Bullitt a chance to collect the scattered fugitives and retreat to Loyal Hanna.

This rash movement cost Bouquet nearly three hundred men, of whom twenty-one were officers. The conduct of the Highlanders, and especially of the Virginians, was highly applauded and publicly acknowledged by General Forbes, and Bullitt was rewarded with a major's commission.

Forbes reached Loyal Hanna with his army on the 5th of November, when a council of war was held, and it was resolved not to proceed that year, since the season was far advanced, the road yet lacked fifty miles of completion, and the Indians had deserted. But some prisoners who were taken and brought into camp gave information that led to a change of plan; the garrison was weak and the provisions low, and the capture of Fort Frontenac by Bradstreet had cut off all hope of supplies.

The heavy baggage was left behind, and the army pushed forward, Washington leading the advance. The route was strewn with the dead bodies of Grant's men, and it is said that a row of stakes was found fixed in the ground, on each of which was displayed the head of a Highlander, and beneath it his kilts. When the Scotch regiment saw this, they broke into a low murmur of rage and fury, constantly increasing in volume and violence, as they rushed forward, breaking their ranks and brandishing their claymores, to take swift and terrible vengeance.

But vengeance was beyond their reach. As the army marched cautiously on, passing the bleaching bones of the unburied dead who had fallen three years before on Braddock's disastrous field, and on the 24th of November were within a day's march of Fort Du Quesne, they heard a heavy explosion from the direction of the fort, and saw smoke and flames rising into the air. The *commandant*, having no hope of a successful resistance, with only five hundred men and no provisions, had abandoned the fort, blown up the magazine, set fire to the buildings, and had his men on the way down the Ohio in boats.

The next day, Washington's troops marched in and took possession of the ruined fort. The defences were put into the best possible condition, and Fort Du Quesne was re-named Fort Pitt, in honour of the English minister who had planned the campaign for the year, and to whose vigorous measures its successes had been largely due. The name survives in that of the city, Pittsburg, which has grown up around the spot where stood the old fort. The Indians submitted quietly to the new domination, and the English had at last gained a foothold west of the Alleghanies.

A curious story is told of the device of a Highlander, Allan Macpherson, to escape torture by his Indian captors. He and several companions had been captured near Fort Du Quesne, and he had witnessed the horrible tortures undergone by some of his comrades before the merciless savages would put them to death. He told an interpreter to tell them that he knew how to make a medicine from herbs which would render the skin proof against all kinds of weapons, and he offered to prove it at the risk of his own neck.

The Indians eagerly consented, and, gathering a quantity of herbs, he made a decoction which he applied to his neck; then laying his head on a block, he challenged them to strike. One of the strongest warriors came forward and dealt a mighty blow. Not until they saw his head flying from his shoulders did the savages suspect Macpherson's design; and it is said they were so pleased at the Highlander's cunning that they remitted the tortures intended for the rest of his companions.

CHAPTER 18

Niagara and Lake Champlain

For the campaign of 1759, the British Parliament voted liberal supplies of men and money, and the American colonies, encouraged by the successes of the preceding year, raised large numbers of troops. Amherst superseded Abercrombie as commander-in-chief. The plan for the year embraced three expeditions: Fort Niagara was to be attacked by Prideaux, assisted by Sir William Johnson; Amherst was to march his force against Ticonderoga and Crown Point; and Quebec was to be assailed by an army under Wolfe and a fleet under Saunders. Prideaux and Amherst, after the capture of the forts, were to descend the St. Lawrence, take Montreal, and join the army before Quebec.

At this time Canada was much weakened; its resources were nearly exhausted, and the French Government, absorbed with the war in Europe, sent but scanty assistance. The occupation of Louisbourg by the English rendered it difficult for ships to ascend the St. Lawrence; a large amount of stores had been destroyed at Fort Frontenac, the French reverses had cooled the ardour of the Indians, and Canada had not a strong reserve force in its colonists, as had the British provinces. There were not over fifteen thousand Canadians able to bear arms, and the French soldiers in the country numbered but little more than three thousand. To add to the distresses of the Canadians, they had been plundered by traders and contractors.

It is said that the worst swindling was in the interest of a company which operated under the name of one of its agents, Cadet. Having the contract to furnish the army with provisions, they collected all the worn-out horses in the country, and served them up to the starving soldiers; and from this, whenever the men saw a jaded skeleton of a horse, they called him "a cadet."

Vaudreuil, the governor, having received warning from France of the intentions of the English, sent a small force to Niagara under the engineer Pouchot, not expecting to be able to hold the post, and not wishing to sacrifice many men, or to spare the troops from the more important points. Pouchot repaired the defences, and when the alarm was given that the English were near, sent for men from Presqu' Isle, Venango, and Detroit.

Prideaux, in command of two British regiments, a battalion of Royal Americans, two battalions from New York, and a train of artillery, was joined by Johnson with a detachment of Indians. They began their march from Schenectady on the 20th of May, and, after a difficult journey, reached Oswego, where a detachment under Colonel Haldimand was left to take possession and form a post, and the remainder of the force embarked on Lake Ontario,, and on the 1st of July landed without opposition about six miles east of the mouth of the Niagara.

The fort was on a narrow promontory between the lake and the river. Prideaux made preparations to invest it by planting batteries on the land side, while his boats cut off the approach by water. To a summons on the 8th to surrender, Pouchot answered that the king had entrusted him with the place; that he was in condition to defend it; and that if General Prideaux were ever to enter it, he should at least gain his esteem by a courageous defence, before making any terms with him.

Prideaux began his trenches on the 10th, and on the 11th a sally was made from the fort; but the English placed themselves in line of battle, and the French were obliged to retire. Prideaux was steadily advancing the work, opening trenches and placing batteries, when, on the 19th, he was killed by the bursting of a shell from a Coehorn mortar in one of the trenches, where he had gone to issue orders. Amherst appointed General Gage to succeed him, but before the arrival of Gage the command devolved upon General Johnson, who carried on the siege according to the plans of Prideaux.

On the 23rd, Pouchot, receiving intelligence that about sixteen hundred French and Indians were on the way to his relief under D'Aubry and De Lignery, sent word that if they did not feel strong enough to attack the enemy, who were four or five thousand strong, they should approach on the other side of the river, where the English were only two hundred strong, and could not easily be re-enforced. After driving them back, they could reach the fort by *bateaux* which would be sent over to them.

The besieged then awaited anxiously the approach of the re-enforcement, on which all their hopes depended. The defences were steadily giving way under the heavy fire from the batteries, and the garrison were picked off by the marksmen in the trenches. Johnson had placed his main army above the fort to intercept the approach from the south. On the 24th, being informed by scouts that the force of French and Indians under D'Aubry and De Lignery was approaching, he detached a force of grenadiers and light infantry and some Mohawks under Colonel Massey, to meet them. A regiment under Colonel Farquhar was placed midway between them and the fort, ready to assist the advance, or go to the aid of the besieged in the event of a sally.

The Mohawks advanced and gave the signal for a *parley* with De Lignery's Indians; but as it was not answered, they fell back and took their station on the flanks of the British regiments. D'Aubry formed his men, and gave the order for attack. His Indians attempted to break up the English ranks by the tactics which had succeeded at Braddock's defeat; but the grenadiers scattered them with a few volleys, and they disappeared so suddenly that the French believed they had previously agreed to desert.

D'Aubry led on his men to attack the English front, but the Mohawks threw themselves on the flanks of the French Army, and plunged them into disorder, while the English made an impetuous charge. The French fought desperately for about half an hour, when they were broken and completely routed. They fled through the woods, and were pursued by the victorious army. Many were slain, and a few escaped; the remainder were captured, D'Aubry and sixteen other officers being among the prisoners.

The firing had been heard at the fort in the morning, and the besieged had anxiously awaited the event of the battle which was to decide the fate of the fort. At first the rattle of musketry seemed to be drawing near, and the beleaguered garrison believed the English were driven before the relieving force. Then the noise of the firing fluctuated, sometimes nearer the fort and again farther away and fainter. At length it receded rapidly, grew fainter, and ceased.

Then the garrison knew that their re-enforcements had been driven back; but how disastrously they were defeated, they did not know till an Onondaga Indian, who had asked leave to go out from the fort to fight with them, returned with great difficulty through the lines of the besiegers at two o'clock, and reported that the survivors had all

BRITISH INFANTRY SOLDIER

HIGHLAND REGIMENT UNIFORMS

been put to flight, and every officer was either killed or captured. At four o'clock Sir William Johnson sent Major Harvey to inform Pouchot of the result of the battle, and ask him to surrender without more bloodshed. Pouchot professed to doubt the report, and sent one of his officers with Major Harvey to see if D'Aubry and his subordinates were really in the hands of the enemy. On their report, the garrison became disorderly, and ready to abandon everything in confusion, and it was with difficulty that Pouchot restrained them until the terms of capitulation were arranged. They marched out with the honours of war, on the 25th, and laid down their arms on the shore of the lake. They were in great fear of the Indians, remembering the scene at Fort William Henry; but Johnson kept his word that they should not be molested, and restrained the savages from any assault on the conquered garrison.

As the stations beyond Niagara were now completely cut off from communication with the east, and had given up a large part of their men to join D'Aubry, they were no longer capable of resistance. Presqu' Isle, Venango, and Le Boeuf were easily taken by Colonel Bouquet, who had been sent to summon them to surrender.

Colonel Haldimand had been left at Oswego with five or six hundred men. They had not had time to entrench themselves fully, but had formed a sort of wall about their camp with the barrels of pork and flour that had been provided and stored there in great profusion, when De la Corne came down from La Presentation (Ogdensburg) with five or six hundred Canadians and a large body of Indians, accompanied by the zealous Abbé Picquet, founder of the mission at that point.

Haldimand's men, having no apprehension of danger, were scattered through the woods, cutting trees for their entrenchments, when they were fired upon by De la Corne's scouts, who then pressed on to the camp. What followed is related by a French writer who was present:—

> If De la Corne had followed his advance-guard, the English would have lost everything. But the Abbé Picquet, who heard the beginning of the firing, thought it was his duty, before his troops should attack, to make a short exhortation and give them absolution. This led to the loss of their opportunity; and the English ran to arms and placed themselves behind the barrels. De la Corne arrived after his detachment, who were scattered

around the English, but did not approach nearer, on account of their superiority. He wished to have them renew the attack, but some Canadians, who would rather retreat than fight, cried out that the blow had failed, and, in spite of their officers, regained their boats as soon as possible. The Abbé Picquet, who tried to rally them, was thrown down, when he caught hold of one and called out, 'Save at least your chaplain!' We sustained but a small loss, as the English did not pursue. Had this body been defeated, Niagara might have been saved, for their army could not have received the troops and supplies.

The English lost only two killed and eleven wounded. The French commandant at Toronto set fire to his buildings and took his small garrison to Montreal, as soon as he heard of the fall of Niagara.

Fearing the army from Niagara would next be marched on Montreal, Vaudreuil sent De Levis up the river to guard the approach to that city from the lake. He took possession of Oswegatchie, or Ogdensburg, to defend the passes of the St. Lawrence, but had only few men. Amherst ordered General Gage to go and get possession of that important post. But Gage found difficulties and made excuses until the season was so far advanced that it was impossible. He had been appointed to succeed Prideaux, but did not reach Niagara until after Johnson had taken the fort. He was afterward, in 1763, appointed commander-in-chief of the British forces in America, and was royal Governor of Massachusetts when the Revolutionary War broke out.

For the reduction of the forts at Ticonderoga and Crown Point, Amherst had somewhat more than eleven thousand men. He began preparations early in May at Albany, preparing boats, gathering stores, and disciplining the new recruits. He sent Major West with a detachment to build a small stockade fort between Fort Edward and Lake George, and in June his army was slowly moved on to encampments near Fort Edward.

On the 21st of June, the general marched six thousand troops to the border of the lake, and traced the plan of a fort on the spot where Fort William Henry had stood. The remainder of the troops and the boats were now brought up; but the embarkation did not take place until the 21st of July; but in the interval, the sloop *Halifax* and a floating battery of eight guns which had been sunk the previous year, were raised from the lake and prepared for service.

The army moved down the lake in four columns, in a fleet of

whale-boats, *bateaux*, and artillery-rafts, very much as Abercrombie's men had gone to their defeat the year before, and left the boats nearly opposite the former landing-place. The vanguard, pushing on rapidly over the road to the falls, met a detachment of French and Indians, whom they overpowered and scattered after a slight skirmish, and the main body pressed on and took a position at the saw-mills. From prisoners it was learned that Bourlamaque commanded at Ticonderoga with thirty-four hundred men. Montcalm was at Quebec.

The next morning, Amherst prepared to attack where the British army had suffered defeat in 1758. But the French, conscious of their inability to defend the lines against so overwhelming a force, abandoned them, and withdrew into the fort, while the lines were taken possession of by the grenadiers, and the remainder of the army encamped in the rear.

In the centre they found a lofty cross surmounting a grave, and on the cross a plate of brass with the inscription:

Pone principes eorum sicut Oreb et Zebec et Zalmanna,
"Make their nobles like Oreb and Zebah and Zalmunna;"—a quotation from the eighty-third psalm.

The French kept up a fire through the 23rd, which fell harmless on the well-protected lines. Bourlamaque, then, seeing the uselessness of a defence, silently withdrew most of his men in the night, leaving four hundred to keep up the firing and conceal the retreat of their comrades. During the two following days, they maintained a vigorous fire, doing some damage to the British, who were advancing their lines toward the fort; then they too abandoned the place, having first loaded and aimed the guns, charged some mines, and placed a lighted fuse to the powder magazine.

An explosion and the light of the burning works assured the English of the retreat of the French, of which they had already heard from a deserter, and Colonel Haviland pursued them down the lake with a few troops, and took sixteen prisoners and some boats laden with powder. At daybreak, a sergeant volunteered to enter the burning fort, and raise the English flag in place of the white banner of France.

After the flames were extinguished, Amherst, who had lost about seventy-five men, went to work to repair the fortifications and complete the road from the lake. Some sunken French boats were raised, and a brig was built. Amherst was slowly preparing to attack Crown Point, and sent Rogers with his rangers to reconnoitre. But on the 1st

PLAN
de la Ville de
QUEBEC

of August they learned that the French had abandoned that fort also; and on the 16th that Bourlamaque's men were encamped on the Isle aux Noix, at the northern extremity of Lake Champlain, commanding the entrance to the Richelieu. They had been joined by some small detachments, and numbered about thirty-five hundred men.

Amherst spent his time fortifying Crown Point, and building boats and rafts, and on the 11th of October he had the brig from Ticonderoga, a raft for artillery, and a new sloop ready to sail, and embarked his troops. One boat with twenty-one men was captured; and with this prize the French vessels disappeared, and carefully avoided an action. Three of them, chased by Amherst's vessels under Captain Loring, were so hard pressed that the crews ran one aground and sank the others. But a storm with contrary winds kept back the English vessels. It was too late to descend to Montreal and go to the help of Wolfe; the time for that had been passed in elaborate and useless preparations.

The repair of the forts, if not unnecessary, was not at all pressing. It was not probable that the French with their exhausted army would very soon attempt to recover the forts on Lake Champlain; if the English were to conquer and keep Canada, they would be of no use; if another campaign had still to be fought, there would be time enough to fortify. The immediate and pressing need was, to sustain Wolfe.

Amherst was very fortunate in his enterprises; he had overwhelming numbers and an exhausted foe, so that his generalship was not put to any severe test. He was cautious to excess, slow and sure in what he attempted; the trouble was, that he did not attempt enough. With the help of the great army lying useless at Lake Champlain, Wolfe's victory might possibly have been more speedy, and would almost certainly have closed the struggle.

In September, General Amherst sent Captain Kennedy with a flag of truce to offer peace and friendship to the St. Francis Indians, living at the lake of that name. These Indians were steadfast friends of the French, and had long harassed the frontier settlements of New England. Rogers says that, to his own knowledge, they had killed or carried off four hundred persons within six years. They kept Captain Kennedy and his whole escort as prisoners, and sent no answer to the message.

Amherst then sent Robert Rogers with two hundred men to attack their settlements, with orders to take complete vengeance on the warriors for their cowardly attacks on defenceless settlements, but by no means to injure any women or children.

St. Francis is within three miles of the St. Lawrence, and about midway between Montreal and Quebec. The route lay through an almost unbroken forest. Rogers says in his journal:—

> We marched nine days through wet, sunken ground, the water most of the way near a foot deep; it being a spruce bog. When we encamped at night, we had no way to secure ourselves from the water but by cutting the boughs of trees, and with them erecting a kind of hammocks. (See *Journals of Robert Rogers of the Rangers* by Robert Rogers; Leonaur 2005.)

It was twenty-two days before they came in sight of the Indian town, and the party was by that time reduced one fourth through the hardships and accidents of the march.

In the evening, Rogers reconnoitred the town. The warriors were holding a feast, dancing, singing, and carousing. Waiting till they had lain down to sleep, at three o'clock in the morning, Rogers marched his men within five hundred yards of the village, where they laid aside their baggage and made ready for the attack.

Just before sunrise he gave the order, and his men burst into the sleeping town. The Indians, who had gone to sleep without placing sentinels, were completely surprised. Bewildered with their excesses and the sudden awakening, they could make no resistance. Many were slain in their sleep, others struck down as they were attempting to fly. Some reached the river and embarked in canoes; but they were pursued, and the boats were sunk. Some concealed themselves in the cellars and lofts of their houses, and were consumed in the flames when the town was fired. By seven o'clock in the morning the ruin was complete. All the houses were burned but three, which were saved because they were stored with corn, that Rogers needed for his men. Two hundred Indians had been killed, and twenty women and children were made prisoners, of whom all but five were released. Rogers had lost but one friendly Indian killed, and a captain and six privates wounded.

He was now, however, in a very dangerous position, for he learned that there was a party of three hundred Frenchmen with some Indians below him on the river, that his boats had been taken, and that a smaller force was lying in wait for him farther up the stream. There seemed to be no way to extricate his men from this peril except by following the upper branches of the Connecticut, and descending that river to Fort Number Four. The route was rugged and difficult, and they were poorly supplied with provisions.

They had marched eight days, and their food was nearly exhausted, when Rogers divided them into small companies to take different routes and sustain themselves on the way as best they could. All were to meet at the mouth of the Ammonoosuc, where provisions were expected; but when Rogers's own party reached the place, they were not there. Rogers, with three others, embarked on a pine raft and dropped down to Fort Number Four, whence he speedily sent food to the starving men above. One party lost the way, and was four days without food; some died, and some lost their reason; the remnant, after devouring their leather straps and the covers of their cartridge-boxes, found a few roots that kept them alive until they reached the Connecticut and met one of the supply-boats sent by Rogers.

CHAPTER 19

The Siege of Quebec

To watch for and signal the approach of the British fleet which was hourly expected at Quebec, three stations were chosen by the French: the first at Isle du Portage, the second on a height near Kamouraska, and the third on the Isle of Orleans.

On the east, and partially on the south of the promontory on which the city is built, sweeps the deep and rapid current of the St. Lawrence, at the north is the embouchure of the St. Charles, and slightly to the west a sudden curve of the same stream. The promontory is very steep along the St. Lawrence, and may be described as a bluff varying in height from one hundred and sixty to three hundred feet. In that direction nature seemed to have anticipated the work of the military engineer. The Lower Town, at the foot of the cliff, was defended by batteries on the quays; and the avenues leading from the river were barricaded. The communication between the Lower Town and the Upper Town was secured by a strong picketing, and commanded by a battery.

To prevent the approach of the enemy from the valley of the St. Charles, it was determined to close the entry to that stream. At a point opposite the gate of the bishop's palace, a boom was run across, consisting of logs chained together and kept in place by anchors. Above this boom three merchant vessels were sunk; and on a platform built upon them was placed a battery of heavy guns, commanding the entire bay. In front of the boom five barges were set, each armed with a cannon. On the left bank was placed a battery of four guns to protect the whole. Farther up, near the Charlesbourg road, a bridge of boats was thrown across the St. Charles, and defended at each end by a horn work.

On the city side, a line of entrenchments, with artillery, ran from the bridge to the palace gate. From the opposite bank of the St.

Charles, the northern shore of the St. Lawrence, to the mouth of the Montmorenci, eight miles below, was entrenched and at all accessible points fortified, the line being continued for a short distance along the right bank of the Montmorenci.

On the landward side, the defence of the city was not formidable, consisting only of a rampart of moderate height, with neither parapet nor embrasures, and unprotected by fosse or glacis. For nine miles above the city, every apparently accessible point was entrenched and guarded; among others the spot then called the Anse du Foulon (the fuller's bay), but now known as Wolfe's Cove.

There were gathered for the defence of Quebec about thirteen thousand men, of whom only six worn battalions were French regulars, the rest being raw Canadian militia; so that the generous Wolfe afterward hesitated to call such a force an army. A council of war was held toward the close of May, when the order of battle was issued and general regulations given for the conduct of the campaign.

Vauquelin was made commander of the bay, with authority over craft of all kinds. The army occupied its entrenched camp from the redoubt on the left bank of the St. Charles to a point on the Montmorenci above the great falls. The right, consisting of the brigades of Quebec and Three Rivers under St. Ours and De Borne, forty-four hundred and twenty men in all, was placed along the plain to the River Beauport. The centre consisted of the regulars, two thousand strong, under Senezergues, and the Montreal militia, eleven hundred and fifty strong, under Prudhomme, and was placed on the heights of Beauport. The brigade of the Island of Montreal, under Herbin, twenty-three hundred strong, formed the left, and was placed along the high ridge down the St. Lawrence. A reserve force of three hundred and fifty cavalry, fourteen hundred volunteers of Canada and Acadia, and four hundred and fifty Indians, under Boishebert, stretched down to the Montmorenci and along its right bank. The artillery was under the command of Mercier, and the militia of the city was left as a garrison under the king's lieutenant, De Ramsay.

It was the opinion of the French commander that no attack would be made directly on the town from the river front, but that an attempt would be made to pierce his extended lines somewhere between the Montmorenci and Beauport River, and possibly between the latter and the left bank of the St. Charles. For the event of a successful assault in either neighbourhood—and Montcalm was by no means overconfident—lines of retreat were carefully marked out, all arranged with the general design of swinging the army back behind the St. Charles as a new line of defence, with the right on the city fortifications, and the left extended as far as possible.

That the authorities were not sanguine, is clear from the final sentence of their instructions:—

It is incumbent on us to exert our most strenuous efforts to defend and preserve Quebec, or at least to retard the reduction of it as long as possible, because it is evident that the fate of the colony will depend entirely on that of its capital.

These precautions were taken in good time. In the middle of February, a powerful squadron set sail from England, under command of Admiral Saunders, described by Walpole as "a pattern of most sturdy bravery united with the most unaffected modesty." With him sailed General James Wolfe, chosen to command the expedition to Quebec. The fleet arrived off Louisbourg on the 21st of April, but the port was blocked with ice, and the squadron rendezvoused at Halifax, and proceeded to Louisbourg a few days later. The naval force consisted of twenty-two ships of the line, five frigates, and nineteen smaller war-vessels, together with a crowd of transports, on which the land forces were embarked on the 1st of June. These were divided into three brigades, under command of Generals Monckton, Townshend, and Murray, all in the prime of manhood, eager for personal glory and zealous in the service of their country.

Colonel Guy Carleton, afterward Lord Dorchester, was quartermaster-general, Major Isaac Barré was adjutant-general, and Richard Montgomery was among the captains. The whole military force is commonly estimated at something more than eight thousand men, though some French writers put its strength at eleven thousand. It might be described as a corps of picked men; braver or better disciplined troops have seldom embarked in a more hazardous enterprise, or been more ably commanded.

Admiral Durell was sent forward with the van, in the hope that he would intercept a squadron of supply-ships from France, but was too late. The whole fleet got under way by June 4th and joined Durell on the 23rd, at Isle aux Coudres. It is said that as the vessels of the latter hove in sight at this point on their way up the river, they were flying the French flag; and the watchers at the signal-stations, seeing the welcome ensign, despatched hasty expresses to Quebec to announce that succour was at hand. But after pilots had put off to the ships in canoes, the white colours were struck, and the Union Jack run up in their place, to the dismay of the Canadians along the shore. A priest who saw the change through a glass dropped dead at the sight, from the sudden revulsion of feeling. On the 26th the squadron anchored off the Isle of Orleans.

The passage up the river had been unusually fortunate, and surprised the French greatly, since they had taken pains to remove the buoys from the channel, and expected that the heavy ships of the line would run aground at various difficult points. The rapidity of the passage was long explained by the fact that charts of the St. Lawrence had been found in one of two French vessels captured by Admiral Durell near the mouth of the river; but French authorities assert that a certain Denis de Vitré, captain of a French frigate taken during the war, consented to pilot the fleet to Quebec for a commission in the British navy.

During the night of the 26th forty rangers landed on the island, and, pushing cautiously into the interior, came upon a party of armed peasants, engaged in burying their valuables. There was a hasty skirmish, in which both parties were badly frightened; a fight in the woods at midnight between a band of marauders and a party of men concealing their treasures being by no means a cheerful kind of encounter.

The next day troops were landed, debarking at a cove under the Church of St. Lawrence, on the walls of which was a placard asking "the worthy officers of the British Army" that the place might be spared. Wolfe probably pushed on at once to the point of the island nearest Quebec.

Above the island, and nearly opposite the city, lay Point Levi, the only unprotected spot within easy reach of the invaders. Montcalm had urged in the council of war that it should be fortified and garrisoned with four thousand troops, but his opinion was overruled by the Governor-General. Wolfe instantly chose it as an available point from which to attack Quebec, though it was said to be held by a strong detachment, and he also selected the spot on which he stood as the site of fortifications to cover the hospitals and army-stores, which might find perfect security in that beautiful island with the fleet at anchor in front.

The day had been stormy, but the evening came on clear though dark; and the French chose it for their first attempt to burn the English fleet. They put fire-ships afloat with the ebbing tide, each laden with grenades, shells, useless muskets loaded to the muzzle, and tar-barrels.

As they were swept in the direction of the transports, the flames broke out among them and spread rapidly and fiercely, to the accompaniment of a random fusillade. A panic arose among the soldiers on the beach, for the unaccustomed character of the danger terrified them; but the sailors were cool, and ready with a remedy. Well-manned boats set out, and, after waiting for the subsidence of the irregular firing, pushed on and grappled the fire-ships, turning them ashore, where they burned harmlessly away, and served as a cheerful illumination to the warlike scene.

On the morning of the 28th, Wolfe issued a proclamation to the inhabitants of Canada. He set forth the determination of the English king to deprive France of her American settlements; enumerated the advantages of Great Britain in the struggle; alluded to the cruelties practised by the French on the English colonies, as justifying severe reprisals, but promised the most considerate treatment if the Canadians would accept the protection of England, and abandon France, which had practically abandoned them. Speaking in the name of his master, he said:—

> It is not against the industrious peasants, their wives and children, nor against the ministers of religion, that he designs making war. He laments the misfortunes to which this quarrel exposes them, and promises them his protection, offers to maintain them in their possessions and permit them to follow the worship of their religion, provided that they do not take any part in the differences between the two crowns, directly or indirectly.

Of course, all these fair promises were worthless, for the conditions on which they were made were not such as the Canadians were very likely to comply with. As a natural consequence, the struggle was destined to degenerate into a cruel and bloody one at all points save the regular field of battle, where it was bloody without being unnecessarily cruel.

On the night of the 29th of June, Monckton, to whom the movement against Point Levi was entrusted, sent over a detachment which took possession of Beaumont Church and barricaded it. Early in the morning more men passed over, and before evening the British troops had possession of the pretty village of Point Levi. The opposition amounted to nothing more than skirmishing, as the force in possession of the position was neither strong enough nor skilful enough to make an obstinate defence, though the nature of the ground was favourable to it.

During the morning occurred one of those tragedies that exhibit the brutality of war. A party of rangers had pushed forward from Beaumont Church to reconnoitre, and had taken possession of a large and fine, but apparently deserted, farmhouse. The soldiers heard the sound of voices, and, after a hasty search, set fire to the buildings and fell back, but were recalled by the shrieks of women and children who had hidden in the cellar and were perishing in the flames. We are told that they worked gallantly though ineffectively to rescue their victims, and it would be pleasant to believe the best; but so many strange things happened during the campaign that the historian grows weary of trying to explain away atrocities.

On the morning of July 1st; the French pushed over their floating batteries to attack the post at Point Levi, but the frigate *Trent* interposed, and easily drove them off. Monckton's and Townshend's men were set at work on the heights opposite Quebec and on the western end of the island, raising fortifications and planting batteries; and by the 9th everything was ready for action at those places.

In the meanwhile, scouting and skirmishing went on constantly. Major Scott pushed up along the right bank of the St. Lawrence as far as the Chaudière, but to no purpose. On one occasion, about twenty of the command, under a lieutenant, coming across a man and his three sons in a log hut, dragged them off out of pure wantonness, though two of the boys were mere children. The man and the oldest boy, a lad of fifteen, went quietly enough, but the frightened children screamed convulsively; and the scouting-party grew alarmed lest the screams should attract pursuit. It is said that they actually saw a band of Indians on their trail and heard the war-whoop ringing through the woods. They endeavoured to calm the children, but the poor things screamed the louder; then they tried to cast them off in the woods, but they clung to their captors all the tighter; and, as a last resource, to silence their hysterical sobs, the soldiers murdered them.

With his supplies in safety and a point secured from which an active bombardment could be maintained against the city, Wolfe began his first effort to break the enemy's lines. Under cover of the fleet, which swung into place on the 9th of July, and commanded the French position along the river below the city, Wolfe moved the bulk of his army, under Townshend and Murray, to the north bank of the St. Lawrence, just below the mouth of the Montmorenci. The east or left bank of this stream is higher than the opposite one; and along these heights the British troops encamped, facing the left of the French line, with nothing but the river intervening. Artillery was placed in position, and the men were ordered to entrench.

On the morning of the 10th, Captain Dank's company of rangers, which had been sent into the woods to protect men engaged in making fascines, was suddenly attacked by Indians, and nearly destroyed. The action took place so close to the lines that the men who rushed to the rescue could actually see the savages scalping their dead comrades and murdering the wounded.

Wolfe reconnoitred the Montmorenci upward in the hope of finding a crossing that he might force, and so turn the left of the French position, but without success. There were two Indian attacks on the reconnoitring party, but they were easily repulsed, though not without the loss of forty officers and men.

It was found that the only pathway to the French lines on the Montmorenci side lay through the ford below the falls, which was practicable at low tide, and might be covered by the fire of the batteries on the heights above, and of such light-draught vessels as could get close to the shore. The prospect for an attack at this point was so unpromising, that Wolfe waited until he should have studied other points before he determined to strike there. It is said that Montcalm, when urged by De Levis to attempt to dislodge his enemy, remarked: "While there, he cannot hurt us. Let him amuse himself."

Meanwhile, on the night of the 12th of July, a body of sixteen hundred French, under Dumas, crossed the St. Lawrence above the city and set out for Point Levi, doubtless with the expectation of finding it held by a weak force. The French marched in two columns, and, in the excitement of the night movement, the rear body mistook that in front for the enemy, and poured a volley into it, which was promptly returned. There was an instant panic, and both parties set off in the wildest disorder for the boats, reaching the beach in time to recross the river early in the morning of the 13th, with a loss of seventy killed and wounded. Wolfe regretted that they got away without making an attack and giving him an opportunity to defeat them. This affair is known among Canadians as "The Scholars' Battle," because the firing was begun by some of the boys from the city schools, who were in the ranks.

A lively bombardment of the city followed, which was especially effective from the Point Levi batteries, and on the 16th the town was set on fire. The firing was renewed at intervals, and four times the city was in flames. To sum up at once the results of weeks of cannonading, it may be said, in the words of Wolfe himself, that the Upper Town was considerably damaged, and the Lower Town entirely destroyed. The destruction fell heaviest upon the church and private individuals; the cathedral and most of the finest residences were in ruins within a month. Of course, all this was useless, except in so far as it kept up the appearance of activity on the part of the besiegers. It did not at all affect the military strength of the place.

On the night of the 18th of July occurred one of the most significant events of the expedition. Two men-of-war, two armed sloops, and two transports filled with troops, the whole under the command of Captain Rous, ran up the river past the town, escaping without injury, as the French failed to notice them in time to bring their guns to bear; and the next day two hapless sentinels who were held responsible were hanged in sight of both armies. A battery in position at Sillery dropped a few shots among the English vessels and made them move on up the river, and the gunners of the city, grown unusually vigilant, struck the mast out of Wolfe's barge, which was skirting the southern shore to join the ships that had run the gauntlet.

The passage of the forts opened up the whole river, and rendered the English masters of the stream above and below. But the first fruits of the achievement were not promising. Wolfe said in his report to Pitt:—

> This enabled me to reconnoitre the country above, where I found the same attention on the enemy's side, and great difficulties on ours, arising from the nature of the ground, and the obstacles to our communication with the fleet. But what I feared most was, that if he should land between the town and the River Cape Rouge, the body first landed could not be re-enforced before they were attacked by the enemy's whole army.

He thought of landing three miles above the town, but the enemy brought cannon and a mortar to play on the shipping, to use his own words:—

> And, as it must have been many hours before we could attack them—even supposing a favourable night for the boats to pass by the town unhurt—it seemed so hazardous that I thought best to desist.

Merely to divert the attention of the enemy, Wolfe sent Colonel

Carleton up the river with the troops that had already passed the town. On the 22nd he landed at Point aux Trembles, dispersed a party of Indians, captured a few civilians, and procured correspondence, which plainly showed that the people in Quebec were hungry and disheartened, and almost as disgusted with the defence as the English were with the attack.

Wolfe returned to the position on the Montmorenci after his trip above the town, convinced that he would have to make an attempt to break into Montcalm's entrenched camp somewhere between the St. Charles and the Montmorenci. He says:—

> I now resolved to take the first opportunity which presented itself of attacking the enemy, though posted to great advantage and everywhere prepared to receive us.

If he was somewhat daunted at the prospect, it is probable that there was much discontent and discouragement throughout the expedition. Indeed, there are extant letters written to the Governor of Nova Scotia by a minister who accompanied the expedition, expressing the greatest contempt for the capacity of the commander-in-chief, and repeating the criticisms on his conduct which were current on shipboard.

But the young general was not the man to give up an enterprise merely because it looked desperate. On the shore of the St. Lawrence, near the mouth of the Montmorenci, was a detached redoubt, apparently out of reach of musketry from the hill and Wolfe determined to make this the key of an attack. His design was to seize it; then, if the French disputed its possession, a general engagement would be brought on, which was what he aimed at. If they gave it up without a struggle, it might afford a point from which to reconnoitre their lines in security.

As the water shoaled along the northern shore so that the men-of-war could not get into position to bring their guns to bear, the admiral armed two light-draught transports which might be run aground to cover a descent on the redoubt, and the frigate *Centurion* was brought close to the mouth of the Montmorenci to cover the ford below the falls. The artillery on the height along the left bank of that stream was placed in position to enfilade the left of the enemy's entrenchments.

The plan of action was, to put a part of Monckton's brigade from Point Levi, and the grenadiers of the army, on the boats, and make a dash for the redoubt; while the brigades of Townshend and Murray

213

were to be ready to march from their camp on the left bank of the Montmorenci, and cross the ford in support of their comrades.

At ten o'clock in the forenoon of July 31st, the 15th and 78th regiments of Monckton's brigade, thirteen companies of grenadiers, and two hundred Royal Americans, embarked in small boats, and the flotilla moved into the northern channel of the St. Lawrence. The two armed transports, Wolfe being on one of them, were run aground at about eleven o'clock; and the cannon from those vessels, from the *Centurion*, and from all the fleet, from the heights of Montmorenci and from Point Levi, opened fire, every available gun in the circle of the British position about Quebec joining in the chorus.

Close inspection showed Wolfe that the detached redoubt was really covered by fire from the French lines, and that musketry from the grounded vessels would be of no avail in helping the attack. This was a disappointment; but he was not to be diverted from his purpose. Some delay was occasioned by a feint on the left of the French line, which looked like a movement to cross the Montmorenci above the falls, and make a counter attack; but this was checked by a display of the 48th regiment in motion beyond Point Levi, which caused Montcalm to send two battalions to guard against a crossing above the town.

It was four o'clock in the afternoon when Wolfe signalled for a renewal of the cannonade, and at five he ran up a red flag at the mizzen peak of one of the stranded transports, as the sign to advance. The flotilla dashed forward with a will, and the troops of Townshend and Murray set out for the ford. The French met the advance of the boats with a lively shower of shot and shell, which, however, did little damage; but the advance was checked by a reef running out from the shore, on which many of the small craft ran aground; and, as a consequence, the whole flotilla of fifteen hundred boats was thrown into confusion.

Order was soon restored, and the general and several naval officers took a flat-bottomed boat, and examined the shore for a landing-place, signalling in the mean time for Townshend to halt. An opening in the reef was found in the course of half an hour, and the flotilla was put in motion once more. The grenadiers and Royal Americans were first on shore. The orders were for the grenadiers to form in four divisions, wait for the landing of Monckton's troops and the approach of Townshend to within supporting distance, and then attack.

But they attacked without waiting or forming—"ran on," to use Wolfe's words, "toward the enemy's entrenchments in the utmost disorder and confusion." This excess of valour and lack of steadiness was fatal. The French had abandoned the detached redoubt, and the mass of grenadiers pushed boldly up the slope at the entrenchments. It was an assault which would have been useless, even if successful, as Monckton had not landed, and Townshend and Murray were not within reach; but it was not destined to succeed. The Canadians received the grenadiers with a close and effective fire, which not only checked their advance, but drove them back in dismay, leaving some scores of scarlet-clad bodies along the green hillside.

The grenadiers sought shelter behind the abandoned redoubt, while their officers exposed themselves to no purpose, in the endeavour to re-form them under fire. Wolfe says:—

I saw the absolute necessity of calling them off, that they might form themselves behind Brigadier Monckton's corps, which was now landed and drawn up on the beach in extreme good order.

Not only were the grenadiers withdrawn, but it was resolved to abandon the attack. It was growing late in the evening, the state of the tide was such that the line of retreat by the ford would be cut off in case of disaster, and a storm which had been threatening for some time broke in fury. But these were, perhaps, the mere pretexts for a retreat. The main reason was, the rapid repulse of the picked troops of the army, who were beaten without getting an opportunity to fight.

The French made no attempt to interrupt the movement, as Monckton's men re-embarked, and Townshend withdrew, but says Wolfe:—

Some of their savages came down to murder such wounded as could not be brought off, and to scalp the dead, as their custom is.

Wolfe lost in this affair thirty-three officers and four hundred and ten men, killed or wounded. In his honest and straightforward account, he argues that the place chosen for the attack was well covered by British artillery, and afforded opportunity for the employment of all the troops at once, and the line of retreat, in case of repulse, was secure. The disadvantages were no less marked. He said:—

The beach upon which the troops were drawn up was of deep mud with holes, and cut by several gullies, the hill to be ascended very steep and not everywhere practicable, the enemy remaining in their entrenchments, and their fire hot. If the attack had succeeded, our loss must certainly have been great and theirs inconsiderable, from the shelter which the neighbouring woods afforded them. The River St. Charles still remained to be passed before the town was invested. All these circumstances I considered; but the desire to act in conformity with the king's instructions induced me to make this trial, persuaded that a victorious army finds no difficulties.

In a general order, the commander rebuked the grenadiers sharply for their undisciplined enthusiasm.

CHAPTER 20

The Capture of Quebec

Notwithstanding Wolfe's proclamation enjoining neutrality upon the Canadians, they withstood the depredations of the soldiery, and in some instances joined with the Indians in murdering and scalping scouting-parties. A protest from Wolfe to Montcalm brought the usual answer that the French officers could not control their wild auxiliaries—the same answer that in after-years the British themselves used to make when American commanders complained of Indian atrocities. As a curious measure of retaliation, the English troops were allowed to scalp all Indians, and Canadians fighting disguised as Indians, which was practically only an exemption of the regular troops. The foraging parties had been ordered to burn and lay waste the country, sparing nothing but churches, but molesting women and children "on no account whatsoever."

On the 28th of July, when the French renewed their attempt to burn the English fleet by casting loose a huge fire-raft of light vessels bound together, Wolfe sent a flag of truce to the garrison with this message:—

> If the enemy presume to send down any more fire-rafts, they are to be made fast to two particular transports, in which are all the Canadian and other prisoners, in order that they may perish by their own base inventions.

The defeat at Montmorenci tended to increase the existing irritation. The whole of August was spent in mere raiding. It was estimated, by one who took part in the devastation, that fourteen hundred farmhouses were burned and their orchards ruined. An expedition against St. Paul's Bay encountered some resistance, but succeeded in burning several pretty villages. The Louisbourg grenadiers, coming across a priest who had thrown himself into a house with a party of his parishioners, drew them out by a stratagem, and then killed and scalped thirty-one of them.

The only serious bit of campaigning that relieved this petty marauding was the expedition of General Murray up the river. He set out with twelve hundred men for the purpose of aiding Admiral Holmes in an attempt to destroy the French ships above the town, and to open communication with Amherst; but they escaped him by lightening and running into shallows, out of the way.

Murray found the north shore carefully watched at all points, and was beaten off twice in attempting to land. The third time he got a foothold at Dechambault, burned a magazine, captured a few prisoners, and discovered, by letters which fell into his hands, that Johnson had captured Niagara, and that Amherst was in possession of Crown Point. He then returned without having accomplished anything of importance.

During August, Wolfe, never in robust health, was stricken with a fever. As soon as he began to recover, he called together his brigadiers, and directed them to take into consideration the problem of the siege. He gave it as his opinion that the town would surrender if the French Army were defeated; that the army, and not the town, should be attacked; and submitted three plans, all looking toward an attempt to carry the entrenched camp at some point between the St. Charles and the Montmorenci.

But General Townshend proposed an alternative which met the approval of his associates, was finally adopted by the commander-in-chief, and resulted in the capture of Quebec. In support of the idea of getting a position on the heights of Abraham, he said:—

> If we can maintain a new position on that side, we shall force Montcalm to fight where we choose; we shall then be not only situated between him and his magazines, but also between his camp and the forces opposed to Amherst. If he offer us battle and he should lose the day, then Quebec, probably all Canada, would fall into our hands, a result far greater than could occur from a victory at Beauport; and, again, if he cross the River St. Charles with forces enough to confront us in the position we have supposed, the Beauport camp, thereby weakened, might be all the more easily attacked.

However, there was nothing sanguine in the tone of Wolfe's mind at this juncture. He had been two months before the city, the summer was rapidly passing away, and little was accomplished. The whole case is summed up frankly in his own letter to Pitt, in which he gave Townshend's plan, and said he had acquiesced in it; but he detailed the difficulties in the way of carrying it out and recapitulated the elements that had hitherto retarded success—the vigilance of the Indian scouts preventing surprise, the batteries on the heights commanding the fleet in case of a direct assault on the town from the river, and the difficulty of receiving any help from the fleet in the position it must necessarily take, if the Upper Town were chosen for the attack. He said:—

In this situation, there is such a choice of difficulties that I own myself at a loss how to determine.

Curiously enough, we have what is supposed to be a record of Montcalm's opinions at about the same time, in a letter sent to Paris. After describing the ill success of the besiegers, he says their only hope is in:—

Effecting a descent on the bank where the city is situated, without fortifications and without defence. They would then be in a position to offer me battle, which I could not refuse, and which I should not gain. . . . My Canadians, without discipline, deaf to the voice of the drum and martial instruments, disordered by this movement, could not form their ranks again. Moreover, they are without bayonets to oppose to those of the enemy; they could only fly, and there I should be, beaten without remedy.

This remarkable military prophecy was followed by a still more remarkable political prophecy which is quoted elsewhere. It is to be regretted that the authenticity of so wonderful a document as this letter should be questioned; but Carlyle, who quotes it in his *Frederick the Great*, declares in a note to the last edition of the work that it is a forgery. His reasons are not given; but the fact that the letter was first published in London, in 1777, is suspicious, as its fabrication might then have had a political end in view. Moreover, it is hard to understand why Montcalm should have written a long letter of this sort at a time when there was very little prospect of getting it to France. But something stronger than mere conjecture is needed to overturn the authority of the document.

On the 29th of August, five vessels ran past the town, and the next day four more. On the 1st of September the sick and wounded were brought to the Isle of Orleans; on the 2nd, a large body of the troops in position there withdrew; on the 3rd, the main body set all the houses and fortifications on fire, embarked in flat-bottomed boats, and moved to Point Levi; and on the 4th, the troops on the Island of Orleans were shifted to the same place. The whole available force of the army was then on the south side of the river.

On the 7th, 8th, and 9th, Admiral Holmes, commanding the squadron above the city, stretching from Sillery to Point aux Trembles, manoeuvred to divert the attention of the French. Montcalm was on the alert, and sent Bougainville up the river with about three thousand men to watch the enemy's movements. The bank was regularly patrolled, and guards were stationed at the Anse des Mères, Anse du Foulon, and the Cove of Samos, all of which the French general persisted in regarding as impracticable, probably because he was urged to take additional precautions by Vaudreuil. A month earlier, he had said in a letter to the governor touching these points:—

> Vigilant patrolling is all that is needed in addition; for we need not suppose that our enemies have wings to enable them in one night to cross the flood, debark, ascend broken up; steep ways, and resort to escalade—an operation all the more unlikely to take place, as the assailants would have to bring ladders.

On another occasion he wrote to Vaudreuil, who was concerned about the Anse des Mères:—

> I swear to you that one hundred men posted will stop an army, give us time to wait till daylight, and then come up from the right. At the slightest nocturnal alarm, I shall march to your relief with the regiments of Guyenne and Bearn, which encamp in line tomorrow. Show light tonight in canoes; and if darkness be great, light up fires.

It seems singular that he who had left nothing to chance below the city, should have trusted so much to chance above it.

After a careful examination of the northern bank, Wolfe and his officers had chosen for the contemplated descent a spot about three miles above the city, called the Anse du Foulon, now known as Wolfe's Cove. There a narrow path ran up the bank, and was defended at the top by an escarpment. The position was guarded by about one hundred men; but, unfortunately for the French, the place was in command of Vercors, who, three years before, had surrendered Beau Séjour, and was more notable for his skill in peculation than for his soldiership.

Some of the English troops marched on the south bank to a point eight miles up the river, and there embarked, but were set ashore again. On September 11th, Wolfe issued an order warning the army to be in readiness to land and attack the enemy, and hinting at a night's service in the boats. On the 12th, a deserter from Montcalm's camp reported the bulk of the French Army below the town, and the general incredulous as to any serious design at any point above. On the evening of that day, Wolfe issued his last general order, declaring that the Canadians were disheartened, that Amherst was advancing, and that a vigorous blow would determine the fate of Canada. Those first ashore were enjoined to form with expedition, march straight on the enemy, and charge whatever appeared. Much was to be expected from them in dealing with "five weak French battalions mingled with a disorderly peasantry."

The same evening, the heavier vessels below the city stood in toward Beauport shore and lowered away their boats filled with seamen and marines, as if for an attack. The rest of them set all sail and moved rapidly up to join Holmes's squadron at Cape Rouge, eight miles above the city, to which point Murray and Monckton marched from Point Levi, and the whole army embarked.

It was nine o'clock when the first division of sixteen hundred men, composed of the light infantry commanded by Colonel Howe, the regiments of Bragg, Kennedy, Lascelles, and Anstruther, a detachment of the Highlanders, and the American Grenadiers, took their places in the flat-bottomed boats, and the flotilla dropped down the river with the tide, Holmes's squadron following with the rest of the troops at an interval of forty-five minutes. Wolfe, though scarcely recovered from his illness, was as usual in the lead; and there is a tradition that, as he sat in the boat, floating along between the clear water and the starlit sky, the sense of the nothingness of that glory for which he had so thirsted came over him, and he repeated these lines from Gray's *Elegy*:—

The boast of heraldry, the pomp of power,
And all that beauty, all that wealth e'er gave,
Await alike the inexorable hour:
The paths of glory lead but to the grave.

He said: —

Now, gentlemen, I would rather be the author of that poem than take Quebec.

And doubtless the capture of the Canadian citadel was an easier task than the composition of that almost faultless threnody.

It was a circumstance in favour of the English expedition, that the French were expecting a convoy of provisions from Bougainville, and, warned of the fact, the boats gave the proper answer when the French sentinels challenged along the shore. One of the English vessels, however, unaware of the attempt to land, and on the watch for the convoy, came near ruining the enterprise by firing on the flotilla. The rapidity of the ebbing tide carried part of the boats a little below the appointed landing.

An hour before daylight, the light company of the 78th Highlanders, which was the first to land, began to scramble up the wooded precipice. The captain, Donald Macdonald, answered the challenge of the sentinel in French, and gained a few moments. But the noise of the advance startled the guard, which turned, fired an irregular volley down the precipice, and fled. According to an English account, Vercors, the captain, alone stood his ground and resisted stoutly; according to a French account, he was captured in his bed.

With very little loss, the troops reached the heights and formed on the Plains of Abraham, the tableland stretching away for nine miles above the city. As fast as a boat was emptied, it was despatched to the fleet, and reloaded with the men of Townshend's division. The battalions formed on the narrow beach, marched up the winding path, and reformed on the open ground above. At dawn, the whole army was in line, but only one gun had been brought up the hill.

Montcalm had been deceived by the movements of the boats below the town during the night, as they seemed to be threatening different points between Beauport and Montmorenci; and, though he heard the sound of a cannon and the rattle of musketry from the westward after daylight, he had no notion of what had happened, until couriers galloped into the camp at six o'clock with the intelligence.

"It can be but a small party come to burn a few houses and retire," he said. But when the news was confirmed, he exclaimed:—

Then they have at last reached the weak side of this miserable garrison! We must give them battle and crush them before midday.

Gathering all his available force, he moved rapidly across the St. Charles by the bridge of boats, and past the ramparts of the town, Vaudreuil being left to guard the lines. As early as eight o'clock, the head of the column was in sight, and by nine Montcalm was forming his line of battle. It has been said that he should not have fought at all: Bougainville was within an easy march; the English Army was weak, and could not attempt to attack a superior, or even an equal force, resting on the works of the city; the season was far advanced, and the raising of the siege merely a question of days. To deliver a hasty battle seemed mere madness.

Montcalm may have been fluttered by the appearance of the British in so dangerous a position, and so have made an unwise decision; or it may be that he was convinced he had a fair chance of victory, and saw that victory won under such circumstances meant the complete destruction of his enemy. Perhaps he simply saw the end approaching which he had so long anticipated; and, believing there was nothing effective to be done, determined to do something gallant.

Wolfe's line of battle was formed with the right on the precipice, scarcely a mile from the ramparts of the town. The 35th regiment was on the extreme right, the Louisbourg grenadiers joined them, and the 28th prolonged the line to the 43rd, which constituted the centre. Toward the left, the 47th, the 78th Highlanders, and the 58th followed in succession, the last regiment holding the brow of the ridge overlooking the valley of the St. Charles and completing the first line. In the second line, the 15th regiment rested its right upon the riverbank; the two battalions of the 60th, or Royal Americans, occupied the plain to the left. Colonel Burton with the 48th regiment was held in reserve, and Colonel Howe with the light infantry, grouped in some houses and neighbouring coppices, protected the left flank. Wolfe with Monckton took his station on the right of the first line, Murray commanded on the left, and Townshend had charge of the second line.

Montcalm's right was formed of the regiment of La Sarre and Languedoc, with a battalion of the Colonial troops; the regiments of Bearne and Guyenne were in the centre, supported by a strong body of militia; the Royal Roussillon and a battalion of the marine held the left. The commander took his place in the centre.

The ordinary English historian is accustomed to give the strength of Wolfe's army at forty-eight hundred and twenty-eight men, and that of Montcalm's at seventy-five hundred and twenty, basing the latter figure on the authority of an "intelligent Frenchman," casually mentioned in Knox's *Journal*, but not named. The ordinary French historian allows Wolfe eight thousand and Montcalm four thousand five hundred troops. But the best authorities estimate the strength of

CLIMBING THE CLIFF AT QUEBEC

each army at less than five thousand men, and as nearly numerically equal. The English troops, however, were a solid mass of tried veterans, confident in themselves and confident in their leader; the French troops were an incongruous mixture, part of whom mistrusted themselves, and part of whom mistrusted their comrades, while the commander mistrusted his army as a whole. Artillery played but little part in the battle. To offset the single cannon that Wolfe had dragged up the precipice, Montcalm brought up only two guns.

If it was inconsiderate folly on the part of the French general to risk a battle, it must be acknowledged that he fought it like a bold and skilful soldier. About ten o'clock, after an hour's cannonading, the fighting opened on the right, where the French skirmishers, mainly Canadians and Indians, pushed up the slope from the valley of the St Charles, turned the left flank of Murray's brigade, and attacked Howe's light infantry. The object of the movement, which was gallantly executed, seemed to be to roll back the English line and crowd it over the precipice. Townshend, who exhibited singular ability throughout this campaign, pushed forward the 15th regiment and the Royal Americans to the help of Howe, and restored the fight.

Meanwhile the French centre and left advanced rapidly, driving in Wolfe's skirmishers, whose retreat for a moment disordered the main line. But the disturbance passed away, and the British waited quietly for the approach of the enemy. The French line came on, firing quickly at a distance of a hundred yards. Wolfe, who was moving along his line exhorting the men to reserve their fire till they could deliver a volley at a distance of forty yards, was struck in the wrist with a bullet; but he wrapped his handkerchief about his hand, and paid no further attention to the wound. When at last the English troops received the order to fire, they delivered one of those close and deadly volleys for which they are celebrated, and under the crash of that battle-bolt the French column staggered.

St. Ours was killed, Senezergues fell mortally wounded, and many minor officers and men were stretched upon the field. The pressure of the fire, was so fierce that the Canadian militia broke, notwithstanding the efforts of Montcalm to keep them steady; and while the French left and centre hesitated and wavered, the right, checked by Townshend's dispositions, began to recoil before a counterattack of the 58th and 78th regiments.

Wolfe, seeing that the crisis of the fight was at hand, ordered an advance along the whole line. The movement, which began as a slow but steady advance, with deadly volleys clearing the way, soon took the form of a triumphant charge, the French breaking away in all directions. At this juncture Wolfe was struck a second time, somewhat more seriously, and as he pressed on in the pursuit at the head of the Louisbourg grenadiers, he was struck in the breast by a shot from a redoubt. He staggered, but catching hold of Lieutenant Brown, of the 22nd, murmured:—

Support me, that my brave fellows may not see me fall.

The lieutenant, a volunteer named Henderson, and a private soldier of the 22nd, carried him a little way to the rear, with the help of Captain Williamson of the Royal Artillery. There he asked to be laid down. They wanted to know if he would have a surgeon, but he said: "It is needless; it is all over with me."

One of the group about him cried out: "They run, see how they run!"

Like a man roused from sleep, Wolfe, who had been sinking rapidly, asked: "Who runs?'"

"The enemy, sir," was the answer. "Egad! they give way everywhere."

"Go one of you, my lads," said Wolfe, "to Colonel Burton. Tell him to march Webb's regiment with all speed down to the St. Charles, to cut off the retreat of the fugitives from the bridge."

Then, turning on his side, he died with the exclamation:—

Now, God be praised! I will die in peace.

About the same time that Wolfe was struck down, Carleton fell severely wounded, and Barré received a ball in the head, from the effect of which he afterward lost the sight of one eye. Monckton also fell, disabled but not dangerously hurt, as he was advancing between the 43rd and 47th regiments, and the command devolved upon Townshend, who, after disposing of the last organised resistance in a coppice toward the left of the victorious forces, took measures to withdraw from the pursuit and re-form the troops to meet the expected advance of Bougainville from up the river.

The 47th and 58th regiments had pushed the fugitives up to the very gates of St. Louis and St. John, while the 78th Highlanders, drawing their broadswords, followed the stragglers, slaughtering as they went; many of the Frenchmen joining to the cry for quarter the protest that they had not been at Fort William Henry. The remnants of

DEATH OF GENERAL WOLFE AT QUEBEC

the left and centre of Montcalm's army found refuge within the fortifications of the city, while all that was left of the right wing fell back in confusion beyond the St. Charles.

Montcalm had been mortally wounded while taking a gallant effort to rally his men. Death came to him more slowly than to Wolfe; but he met it with a Christian resignation not less admirable than the fiery heroism of the British commander. When he had been carried to the general hospital, a convent of the Augustine nuns on the St. Charles, about a mile from the town, and put to bed, with his wound dressed, he asked the surgeon if his hurt was mortal. When told that it was, he said: "I am glad of it." He then inquired:

"How long can I survive?"

"About a dozen hours; perhaps more, peradventure less," was the answer.

"So much the better," said Montcalm; "I shall not live to see the surrender of Quebec."

Shortly afterward Monsieur de Ramsay, the king's lieutenant, in command of the fortifications of the city, called upon the general and asked his advice on various points touching the defence. The dying man made answer:—

I'll neither give orders nor interfere any further. I have business that must be attended to of much greater moment than your ruined garrison and this wretched country. My time is very short; therefore, pray leave me. I wish you all comfort, and to be happily extricated from your present perplexities.

He then called for his chaplain and prepared for death, which came to his relief on the evening of September 14th.

The battle was scarcely over when Bougainville appeared upon the field; but the resolute front and superior numbers of Townshend dismayed him, and he fell back unpursued to Cape Rouge. There he was joined the same evening by Vaudreuil, who had abandoned the entrenched camp below the St. Charles with the remnants of the French Army. Word was sent to M. de Levis, then at Montreal, to come and assume command in Montcalm's place, and it is not improbable that an energetic leader such as he was might have done something to retrieve the evil effects of the first Battle of the Plains of Abraham; but by the time he was ready to move, Quebec had surrendered.

On the day succeeding the action, Townshend began the construction of works against the city and cut it off from communication with the surrounding country; and on the 17th the fleet moved up for an attack on the Lower Town. Provisions were scarce, the inhabitants of the city were disheartened, and the prospects of a protracted defence were gloomy. Consequently, M, de Ramsay completed negotiations for the surrender of the place at once. The capitulation was proclaimed on the morning of the 18th, and in the afternoon the representatives of the army took possession of the Upper Town, the representatives of the navy assuming the honour of occupying the Lower Town. The terms granted were honourable, as Townshend and Admiral Saunders were only too glad to secure their easy conquest by liberal concessions.

The garrison marched out with the honours of war, the people were secured in all their rights and privileges, and the Catholic church was guaranteed the enjoyment of freedom and the possession of its property. On the part of the French commander, the surrender must, on the whole, be regarded as somewhat pusillanimous, since a messenger from De Levis arrived on the 18th with a promise of help, which that officer would certainly have tried desperately to make good.

So ended the memorable siege of Quebec. The battle which decided the result was a mere skirmish, if we consider only the numbers engaged and the losses; for the English acknowledge a loss on their own part of but fifty-five killed and six hundred and seven wounded of all ranks, and only claim a loss on the part of the French of fifteen hundred killed, wounded, or missing. But the romantic circumstances attending the action—the night movement on the great river, the ascent of a precipice to find a field of battle, the fall of the two commanders, one so heroic in his victory, and the other so manly in his defeat, the decisive results of the brief struggle—all these things make the story of the capture of Quebec a favourite with the historian and the artist. (*See Musket & Tomahawk* by Francis Parkman; Leonaur, 2007.)

To be sure, the decisive character of the engagement on the Plains of Abraham was mainly due to the fact that it was England that won the victory; for the result gave her one of those strong natural positions on a great commercial channel which her mastery at sea has enabled her to hold in different parts of the world. Though the war was still to linger on, the event was no longer doubtful, as the possession of Quebec afforded the means of bringing the naval power of Great Britain to bear effectively; and the support of that power rendered Quebec invulnerable. The French might win another battle on the spot where Wolfe had defeated them, but it was destined to be a barren victory.

The news of the fall of the capital of Canada reached England two days after the news of the defeat at Montmorenci, and caused the wildest rejoicings—save in one small Kentish village, where sympathy with the widowed mother of the dead victor restrained the expression of public gratification. The remains of Wolfe were taken to England for interment, and his memory was honoured by his countrymen with lavish gratitude. Montcalm was buried in a church in Quebec, in a tomb scooped out by a hostile shell. Today a monument erected to the honour of both heroes looks down on the scene of their struggle—a memorial of one of those few conquests in the history of the world in which the vanquished have preserved possessions, language, religion, and the fair fame of the men who died for the lost cause.

CHAPTER 21

The Surrender of Canada

Notwithstanding the successes of 1759, Canada was not yet completely conquered. If Amherst had moved on faster and taken Montreal, the work would have been finished; but his failure to do so gave the French forces an opportunity to rally, and the indefatigable De Levis, who had succeeded Montcalm, gathered what remained of the army at Montreal, and made preparations for attempting the recovery of Quebec. The people of Canada were still more pressed with want than the year before; wheat sold at from thirty to forty *livres* a bushel (six or eight dollars), a cow was worth nine hundred *livres*, and a sheep from two to three hundred. (See also *The War for North America*: The Struggle between France & Britain for a Continent, containing *The Conquest of New France* and *The Fall of Canada* by George M. Wrong; Leonaur, 2016.)

After several fruitless attacks had been made on the British outposts during the winter, De Levis refitted all the vessels yet remaining early in the spring and gathered the stores still left at the forts on the Richelieu. On the 17th of April, he left Montreal with all his force, and descended the river, gathering up the detached troops on the way; the whole amounting to more than ten thousand men.

Quebec had been left in charge of Murray, with seven thousand men, a supply of heavy artillery, and stores of ammunition and provisions; but the number of men had been much reduced by sickness and by hardship encountered in bringing fuel to the city from forests, some as far as ten miles away. Their position, however, had been very much strengthened; Murray had erected redoubts, with artillery, outside the fortifications, and repaired five hundred of the injured houses for the accommodation of his troops.

De Levis encamped at St. Foy, and on the 27th advanced to within three miles of the city. Murray took the unaccountable resolution of sallying out with his reduced and dispirited army to meet the enemy in the open field—a measure which he afterward attempted to explain in a letter to the Secretary of State:—

> Well weighing my peculiar position, and well knowing that in shutting myself up within the walls of the city, I should risk the whole stake in the chance of defending a wretched fortification, which could not be lessened by an action in the field.

On the morning of the 28th of April, Murray marched his wasted army out to the Plains of Abraham, with twenty pieces of artillery, and formed his line of battle. Riding out to observe the position of the enemy, he found that they were unprepared for action, and returning he gave orders for an immediate attack, and the army marched down the slope from the heights and into the plains near Sillery Wood.

Two companies of the French grenadiers advanced and met the vanguard of the British, and then drew back; whereupon some of Murray's men pursued them, but were thus exposed to the fire of their own cannon, which obliged the gunners to cease firing, and they were repelled in turn by the French, who were now in battle array. The engagement immediately became general. The British left soon gave way, and drew back in confusion; the right followed; the artillery was lost; and at length only two regiments held the forlorn hope, and Murray's men were forced to fly, leaving three hundred dead upon; the field.

The wounded amounted to about seven hundred, many of whom were left in the hands of the enemy. It is charged that only twenty-eight of these were sent to the hospitals, and the rest given up to the Indians; but the French accounts say that the Indians, who had taken no part in the action, but had been skulking in the rear, came to the field during the pursuit and killed many of the wounded, while those that survived were protected from the Indians, whom De Levis quickly dispersed, and received the same treatment as the wounded French. The loss of De Levis has been variously given at from four hundred to eighteen hundred.

The French made immediate preparations for a siege by opening trenches. The English garrison was so reduced that not more than twenty-two hundred were fit for service; but they all went to work with alacrity, hoping to hold out until relief should come. Five hundred men who could not walk without crutches, made sand-bags and cartridges; and the women who were not employed in the care of the wounded assisted in the light work of the garrison. One hundred and thirty-two cannon were mounted, and opened fire on the French lines.

On the 9th of May, a ship was seen turning the bend below and advancing toward the city. Both armies were expecting relief, and their strength was so nearly balanced that the turning of the scale depended on the approaching ship. One of them wrote:—

> Such was the garrison's anxiety, that we remained some time in suspense, not having eyes enough to look at it; but we were soon convinced that she was British, although there were some among us who, having their motives for appearing wise, sought to temper our joy by obstinately insisting that she was French. But the vessel having saluted the fort with twenty-one guns, and launched her small boat, all doubts vanished. It is impossible to describe the gayety that seized upon the garrison. Officers and men mounted the ramparts, mocked at the French, and for an hour raised continual hurras, and threw their caps into the air. The city, the enemy's camp, the harbour, and the country around for miles in extent, re-echoed our cries and the roar of our batteries.

Other vessels arrived on the 15th, and on the following day they attacked and quickly destroyed the little French fleet under Vauquelin. De Levis, having nothing more to hope for, raised the siege in haste, abandoned his stores, and retreated to Montreal. A detachment of English troops pursued, and brought back a few prisoners.

All this time, Amherst was ponderously preparing to go to the aid of Quebec, and early in May he was ready to move from New York. Captain Loring was sent to drive the French cruisers from Lake Ontario, to prevent the French forces from retiring to the west, and making another stand.

Amherst had chosen to reach Montreal by the roundabout way of Oswego and the St. Lawrence. Colonel Haviland was to take the direct route by way of Lake Champlain, with about thirty-five hundred men; and Murray, aided by Lord Rollo and two battalions from Louisbourg, had been directed to ascend the river, and meet Amherst and Haviland before the doomed city.

It was the 9th of July when Amherst reached Oswego with part of his army; Gage brought the rest on the 22nd, and Johnson and his Indians joined the encampment the following day. There were over ten thousand soldiers and seven hundred Indians.

On the 7th of August, Amherst sent a detachment under Haldimand to take possession of the post at the head of the river, where Kingston now stands; and by the 12th the last of the army were embarked, and an armed vessel was captured on the river by a detachment of men in barges, under Colonel Williamson.

On Isle Royale was a small work called Fort Levi, under the command of Pouchot, which the English expected to pass "like a beaver's hut." But learning that there were some skilful pilots there, Amherst determined to capture it. Batteries were therefore placed, and on the 23rd the vessels opened a vigorous fire, and were soon joined by the batteries. Pouchot waited till the ships were within pistol-shot, and then returned the fire with such spirit that two of them were forced to run aground, and one to strike her colours.

Many of the English ships bore Indian names—the *Ottawa, Oneida, Onondaga*, etc.—and the Catholic Indians of Father Picquet's, mission, who were watching the contest from the fort, regarding the ships as on their side on account of the names, and because they carried Indians painted on their flags, became very much excited at seeing them faring badly, and especially when the *Ottawa* and the *Oneida* drifted off and ran aground.

On the 25th, Pouchot, being nearly at the end of his resources, surrendered to Amherst, with his garrison of nearly three hundred men. Selecting some guides for his ships down the dangerous course of the river, Amherst despatched the remainder of the garrison to New York by way of Oswego. The Indians had secretly planned to destroy the garrison when the fort should be given up; but Amherst, hearing of the plan, told Sir William Johnson to dissuade them from it, promising them all the stores in the fort, and threatening that his own soldiers would turn upon them if they attempted a massacre. The Indians submitted, but were sulky and dissatisfied, and Johnson told Amherst they would probably leave the army—as, indeed, most of them did. Amherst threatened them with vengeance on his return if they should commit any acts of violence on their way to their homes; and they were forced to content themselves with a peaceable journey.

On the way through the rapids, sixty-four boats, eighty-eight men, and a quantity of stores were lost. Amherst invested Montreal on the 6th of September, and was met by Murray, whose progress up the river had been a continual skirmish. Nearly every village assailed him with a fire of musketry; and he had taken vengeance on some by burning them. Haviland, coming up from Crown Point, had forced Bougainville to draw off most of his men from Isle aux Noix, and received the surrender of the remainder, and reached Montreal a day later than Amherst.

Vaudreuil had resolved not to make any useless resistance, but to give up the city as soon as the English Army should arrive; and on the 8th of September, not only Montreal, but all Canada—from the fishing stations on the Gulf of St. Lawrence to the crest dividing the rivers that flow into lakes Erie and Michigan from those that find their way to the Mississippi and the Gulf of Mexico—was surrendered to England.

The provincial troops were to return to their homes, and the regulars to march out from their posts with all the honours of war, and be sent to France in British vessels, under pledges not to serve again before the conclusion of peace. The civil officers were also to be conveyed to France with their families and baggage; and only such papers were to be retained as would be useful for the future regulation of the affairs of the colony. Religious liberty was granted, private property was to be respected, and the French colonists were to enjoy the same civil and commercial rights as the British.

An armament had been ordered from France to the aid of the French troops in Canada, consisting of a thirty-gun frigate, two large supply-ships, and nineteen smaller vessels; but, learning that British ships were in the St. Lawrence, the officers thought best to put into the Bay of Chaleurs, whither Captain Byron, in command at Louisbourg, sailed with five vessels and destroyed the entire fleet, together with two batteries and two hundred houses.

After long negotiations, the preliminaries of peace were signed on the 3rd of November, 1762, and ratified February 10th, 1763. By this, called the Treaty of Paris, Canada, Nova Scotia, and Cape Breton were ceded to Great Britain. France reserved New Orleans and the territory west of the Mississippi, but immediately afterward ceded them to Spain. They did not, however, remain long in Spanish possession, but were returned to France, and finally conveyed to the United States in 1803.

Thus, Great Britain gained possession of nearly all the inhabited portion of North America. The struggle to found a French Empire in the west was over, and New France disappeared from the map, while the boundary of British America was moved northward to the Polar Sea. It looked as if the lines of British territory were definitely settled. But already there were predictions that the power of England on the western continent was soon to be assailed by her own children in the colonies that she herself had planted; that the spirit of independence which had been growing up among them would break into open rebellion against the arbitrary exactions of the old country and the repressions imposed on the growth of trade and manufactures, so soon as the fear of French aggression from the north and Indian hostilities on the frontier should be removed.

Writing after the fall of Canada, a French diplomatist said:—

The colonies will no longer need the protection of England. She will call on them to contribute toward supporting the burdens they have helped to bring on her, and they will answer by Striking off all dependence.

And in the letter before alluded to, said to have been written by Montcalm in 1759, when he knew that the surrender of Quebec was only a question of time, he said:—

If they must have masters, they prefer their countrymen to strangers, taking care, however, to yield as little obedience as possible; but, Canada once conquered, and the Canadians one people with those colonists, let the first occasion come when England seems to interfere with their interests, and do you believe, my dear cousin, that the colonies will obey? And what would they have to fear in revolting?

Some English statesmen also saw the danger, and wished to take it into consideration in arranging the terms of the peace. One of them said:—

If the people of our colonies find no check from Canada, they will extend themselves almost without bound into the inland parts. They will increase infinitely, from all causes. What the consequence will be, to have a numerous, hardy, independent people, possessed of a strong country, communicating little or not at all with England, I leave to your own reflections. By eagerly grasping at extensive territory, we may run the risk, and in no very distant period, of losing what we now possess. A neighbour that keeps us in some awe is not always the worst of neighbours. So that, far from sacrificing Guadaloupe to Canada, perhaps if we might have Canada without any sacrifice at all, we ought not to desire it. There should be a balance of power in America.

The Ohio Indian War

By Thomas Guthrie Marquis

The Times and the Men

There was rejoicing throughout the Thirteen Colonies, in the month of September 1760, when news arrived of the capitulation of Montreal. Bonfires flamed forth and prayers were offered up in the churches and meetinghouses in gratitude for deliverance from a foe that for over a hundred years had harried and had caused the Indians to harry the frontier settlements. The French Armies were defeated by land; the French fleets were beaten at sea. The troops of the enemy had been removed from North America, and so powerless was France on the ocean that, even if success should crown her arms on the European continent, where the Seven Years' War was still raging, it would be impossible for her to transport a new force to America.

The principal French forts in America were occupied by British troops. Louisbourg had been razed to the ground; the British flag waved over Quebec, Montreal, and Niagara, and was soon to be raised on all the lesser forts in the territory known as Canada. The Mississippi valley from the Illinois River southward alone remained to France. Vincennes on the Wabash and Fort Chartres on the Mississippi were the only posts in the hinterland occupied by French troops. These posts were under the government of Louisiana; but even these the American colonies were prepared to claim, basing the right on their 'sea to sea' charters.

The British in America had found the strip of land between the Alleghanies and the Atlantic far too narrow for a rapidly increasing population, but their advance westward had been barred by the French. Now, praise the Lord, the French were out of the way, and American traders and settlers could exploit the profitable fur-fields and the rich agricultural lands of the region beyond the mountains. True, the Indi-

237

ans were there, but these were not regarded as formidable foes. There was no longer any occasion to consider the Indians—so thought the colonists and the British officers in America. The red men had been a force to be reckoned with only because the French had supplied them with the sinews of war, but they might now be treated like other denizens of the forest—the bears, the wolves, and the wild cats. For this mistaken policy the British colonies were to pay a heavy price.

The French and the Indians, save for one exception, had been on terms of amity from the beginning. The reason for this was that the French had treated the Indians with studied kindness. The one exception was the Iroquois League or Six Nations. Champlain, in the first years of his residence at Quebec, had joined the Algonquins and Hurons in an attack on them, which they never forgot; and, in spite of the noble efforts of French missionaries and a lavish bestowal of gifts, the Iroquois thorn remained in the side of New France. But with the other Indian tribes the French worked hand in hand, with the Cross and the priest ever in advance of the trader's pack. French missionaries were the first white men to settle in the populous Huron country near Lake Simcoe.

A missionary was the first European to catch a glimpse of Georgian Bay, and a missionary was probably the first of the French race to launch his canoe on the lordly Mississippi. As a father the priest watched over his wilderness flock; while the French traders fraternised with the red men, and often mated with dusky beauties. Many French traders, according to Sir William Johnson—a good authority, of whom we shall learn more later—were 'gentlemen in manners, character, and dress,' and they treated the natives kindly. At the great centres of trade—Montreal, Three Rivers, and Quebec—the chiefs were royally received with roll of drum and salute of guns. The governor himself—the 'Big Mountain,' as they called him—would extend to them a welcoming hand and take part in their feastings and councils.

At the inland trading-posts the Indians were given goods for their winter hunts on credit and loaded with presents by the officials. To such an extent did the custom of giving presents prevail that it became a heavy tax on the treasury of France, insignificant, however, compared with the alternative of keeping in the hinterland an armed force. The Indians, too, had fought side by side with the French in many notable engagements. They had aided Montcalm, and had assisted in such triumphs as the defeat of Braddock. They were not only friends of the French; they were sword companions.

The British colonists could not, of course, entertain friendly feelings towards the tribes which sided with their enemies and often devastated their homes and murdered their people. But it must be admitted that, from the first, the British in America were far behind the French in Christianlike conduct towards the native races. The colonial traders generally despised the Indians and treated them as of commercial value only, as gatherers of pelts, and held their lives in little more esteem than the lives of the animals that yielded the pelts. The missionary zeal of New England, compared with that of New France, was exceedingly mild. Rum was a leading article of trade. The Indians were often cheated out of their furs; in some instances, they were slain and their packs stolen. Sir William Johnson described the British traders as 'men of no zeal or capacity: men who even sacrifice the credit of the nation to the basest purposes.' There were exceptions, of course, in such men as Alexander Henry and Johnson himself, who, besides being a wise official and a successful military commander, was one of the leading traders.

No sooner was New France vanquished than the British began building new forts and blockhouses in the hinterland. (By the hinterland is meant, of course, the regions beyond the zone of settlement; roughly, all west of Montreal and the Alleghanies.) Since the French were no longer to be reckoned with, why were these forts needed? Evidently, the Indians thought, to keep the red children in subjection and to deprive them of their hunting-grounds! The gardens they saw in cultivation about the forts were to them the forerunners of general settlement. The French had been content with trade; the British appropriated lands for farming, and the coming of the white settler meant the disappearance of game. Indian chiefs saw in these forts and cultivated strips of land a desire to exterminate the red man and steal his territory; and they were not far wrong.

Outside influences, as well, were at work among the Indians. Soon after the French Armies departed, the inhabitants along the St Lawrence had learned to welcome the change of government. They were left to cultivate their farms in peace. The tax-gatherer was no longer squeezing from them their last *sou* as in the days of Bigot; nor were their sons, whose labour was needed on the farms and in the workshops, forced to take up arms. They had peace and plenty, and were content. But in the hinterland, it was different. At Detroit, Michilimackinac, and other forts were French trading communities, which, being far from the seat of war and government, were slow to realise that they were no longer subjects of the French king. Hostile themselves, these French traders naturally encouraged the Indians in an attitude of hostility to the incoming British. They said that a French fleet and army were on their way to Canada to recover the territory. Even if Canada were lost, Louisiana was still French, and, if only the British could be kept out of the west, the trade that had hitherto gone down the St Lawrence might now go by way of the Mississippi.

The commander-in-chief of the British forces in North America, Sir Jeffery Amherst, despised the red men. They were 'only fit to live with the inhabitants of the woods, being more nearly allied to the Brute than to the Human creation.' Other British officers had much the same attitude. Colonel Henry Bouquet, on a suggestion made to him by Amherst that blankets infected with smallpox might be distributed to good purpose among the savages, not only fell in with Amherst's views, but further proposed that dogs should be used to hunt them down. Amherst wrote to Bouquet:

> You will do well to try to inoculate the Indians by means of blankets as well as to try every other method that can serve to extirpate this execrable race. I should be very glad if your scheme for hunting them down by dogs could take effect, but England is at too great a distance to think of that at present.

And Major Henry Gladwyn, who, as we shall see, gallantly held Detroit through months of trying siege, thought that the unrestricted sale of rum among the Indians would extirpate them more quickly than powder and shot, and at less cost.

There was, however, one British officer, at least, in America who did not hold such views towards the natives of the soil. Sir William Johnson, through his sympathy and generosity, had won the friendship of the Six Nations, the most courageous and the most cruel of the Indian tribes. It has been said by a recent writer that Johnson was 'as much Indian as white man.' (Lucas's *A History of Canada, 1768-1812*.) Nothing could be more misleading. Johnson was simply an enlightened Irishman of broad sympathies who could make himself at home in palace, hut, or wigwam. He was an astute diplomatist, capable of winning his point in controversy with the most learned and experienced legislators of the colonies, a successful military leader, a most successful trader; and there was probably no more progressive and scientific farmer in America.

He had a cultivated mind; the orders he sent to London for books show that he was something of a scholar and in his leisure moments given to serious reading. His advice to the lords of trade regarding colonial affairs was that of a statesman. He fraternised with the Dutch settlers of his neighbourhood and with the Indians wherever he found them. At Detroit, in 1761, he entered into the spirit of the French settlers and joined with enthusiasm in their feasts and dances. He was one of those rare characters who can be all things to all men and yet keep an untarnished name. The Indians loved him as a firm friend, and his home was to them Liberty Hall. But for this man the Indian rising against British rule would have attained greater proportions.

At the critical period he succeeded in keeping the Six Nations loyal, save for the Senecas. This was most important; for had the Six Nations joined in the war against the British, it is probable that not a fort west of Montreal would have remained standing. The line of communication between Albany and Oswego would have been cut, provisions and troops could not have been forwarded, and, inevitably, both Niagara and Detroit would have fallen.

But as it was, the Pontiac War proved serious enough. It extended as far north as Sault Ste Marie and as far south as the borders of South Carolina and Georgia. Detroit was cut off for months; the Indians drove the British from all other points on the Great Lakes west of Lake Ontario; for a time, they triumphantly pushed their war-parties, plundering and burning and murdering, from the Mississippi to the frontiers of New York. During the year 1763, more British lives were lost in America than in the memorable year of 1759, the year of the siege of Quebec and the world-famous Battle of the Plains of Abraham.

PONTIAC AND THE TRIBES OF THE HINTERLAND

Foremost among the Indian leaders was Pontiac, the over-chief of the Ottawa Confederacy. It has been customary to speak of this chief as possessed of 'princely grandeur' and as one 'honoured and revered by his subjects.' But it was not by a display of princely dignity or by inspiring awe and reverence that he influenced his bloodthirsty followers. His chief traits were treachery and cruelty, and his pre-eminence in these qualities commanded their respect. His conduct of the siege of Detroit, as we shall see, was marked by duplicity and diabolic savagery. He has often been extolled for his skill as a military leader, and there is a good deal in his siege of Detroit and in the murderous ingenuity of some of his raids to support this view.

But his principal claim to distinction is due to his position as the head of a confederacy—whereas the other chiefs in the conflict were merely leaders of single tribes—and to the fact that he was situated at the very centre of the theatre of war. News from Detroit could be quickly heralded along the canoe routes and forest trails to the other tribes, and it thus happened that when Pontiac struck, the whole Indian country rose in arms. But the evidence clearly shows that, except against Detroit and the neighbouring blockhouses, he had no part in planning the attacks. The war as a whole was a leaderless war.

Let us now look for a moment at the Indians who took part in the war. Immediately under the influence of Pontiac were three tribes— the Ottawas, the Chippewas, and the Potawatomis. These had their hunting-grounds chiefly in the Michigan peninsula, and formed what was known as the Ottawa Confederacy or the Confederacy of the Three Fires. It was at the best a loose confederacy, with nothing of the organised strength of the Six Nations. The Indians in it were of a low type—sunk in savagery and superstition. A leader such as Pontiac naturally appealed to them. They existed by hunting and fishing— feasting today and famishing tomorrow—and were easily roused by the hope of plunder.

The weakly manned forts containing the white man's provisions, ammunition, and traders' supplies were an attractive lure to such savages. Within the confederacy, however, there were some who did not rally round Pontiac. The Ottawas of the northern part of Michigan, under the influence of their priest, remained friendly to the British. Including the Ottawas and Chippewas of the Ottawa and Lake Superior, the confederates numbered many thousands; yet at no time was Pontiac able to command from among them more than one thousand warriors.

In close alliance with the Confederacy of the Three Fires were the tribes dwelling to the west of Lake Michigan—the Menominees, the Winnebagoes, and the Sacs and Foxes. These tribes could put into the field about twelve hundred warriors; but none of them took part in the war save in one instance, when the Sacs, moved by the hope of plunder, assisted the Chippewas in the capture of Fort Michilimackinac.

The Wyandots living on the Detroit River were a remnant of the ancient Hurons of the famous mission near Lake Simcoe. For more than a century they had been bound to the French by ties of amity. They were courageous, intelligent, and in every way on a higher plane of life than the tribes of the Ottawa Confederacy. Their two hundred and fifty braves were to be Pontiac's most important allies in the siege of Detroit.

South of the Michigan peninsula, about the headwaters of the rivers Maumee and Wabash, dwelt the Miamis, numbering probably about fifteen hundred. Influenced by French traders and by Pontiac's emissaries, they took to the war-path, and the British were thus cut off from the trade-route between Lake Erie and the Ohio.

The tribes just mentioned were all that came under the direct influence of Pontiac. Farther south were other nations who were to figure in the impending struggle. The Wyandots of Sandusky Bay, at the south-west corner of Lake Erie, had about two hundred warriors, and were in alliance with the Senecas and Delawares. Living near Detroit, they were able to assist in Pontiac's siege. Directly south of these, along the Scioto, dwelt the Shawnees—the tribe which later gave birth to the great Tecumseh—with three hundred warriors. East of the Shawnees, between the Muskingum and the Ohio, were the Delawares.

At one time this tribe had lived on both sides of the Delaware River in Pennsylvania and New York, and also in parts of New Jersey and Delaware. They called themselves *Leni-Lenape*, real men; but were, nevertheless, conquered by the Iroquois, who 'made women' of them, depriving them of the right to declare war or sell land without permission. Later, through an alliance with the French, they won back their old independence. But they lay in the path of white settlement, and were ousted from one hunting-ground after another, until finally they had to seek homes beyond the Alleghanies. The British had robbed the Delawares of their ancient lands, and the Delawares hated with an undying hatred the race that had injured them. They mustered six hundred warriors.

Almost directly south of Fort Niagara, by the upper waters of the Genesee and Alleghany rivers, lay the homes of the Senecas, one of the Six Nations. This tribe looked upon the British settlers in the Niagara region as squatters on their territory. It was the Senecas, not Pontiac, who began the plot for the destruction of the British in the hinterland, and in the war which followed more than a thousand Seneca warriors took part. Happily, as has been mentioned, Sir William Johnson was able to keep the other tribes of the Six Nations loyal to the British; but the 'Door-keepers of the Long House,' as the Senecas were called, stood aloof and hostile.

The motives of the Indians in the rising of 1763, may therefore, be summarised as follows: amity with the French, hostility towards the British, hope of plunder, and fear of aggression. The first three were the controlling motives of Pontiac's Indians about Detroit. They called it the 'Beaver War.' To them it was a war on behalf of the French trad-ers, who loaded them with gifts, and against the British, who drove them away empty-handed. But the Senecas and the Delawares, with their allies of the Ohio valley, regarded it as a war for their lands. Al-ready the Indians had been forced out of their hunting-grounds in the valleys of the Juniata and the Susquehanna. The Ohio valley would be the next to go, unless the Indians went on the war-path. The chiefs there had good reason for alarm.

Not so Pontiac at Detroit, because no settlers were invading his hunting-grounds. And it was for this lack of a strong motive that Pon-tiac's campaign, as will hereafter appear, broke down before the end of the war; that even his own confederates deserted him; and that, while the Senecas and Delawares were still holding out, he was wandering through the Indian country in a vain endeavour to rally his scattered warriors.

THE GATHERING STORM

When Montreal capitulated, and the whole of Canada passed into British hands, it was the duty of Sir Jeffery Amherst, the commander-in-chief, to arrange for the defence of the country that had been wrested from France. General Gage was left in command at Montreal, Colonel Burton at Three Rivers, and General Murray at Quebec. Amherst him-self departed for New York in October, and never again visited Canada. Meanwhile provision had been made, though quite inadequate, to gar-rison the long chain of forts that had been established by the French in the vaguely defined Indian territory to the west.

★★★★★★★

See the map in the following pages. Except for these forts or trading-posts, the entire region west of Montreal was at this time practically an unbroken wilderness. There were on the north shore of the St Lawrence a few scattered settlements, on Ile Perrot and at Vaudreuil, and on the south shore at the Cedars and Chateauguay; but anything like continuity of settlement westward ceased with the island of Montreal.

★★★★★★★

The fortunes of war had already given the British command of the eastern end of this chain. Fort Lévis, on what is now Chimney Island, a few miles east of Ogdensburg, had been captured. Fort Frontenac had been destroyed by Bradstreet, and was left without a garrison. British troops were in charge of Fort Oswego, which had been built in 1759.

Niagara, the strongest fort on the Great Lakes, had been taken by Sir William Johnson. Near it were two lesser forts, one at the foot of the rapids, where Lewiston now stands, and the other, Fort Schlosser, on the same side of the river, above the falls. Forts Presqu'isle, Le Boeuf, and Venango, on the trade-route between Lake Erie and Fort Pitt, and Fort Pitt itself, were also occupied.

But all west of Fort Pitt was to the British unknown country. Sandusky, at the south-west end of Lake Erie; Detroit, guarding the passage between Lakes Erie and St Clair; Miami and Ouiatanon, on the trade-route between Lake Erie and the Wabash; Michilimackinac, at the entrance to Lake Michigan; Green Bay (La Baye), at the southern end of Green Bay; St Joseph, on Lake Michigan; Sault Ste Marie, at the entrance to Lake Superior—all were still commanded by French officers, as they had been under New France.

The task of raising the British flag over these forts was entrusted to Major Robert Rogers of New England, who commanded Rogers's Rangers, a famous body of Indian-fighters. On September 13, 1760, with two hundred Rangers in fifteen whale-boats, Rogers set out from Montreal. On November 7 the contingent without mishap reached a river named by Rogers the Chogage, evidently the Cuyahoga, on the south shore of Lake Erie. Here the troops landed, probably on the site of the present city of Cleveland; and Rogers was visited by a party of Ottawa Indians, whom he told of the conquest of Canada and of the retirement of the French Armies from the country.

He added that his force had been sent by the commander-in-chief to take over for their father, the king of England, the western posts still held by French soldiers. He then offered them a peace-belt, which they accepted, and requested them to go with him to Detroit to take part in the capitulation and 'see the truth' of what he had said. They promised to give him an answer next morning. The *calumet* was smoked by the Indians and the officers in turn; but a careful guard was kept, as Rogers was suspicious of the Indians. In the morning, however, they returned with a favourable reply, and the younger warriors of the band agreed to accompany their new friends. Owing to stormy weather nearly a week passed—the Indians keeping the camp supplied with venison and turkey, for which Rogers paid them liberally—before the party, on November 12, moved forward towards Detroit.

Detroit was at this time under the command of the Sieur de Belêtre, or Bellestre. This officer had been in charge of the post since 1758, and had heard nothing of the surrender of Montreal. Rogers, to

THE HINTERLAND
1763

Scale of Miles

0   40   80   120

pave the way, sent one of his men in advance with a letter to Belêtre notifying him that the western posts now belonged to King George and informing him that he was approaching with a letter from the Marquis de Vaudreuil and a copy of the capitulation. Belêtre was irritated; the French Armies had been defeated and he was about to lose his post.

He at first refused to believe the tidings; and it appears that he endeavoured to rouse the inhabitants and Indians about Detroit to resist the approaching British, for on November 20 several Wyandot *sachems* met the advancing party and told Rogers that four hundred warriors were in ambush at the entrance to the Detroit River to obstruct his advance.

The Wyandots wished to know the truth regarding the conquest of Canada, and on being convinced that it was no fabrication, they took their departure 'in good temper.' On the 23rd Indian messengers, among whom was an Ottawa chief, arrived at the British camp, at the western end of Lake Erie, reporting that Belêtre intended to fight and that he had arrested the officer who bore Rogers's message.

★★★★★★★★

In Rogers's journal of this trip no mention is made of Pontiac's name. In *A Concise Account of North America*, published in 1765, with Rogers's name on the title-page, a detailed account of a meeting with Pontiac at the Cuyahoga is given, but this book seems to be of doubtful authenticity. It was, however, accepted by Parkman.

★★★★★★★★

Belêtre's chief reason for doubting the truth of Rogers's statement appears to have been that no French officers had accompanied the British contingent from Montreal.

When the troops entered the Detroit River Rogers sent Captain Donald Campbell to the fort with a copy of the capitulation of Montreal and Vaudreuil's letter instructing Belêtre to hand over his fort to the British. These documents were convincing, and Belêtre consented, though with no good grace; and on November 29 Rogers formally took possession of Detroit.

★★★★★★★★

Although Belêtre received Rogers and his men in no friendly spirit, he seems soon to have become reconciled to British rule; for in 1763, he was appointed to the first Legislative Council of Canada, and until the time of his death in May 1793, he was a highly respected citizen of Quebec.

****

It was an impressive ceremony. Some seven hundred Indians were assembled in the vicinity of Fort Detroit, and, ever ready to take sides with the winning party, appeared about the stockade painted and plumed in honour of the occasion. When the lilies of France were lowered and the cross of St George was thrown to the breeze, the barbarous horde uttered wild cries of delight. A new and rich people had come to their hunting-grounds, and they had visions of unlimited presents of clothing, ammunition, and rum. After the fort was taken over the militia were called together and disarmed and made to take the oath of allegiance to the British king.

Captain Campbell was installed in command of the fort, and Belêtre and the other prisoners of war were sent to Philadelphia. Two officers were dispatched with twenty men to bring the French troops from Forts Miami and Ouiatanon. A few soldiers were stationed at Fort Miami to keep the officers at Detroit informed of any interesting events in that neighbourhood. Provisions being scarce at Detroit, Rogers sent the majority of his force to Niagara; and on December 10 set out for Michilimackinac with an officer and thirty-seven men. But he was driven back by stormy weather and ice, and forced, for the present year, to give up the attempt to garrison the posts on Lakes Huron and Michigan. Leaving everything in peace at Detroit, Rogers went to Fort Pitt, and for nine months the forts in the country of the Ottawa Confederacy were to be left to their own resources.

Meanwhile the Indians were getting into a state of unrest. The presents, on which they depended so much for existence, were not forthcoming, and rumours of trouble were in the air. Senecas, Shawnees, and Delawares were sending war-belts east and west and north and south. A plot was on foot to seize Pitt, Niagara, and Detroit. Seneca ambassadors had visited the Wyandots in the vicinity of Detroit, urging them to fall on the garrison. After an investigation, Captain Campbell reported to Amherst that an Indian rising was imminent, and revealed a plot, originated by the Senecas, which was identical with that afterwards matured in 1763, and attributed to Pontiac's initiative. Campbell warned the *commandants* of the other forts of the danger; and the Indians, seeing that their plans were discovered, assumed a peaceful attitude.

Still, the situation was critical; and, to allay the hostility of the natives and gain their confidence, Amherst dispatched Sir William Johnson to Detroit with instructions 'to settle and establish a firm and lasting treaty' between the British and the Ottawa Confederacy and other nations inhabiting the Indian territory, to regulate the fur trade at the posts, and to settle the price of clothes and provisions. He was likewise to collect information as exhaustive as possible regarding the Indians, their manners and customs, and their abodes. He was to find out whether the French had any shipping on Lakes Huron, Michigan, and Superior, what were the best posts for trade, and the price paid by the French for pelts. He was also to learn, if possible, how far the boundaries of Canada extended towards the Mississippi, and the number of French posts, settlements, and inhabitants along that river.

Sir William left his home at Fort Johnson on the Mohawk River early in July 1761. Scarcely had he begun his journey when he was warned that it was dangerous to proceed as the nations in the west were unfriendly and would surely fall upon his party. But Johnson was confident that his presence among them would put a stop to 'any such wicked design.' As he advanced up Lake Ontario the alarming reports continued. The Senecas, who had already stolen horses from the whites and taken prisoners, had been sending ambassadors abroad, endeavouring to induce the other nations to attack the British.

Johnson learned, too, that the Indians were being cheated in trade by British traders; that at several posts they had been roughly handled, very often without cause; that their women were taken from them by violence; and that they were hindered from hunting and fishing on their own grounds near the posts, even what they did catch or kill being taken from them. He heard, too, that Seneca and Ottawa warriors had been murdered by whites near Forts Pitt and Venango, At Niagara he was visited by Seneca chiefs, who complained that one of their warriors had been wounded nearby and that four horses had been stolen from them. Johnson evidently believed the story, for he gave them 'two casks of rum, some paint and money to make up their loss,' and they left him well satisfied.

On Lake Erie, stories of the hostility of the Indians multiplied. They were ready to revolt; even before leaving Niagara, Johnson had it on good authority that the Indians 'were certainly determined to rise and fall on the English,' and that 'several thousands of the Ottawas and other nations' had agreed to join the dissatisfied member 'of the Six Nations in this scheme or plot.' But Johnson kept on his way, confident that he could allay dissatisfaction and win all the nations to friendship.

When Sir William reached Detroit on September 3, he was welcomed by musketry volleys from the Indians and by cannon from the fort. His reputation as the great superintendent of Indian Affairs, the friend of the red man, had gone before him, and he was joyously received, and at once given quarters in the house of the former commandant of Detroit, Belêtre. On the day following his arrival the Wyandots and other Indians, with their priest, Father Pierre Potier (called Pottie by Johnson), waited on him. He treated them royally, and gave them pipes and tobacco and a barbecue of a large ox roasted whole. He found the French inhabitants most friendly, especially Pierre Chesne, better known as La Butte, the interpreter of the Wyandots, and St Martin, the interpreter of the Ottawas.

The ladies of the settlement called on him, and were regaled 'with cakes, wine and cordial.' He was hospitably entertained by the officers and settlers, and in return gave several balls, at which, it appears, he danced with 'Mademoiselle Curie—a fine girl.' This vivacious lady evidently made an impression on the susceptible Irishman; for after the second ball—'there never was so brilliant an affair' at Detroit before—he records in his private diary:

> Promised to write Mademoiselle Curie my sentiments.

While at Niagara on his journey westward Johnson had been joined by Major Henry Gladwyn, to whom Amherst had assigned the duty of garrisoning the western forts and taking over in person the command of Fort Detroit. Gladwyn had left Niagara a day or two in advance of Johnson, but on the way to his new command he had been seized with severe fever and ague and totally incapacitated for duty. On Johnson fell the task of making arrangements for the still unoccupied posts. He did the work with his customary promptitude and thoroughness, and by September 10 had dispatched men of Gage's Light Infantry and of the Royal Americans from Detroit for Michilimackinac, Green Bay, and St Joseph.

The chiefs of the various tribes had flocked to Detroit to confer with Sir William. He won them all by his honeyed words and liberal distribution of presents; he was told that his 'presents had made the sun and sky bright and clear, the earth smooth and level, the roads all pleasant'; and they begged that he 'would continue in the same friendly disposition towards them and they would be a happy people.' His work completed, Johnson set out, September 19, on his homeward journey, leaving behind him the promise of peace in the Indian territory. (It is remarkable that Johnson in his private diary or in his official correspondence makes no mention of Pontiac. The Ottawa chief apparently played no conspicuous part in the plots of 1761, and 1762.)

For the time being Johnson's visit to Detroit had a salutary effect, and the year 1761, terminated with only slight signs of unrest among the Indians; but in the spring of 1762, the air was again heavy with threatening storm. The Indians of the Ohio valley were once more sending out their war-belts and bloody hatchets. In several instances Englishmen were murdered and scalped and horses were stolen. The Shawnees and Delawares held British prisoners whom they refused to surrender. By Amherst's orders presents were withheld. Until they surrendered all prisoners and showed a proper spirit towards the British, he would suppress all gifts, in the belief that 'a due observance of this alone will soon produce more than can ever be expected from bribing them.'

The reply of the Shawnees and Delawares to his orders was stealing horses and terrorizing traders. Sir William Johnson and his assistant in office, George Croghan, warned Amherst of the danger he was running in rousing the hatred of the savages. Croghan in a letter to Bouquet said:

I do not approve of General Amherst's plan of distressing them too much, as in my opinion they will not consider consequences if too much distressed, tho' Sir Jeffery thinks they will.

Although warnings were pouring in upon him, Amherst was of the opinion that there was 'no necessity for any more at the several posts than are just enough to keep up the communication, there being nothing to fear from the Indians in our present circumstances.' To Sir William Johnson he wrote that:

It was not in the power of the Indians to effect anything of consequence.

In the spring of 1763, the war-cloud was about to burst; but in remote New York the commander-in-chief failed to grasp the situation, and turned a deaf ear to those who warned him that an Indian war with all its horrors was inevitable. These vague rumours, as Amherst regarded them, of an imminent general rising of the western tribes, took more definite form as the spring advanced. Towards the end of March Lieutenant Edward Jenkins, the commandant of Fort Ouiatanon, learned that the French traders had been telling the Indians that the British would 'all be prisoners in a short time.'

But what caused most alarm was information from Fort Miami of a plot for the capture of the forts and the slaughter of the garrisons. A war-belt was received by the Indians residing near the fort, and with it came the request that they should hold themselves in readiness to attack the British. Robert Holmes, the commandant of Fort Miami, managed to secure the 'bloody belt' and sent it to Gladwyn, who in turn sent it to Amherst. (Gladwyn's illness in 1761, proved so severe that he had to take a journey to England to recuperate; but he was back in Detroit as *commandant* in August 1762.)

News had now reached the Ohio tribes of the Treaty of Paris, but the terms of this treaty had only increased their unrest. On April 30, 1763, Croghan wrote to Amherst that the Indians were 'uneasy since so much of North America was ceded to Great Britain,' holding that the British had no right in their country, he added:

The Peace, and hearing so much of this country being given up has thrown them into confusion and prevented them bringing in their prisoners this spring as they promised.

Amherst's reply was:

Whatever idle notions they may entertain in regard to the cessions made by the French crown can be of very little consequence.

On April 20 Gladwyn, though slow to see danger, wrote to Amherst:

They (the Indians) say we mean to make Slaves of them by taking so many posts in the country, and that they had better attempt something now to recover their liberty than wait till we are better established.

Even when word that the Indians were actually on the warpath reached Amherst, he still refused to believe it a serious matter, and delayed making preparations to meet the situation. It was, according to him, a 'rash attempt of that turbulent tribe the Senecas'; and, again, he was 'persuaded this alarm will end in nothing more than a rash attempt of what the Senecas have been threatening.' Eight British forts in the west were captured and the frontiers of the colonies bathed in blood before he realised that 'the affair of the Indians was more general than they apprehended.'

The Indians were only waiting for a sudden, bold blow at some one of the British posts, and on the instant, they would be on the warpath from the shores of Lake Superior to the borders of the southernmost colonies of Great Britain. The blow was soon to be struck. Pontiac's war-belts had been sent broadcast, and the nations who recognised him as over-chief were ready to follow him to the slaughter. Detroit was the strongest position to the west of Niagara; it contained an abundance of stores, and would be a rich prize. As Pontiac yearly visited this place during the trading season, he knew the locality well and was familiar with the settlers, the majority of whom were far from being friendly to the British. Against Detroit he would lead the warriors, under the pretence of winning back the country for the French.

In the spring of 1763, instead of going direct to his usual camping-place, an island in Lake St Clair, Pontiac pitched his wigwam on the bank of the River Ecorces, ten miles south of Detroit, and here awaited the tribes whom he had summoned to a council to be held 'on the 15th of the moon'—the 27th of April. And at the appointed time nearly five hundred warriors—Ottawas, Potawatomis, Chippewas, and Wyandots—with their squaws and papooses, had gathered at the meeting place, petty tribal jealousies and differences being laid aside in their common hatred of 'the dogs dressed in red,' the British soldiers.

When the council assembled Pontiac addressed them with fiery words. The Ottawa chief was at this time about fifty years old. He was a man of average height, of darker hue than is usual among Indians, lithe as a panther, his muscles hardened by forest life and years of warfare against Indian enemies and the British. Like the rush of a mountain torrent the words fell from his lips. His speech was one stream of denunciation of the British. In trade they had cheated the Indians, robbing them of their furs, overcharging them for the necessaries of life, and heaping insults and blows upon the red men, who from the French had known only kindness.

The time had come to strike. As he spoke, he flashed a red and purple *wampum* belt before the gaze of the excited braves. This, he declared, he had received from their father the King of France, who commanded his red children to fight the British. Holding out the belt, he recounted with wild words and vehement gestures the victories gained in the past by the Indians over the British, and as he spoke the blood of his listeners pulsed through their veins with battle ardour. To their hatred and sense of being wronged he had appealed, and he saw that every warrior present was with him; but his strongest appeal was to their superstition. In spite of the fact that French missionaries had been among them for a century, they were still pagan, and it was essential to the success of his project that they should believe that the

Master of Life favoured their cause.

He told them the story of a Wolf (Delaware) Indian who had journeyed to heaven and talked with the Master of Life, receiving instructions to tell all the Indians that they were to 'drive out' and 'make war upon' the 'dogs clothed in red who will do you nothing but harm.' When he had finished, such chiefs as Ninevois of the Chippewas and Takay of the Wyandots—'the bad Hurons,' as the writer of the *Pontiac Manuscript* describes them to distinguish them from Father Potier's flock—spoke in similar terms. Every warrior present shouted his readiness to go to war, and before the council broke up it was agreed that in four days Pontiac 'should go to the fort with his young men for a peace dance' in order to get information regarding the strength of the place. The blow must be struck before the spring boats arrived from the Niagara with supplies and additional troops. The council at an end, the different tribes scattered to their several summer villages, seemingly peaceful Indians who had gathered together for trade.

The Siege of Detroit

At the time of the Pontiac outbreak there were in the vicinity of Fort Detroit between one thousand and two thousand white inhabitants. Yet the place was little more than a wilderness post. The settlers were cut off from civilization and learned news of the great world outside only in the spring, when the traders' boats came with supplies. They were out of touch with Montreal and Quebec, and it was difficult for them to realise that they were subjects of the hated king of England. They had not lost their confidence that the armies of France would yet be victorious and sweep the British from the Great Lakes, and in this opinion, they were strengthened by traders from the Mississippi, who came among them. But the change of rulers had made little difference in their lives. The majority of them were employed by traders, and the better class contentedly cultivated their narrow farms and traded with the Indians who periodically visited them.

The settlement was widely scattered, extending along the east shore of the Detroit River for about eight miles from Lake St Clair, and along the west shore for about six miles, four above and two below the fort. On either side of the river the fertile fields and the long row of whitewashed, low-built houses, with their gardens and orchards of apple and pear trees, fenced about with rounded pickets, presented a picture of peace and plenty. The summers of the inhabitants were enlivened by the visits of the Indians and the traders; and in winter they light-heartedly whiled away the tedious hours with gossip and dance and feast, like the habitants along the Richelieu and the St Lawrence.

The militia of the settlement, as we have seen, had been deprived of their arms at the taking over of Detroit by Robert Rogers; and for the most part the settlers maintained a stolid attitude towards their conquerors, from whom they suffered no hardship and whose rule was not galling. The British had nothing to fear from them. But the Indians were a force to be reckoned with. There were three Indian villages in the vicinity—the Wyandot, on the east side of the river, opposite the fort; the Ottawa, five miles above, opposite Ile au Cochon (Belle Isle); and the Potawatomi, about two miles below the fort on the west shore. The Ottawas here could muster 200 warriors, the Potawatomis about 150, and the Wyandots 250, while near at hand were the Chippewas, 320 strong.

Pontiac, although head chief of the Ottawas, did not live in the village, but had his wigwam on Ile à la Peche, at the outlet of Lake St Clair, a spot where whitefish abounded. Here he dwelt with his squaws and papooses, not in 'grandeur,' but in squalid savagery. Between the Indians and the French there existed a most friendly relationship; many of the habitants, indeed, having Indian wives.

Near the centre of the settlement, on the west bank of the river, about twenty miles from Lake Erie, stood Fort Detroit, a miniature town. It was in the form of a parallelogram and was surrounded by a palisade twenty-five feet high. According to a letter of an officer, the walls had an extent of over one thousand paces. At each corner was a bastion and over each gate a blockhouse. Within the walls were about one hundred houses, the little Catholic church of Ste Anne's, a council house, officers' quarters, and a range of barracks. Save for one or two exceptions the buildings were of wood, thatched with bark or straw, and stood close together. The streets were exceedingly narrow; but immediately within the palisade a wide road extended round the entire village. The spiritual welfare of the French and Indian Catholics in the garrison was looked after by Father Potier, a Jesuit, whose mission was in the Wyandot village, and by Father Bocquet, a Récollet, who lived within the fort. Major Henry Gladwyn was in command. He had a hundred and twenty soldiers, and two armed schooners, the *Gladwyn* and the *Beaver*, were in the river nearby.

On the first day of May 1763, Pontiac came to the main gate of the fort asking to be allowed to enter, as he and the warriors with him, forty in all, desired to show their love for the British by dancing

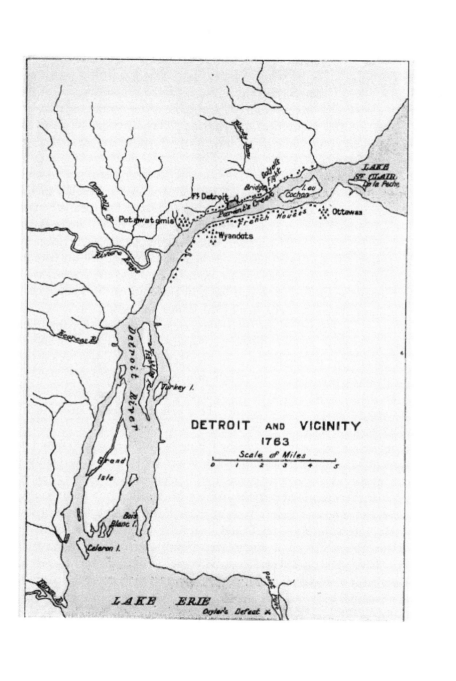

DETROIT AND VICINITY
1763
Scale of Miles
0   1   2   3   4   5

the *calumet* or peace dance. Gladwyn had not the slightest suspicion of evil intent, and readily admitted them. The savages selected a spot in front of the officers' houses, and thirty of them went through their grotesque movements, shouting and dancing to the music of the Indian drum, and all the while waving their *calumets* in token of friendship. While the dancers were thus engaged, the remaining ten of the party were busily employed in surveying the fort—noting the number of men and the strength of the palisades. The dance lasted about an hour. Presents were then distributed to the Indians, and all took their departure.

Pontiac now summoned the Indians about Detroit to another council. On this occasion the chiefs and warriors assembled in the council-house in the Potawatomi village south of the fort. When all were gathered together Pontiac rose and, as at the council at the River Ecorces, in a torrent of words and with vehement gestures, denounced the British. He declared that under the new occupancy of the forts in the Indian country the red men were neglected and their wants were no longer supplied as they had been in the days of the French; that exorbitant prices were charged by the traders for goods; that when the Indians were departing for their winter camps to hunt for furs they were no longer able to obtain ammunition and clothing on credit; and, finally, that the British desired the death of the Indians, and it was therefore necessary as an act of self-preservation to destroy them.

He once more displayed the war-belt that he pretended to have received from the king of France. This belt told him to strike in his own interest and in the interest of the French. He closed his speech by saying that he had sent belts to the Chippewas of Saginaw and the Ottawas of Michilimackinac and of the River La Tranche (the Thames). Seeing that his words were greeted with grunts and shouts of approval and that the assembled warriors were with him to a man, Pontiac revealed a plan he had formed to seize the fort and slaughter the garrison.

He and some fifty chiefs and warriors would wait on Gladwyn on the pretence of discussing matters of importance. Each one would carry beneath his blanket a gun, with the barrel cut short to permit of concealment. Warriors and even women were to enter the fort as if on a friendly visit and take up positions of advantage in the streets, in readiness to strike with tomahawks, knives, and guns, all which they were to have concealed beneath their blankets. At the council Pontiac was to address Gladwyn and, in pretended friendship, hand him a *wampum* belt. If it were wise to strike, he would on presenting the belt hold its reverse side towards Gladwyn. This was to be the signal for attack. Instantly blankets were to be thrown aside and the officers were to be shot down.

At the sound of firing in the council-room the Indians in the streets were to fall on the garrison and every British soldier was to be slain, care being taken that no Frenchman suffered. The plan, by its treachery, and by its possibilities of slaughter and plunder, appealed to the savages; and they dispersed to make preparations for the morning of the 7th, the day chosen for carrying out the murderous scheme.

The plot was difficult to conceal. The aid of French blacksmiths had to be sought to shorten the guns. Moreover, the British garrison had some friends among the Indians. Scarcely had the plot been matured when it was discussed among the French, and on the day before the intended massacre it was revealed to Gladwyn. His informant is not certainly known. A Chippewa maiden, an old squaw, several Frenchmen, and an Ottawa named Mahiganne have been mentioned. It is possible that Gladwyn had it from a number of sources, but most likely from Mahiganne. The *Pontiac Manuscript*, probably the work of Robert Navarre, the keeper of the notarial records of the settlement, distinctly states that Mahiganne revealed the details of the plot with the request that Gladwyn should not divulge his name; for, should Pontiac learn, the informer would surely be put to death. This would account for the fact that Gladwyn, even in his report of the affair to Amherst, gives no hint as to the person who told him.

Gladwyn at once made preparations to receive Pontiac and his chiefs. On the night of the 6th instructions were given to the soldiers and the traders within the fort to make preparations to resist an attack, and the guards were doubled. As the sentries peered out into the darkness occasional yells and whoops and the beating of drums reached their ears, telling of the war-dance that was being performed in the Indian villages to hearten the warriors for the slaughter.

Gladwyn determined to act boldly. On the morning of the 7th all the traders' stores were closed and every man capable of bearing weapons was under arms; but the gates were left open as usual, and shortly after daylight Indians and squaws by twos and threes began to gather in the fort as if to trade. At ten in the morning a line of chiefs with Pontiac at their head filed along the road leading to the river gate. All were painted and plumed and each one was wrapped in a brightly coloured blanket. When they entered the fort, they were astonished to see the warlike preparations, but stoically concealed their surprise. Arrived in the council-chamber, the chiefs noticed the sentinels standing at arms, the commandant and his officers seated, their faces stern and set, pistols in their belts and swords by their sides. So perturbed were the chiefs by all this warlike display that it was some time before they would take their seats on the mats prepared for them. At length they recovered their composure, and Pontiac broke the silence by asking why so many of the young men were standing in the streets with their guns. Answer was made through the interpreter La Butte that it was for exercise and discipline. Pontiac then addressed Gladwyn, vehemently protesting friendship. All the time he was speaking Gladwyn bent on him a scrutinising gaze, and as the chief was about to present the *wampum* belt, a signal was given and the drums crashed out a charge. Every doubt was removed from Pontiac's mind—his plot was discovered. His nervous hand lowered the belt; but he recovered himself immediately and presented it in the ordinary way.

Gladwyn replied to his speech sternly, but kindly, saying that he would have the protection and friendship of the British so long as he merited it. A few presents were then distributed among the Indians, and the council ended. The chiefs, with their blankets still tightly wrapped about them, filed out of the council-room and scattered to their villages, followed by the disappointed rabble of fully three hundred Indians, who had assembled in the fort.

On the morrow, Pontiac, accompanied by three chiefs, again appeared at the fort, bringing with him a pipe of peace. When this had been smoked by the officers and chiefs, he presented it to Captain Campbell, as a further mark of friendship. The next day he was once more at the gates seeking entrance. But he found them closed: Gladwyn felt that the time had come to take no chances. This morning a rabble of Potawatomis, Ottawas, Wyandots, and Chippewas thronged the common just out of musket range. On Pontiac's request for a conference with Gladwyn he was sternly told that he might enter alone. The answer angered him, and he strode back to his followers. Now, with yells and war-whoops, parties of the savages bounded away on a murderous mission.

Half a mile behind the fort an English woman, Mrs Turnbull, and her two sons cultivated a small farm. All three were straightway slain. A party of Ottawas leapt into their canoes and paddled swiftly to Ile au Cochon, where lived a former sergeant, James Fisher. Fisher was seized, killed, and scalped, his young wife brutally murdered, and their two little children carried into captivity. On this same day news was brought to the fort that Sir Robert Davers and Captain Robertson had been murdered three days before on Lake St Clair by Chippewas who were on their way from Saginaw to join Pontiac's forces. Thus began the Pontiac War in the vicinity of Detroit. For several months the garrison was to know little rest.

That night at the Ottawa village arose the hideous din of the war-dance, and while the warriors worked themselves into a frenzy the squaws were busy breaking camp. Before daylight the village was moved to the opposite side of the river, and the wigwams were pitched near the mouth of Parent's Creek, about a mile and a half above the fort. On the morning of the 10th the siege began in earnest. Shortly after daybreak the yells of a horde of savages could be heard north and south and west.

But few of the enemy could be seen, as they had excellent shelter behind barns, outhouses, and fences. For six hours they kept up a continuous fire on the garrison, but wounded only five men. The fort vigorously returned the fire, and none of the enemy dared attempt to rush the palisades. A cluster of buildings in the rear sheltered a particularly ferocious set of savages. A three-pounder—the only effective artillery in the fort—was trained on this position; spikes were bound together with wire, heated red-hot, and fired at the buildings. These were soon a mass of flames, and the savages concealed behind them fled for their lives.

Presently the Indians grew tired of this useless warfare and withdrew to their villages. Gladwyn, thinking that he might bring Pontiac to terms, sent La Butte to ask the cause of the attack and to say that the British were ready to redress any wrongs from which the Indians might be suffering. La Butte was accompanied by Jean Baptiste Chapoton, a captain of the militia and a man of some importance in the fort, and Jacques Godfroy, a trader and likewise an officer of militia.

It may be noted that Godfroy's wife was the daughter of a Miami chief. The ambassadors were received in a friendly manner by Pontiac, who seemed ready to cease hostilities. La Butte returned to the fort with some of the chiefs to report progress; but when he went again to Pontiac, he found that the Ottawa chief had made no definite promise. It seems probable, judging from their later actions, that Chapoton and Godfroy had betrayed Gladwyn and urged Pontiac to force the British out of the country. Pontiac now requested that Captain Donald Campbell, who had been in charge of Detroit before Gladwyn took over the command, should come to his village to discuss terms.

Campbell was confident that he could pacify the Indians, and, accompanied by Lieutenant George M'Dougall, he set out along the river road for the Ottawas' encampment at Parent's Creek.

As the two officers crossed the bridge at the mouth of the creek, they were met by a savage crowd—men, women, and children—armed with sticks and clubs. The mob rushed at them with yells and threatening gestures, and were about to fall on the officers when Pontiac appeared and restored order. A council was held, but as Campbell could get no satisfaction he suggested returning to the fort. Thereupon Pontiac remarked:

My father will sleep tonight in the lodges of his red children.

Campbell and M'Dougall were given good quarters in the house of Jean Baptiste Meloche. For nearly two months they were to be kept close prisoners.

So far only part of the Wyandots had joined Pontiac: Father Potier had been trying to keep his flock neutral. But on the 11th Pontiac crossed to the Wyandot village, and threatened it with destruction if the warriors did not take up the tomahawk. On this compulsion they consented, no doubt glad of an excuse to be rid of the discipline of their priest.

Another attack on the fort was made, this time by about six hundred Indians; but it was as futile as the one of the earlier day. Pontiac now tried negotiation. He summoned Gladwyn to surrender, promising that the British should be allowed to depart unmolested on their vessels. The officers, knowing that their communications with the east were cut, that food was scarce, that a vigorous assault could not fail to carry the fort, urged Gladwyn to accept the offer, but he sternly refused. He would not abandon Detroit while one pound of food and one pound of powder were left in the fort. Moreover, the treacherous conduct of Pontiac convinced him that the troops and traders as they left the fort would be plundered and slaughtered. He rejected Pontiac's demands, and advised him to disperse his people and save his ammunition for hunting.

At this critical moment Detroit was undoubtedly saved by a French Canadian. But for Jacques Bâby, the grim spectre Starvation would have stalked through the little fortress. Bâby was a prosperous trader and merchant who, with his wife Susanne Reaume, lived on the east shore of the river, almost opposite the fort. He had a farm of one thousand acres, two hundred of which were under cultivation. His trading establishment was a low-built log structure eighty feet long by twenty wide. He owned thirty slaves—twenty men and ten women. He seems to have treated them kindly; at any rate, they loyally did his will. Bâby agreed to get provisions into the fort by stealth; and on a dark night, about a week after the siege commenced, Gladwyn had a lantern displayed on a plank fixed at the water's edge. Bâby had six canoes in readiness; in each were stowed two quarters of beef, three hogs, and six bags of meal. All night long these canoes plied across the half-mile stretch of water and by daylight sufficient food to last the garrison for several weeks had been delivered.

From day to day the Indians kept up a desultory firing, while Gladwyn took precautions against a long siege. Food was taken from the houses of the inhabitants and placed in a common storehouse. Timber was torn from the walks and used in the construction of portable bastions, which were erected outside the fort. There being danger that the roofs of the houses would be ignited by means of fire-arrows, the French inhabitants of the fort were made to draw water and store it in vessels at convenient points. Houses, fences, and orchards in the neighbourhood were destroyed and levelled, so that skulking warriors could not find shelter. The front of the fort was comparatively safe from attack, for the schooners guarded the river gate, and the Indians had a wholesome dread of these floating fortresses.

About the middle of the month the *Gladwyn* sailed down the Detroit to meet a convoy that was expected with provisions and ammunition from Fort Schlosser. At the entrance to Lake Erie, as the vessel lay becalmed in the river, she was suddenly beset by a swarm of savages in canoes; and Pontiac's prisoner, Captain Campbell, appeared in the foremost canoe, the savages thinking that the British would not fire on them for fear of killing him. Happily, a breeze sprang up and the schooner escaped to the open lake. There was no sign of the convoy; and the *Gladwyn* sailed for the Niagara, to carry to the officers there tidings of the Indian rising in the west.

On May 30 the watchful sentries at Detroit saw a line of *bateaux* flying the British flag rounding a point on the east shore of the river. This was the expected convoy from Fort Schlosser, and the cannon boomed forth a welcome. But the rejoicings of the garrison were soon stilled. Instead of British cheers, wild war-whoops resounded from the *bateaux*. The Indians had captured the convoy and were forcing their captives to row. In the foremost boat were four soldiers and three savages. Nearing the fortress one of the soldiers conceived the daring plan of overpowering the Indian guard and escaping to the *Beaver*, which lay anchored in front of the fort.

Seizing the nearest savage, he attempted to throw him into the river; but the Indian succeeded in stabbing him, and both fell overboard and were drowned. The other savages, dreading capture, leapt out of the boat and swam ashore. The *bateau* with the three soldiers in it reached the *Beaver*, and the provisions and ammunition it contained were taken to the fort. The Indians in the remaining *bateaux*, warned by the fate of the leading vessel, landed on the east shore; and, marching their prisoners overland past the fort, they took them across the river to Pontiac's camp, where most of them were put to death with fiendish cruelty.

The soldiers who escaped to the *Beaver* told the story of the ill-fated convoy. On May 13 Lieutenant Abraham Cuyler, totally ignorant of the outbreak of hostilities at Detroit, had left Fort Schlosser with ninety-six men in ten *bateaux*. They had journeyed in leisurely fashion along the northern Shore of Lake Erie, and by the 28th had reached Point Pelée, about thirty miles from the Detroit River. Here a landing was made, and while tents were being pitched a band of painted savages suddenly darted out of the forest and attacked a man and a boy who were gathering wood. The man escaped, but the boy was tomahawked and scalped.

Cuyler drew up his men in front of the boats, and a sharp musketry fire followed between the Indians, who were sheltered by a thick wood, and the white men on the exposed shore. The raiders were Wyandots from Detroit, the most courageous and intelligent savages in the region. Seeing that Cuyler's men were panic-stricken, they broke from their cover, with unusual boldness for Indians, and made a mad charge. The soldiers, completely unnerved by the savage yells and hurtling tomahawks, threw down their arms and dashed in confusion to the boats. Five they succeeded in pushing off, and into these they tumbled without weapons of defence.

Cuyler himself was left behind wounded; but he waded out, and was taken aboard under a brisk fire from the shore. The Indians then launched two of the abandoned boats, rushed in pursuit of the fleeing soldiers, speedily captured three of the boats, and brought them ashore in triumph. The two others, in one of which was Cuyler, hoisted sail and escaped. The Indians, as we have seen, brought the captured boats and their prisoners to Detroit. Cuyler had directed his course to Sandusky, but finding the blockhouse there burnt to the ground, he had rowed eastward to Presqu'isle, and then hastened to Niagara to report the disaster.

The siege of Detroit went on. Towards the middle of June, Jacques Bâby brought word to the commandant that the *Gladwyn* was returning from the Niagara with supplies and men, and that the Indians were making preparations to capture her. A few miles below Detroit lay Fighting Island; between it and the east shore, Turkey Island. Here the savages had erected a breastwork, so carefully concealed that it would be difficult even for the keenest eyes to detect its presence. The vessel would have to pass within easy range of this barricade; and it was the plan of the Indians to dart out in their canoes as the schooner worked up-stream, seize her, and slay her crew.

On learning this news Gladwyn ordered cannon to be fired to notify the captain that the fort still held out, and sent a messenger to meet the vessel with word of the plot. It happened that the *Gladwyn* was well manned and prepared for battle. On board was Cuyler with twenty-two survivors of the ill-starred convoy, besides twenty-eight men of Captain Hopkins's company. To deceive the Indians as to the number of men, all the crew and soldiers, save ten or twelve, were concealed in the hold; to invite attack, the vessel advanced boldly upstream, and at nightfall cast anchor in the narrow channel in front of Turkey Island. About midnight the Indians stealthily boarded their canoes and cautiously, but confidently, swept towards her with muffled paddles.

The *Gladwyn* was ready for them. Not a sound broke the silence of the night as the Indians approached the schooner; when suddenly the clang of a hammer against the mast echoed over the calm waters, the signal to the soldiers in the hold. The Indians were almost on their prey; but before they had time to utter the war-whoop, the soldiers had come up and had attacked the savages with bullets and cannon shot. Shrieks of death arose amid the din of the firing and the splash of swimmers hurriedly making for the shore from the sinking canoes. In a moment fourteen Indians were killed and as many more wounded. From behind the barricade the survivors began a harmless musketry fire against the schooner, which simply weighed anchor and drifted downstream to safety.

A day or two later she cleared Turkey Island and reached the fort, pouring a shattering broadside into the Wyandot village as she passed it. Besides the troops, the *Gladwyn* had on board a precious cargo of a hundred and fifty barrels of provisions and some ammunition. She had not run the blockade unscathed, for in passing Turkey Island one sergeant and four men had been wounded. There was rejoicing in the fort when the reinforcement marched in. This additional strength in men and provisions, it was expected, would enable the garrison to hold out for at least another month, within which time soldiers would arrive in sufficient force to drive the Indians away.

In the meantime, Pontiac was becoming alarmed. He had expected an easy victory, and was not prepared for a protracted siege. He had drawn on the French settlers for supplies; his warriors had slain cattle and taken provisions without the consent of the owners. Leaders in the settlement now waited on Pontiac, making complaint. He professed to be fighting for French rule, and expressed sorrow at the action of his young men, promising that in future the French should be paid. Acting, no doubt, on the suggestion of some of his French allies, he made a list of the inhabitants, drew on each for a definite quantity of supplies, and had these deposited at Meloche's house near his camp on Parent's Creek. A commissary was appointed to distribute the provisions as required. In payment he issued letters of credit, signed with his totem, the otter. It is said that all of them were afterwards redeemed; but this is almost past belief in the face of what actually happened.

From the beginning of the siege Pontiac had hoped that the French traders and settlers would join him to force the surrender of the fort. The arrival of the reinforcement under Cuyler made him despair of winning without their assistance, and early in July he sent his Indians to the leading inhabitants along the river, ordering them to a council, at which he hoped by persuasion or threats to make them take up arms. This council was attended by such settlers as Robert Navarre, Zacharie Sicotte, Louis Campau, Antoine Cuillerier, François Meloche, all men of standing and influence. In his address to them Pontiac declared:

> If you are French, accept this war-belt for yourselves, or your young men, and join us; if you are English, we declare war upon you.'

The *Gladwyn* had brought news of the Peace of Paris between France and England. Many of the settlers had been hoping that success would crown the French arms in Europe and that Canada would be restored. Some of those at the council said that these articles of peace were a mere ruse on the part of Gladwyn to gain time. Robert Navarre, who had published the articles of peace to the French and Indians, and several others were friendly to the British, but the majority of those present were unfriendly. Sicotte told Pontiac that, while the heads of families could not take up arms, there were three hundred young men about Detroit who would willingly join him. These words were probably intended to humour the chief; but there were those who took the belt and commenced recruiting among their fellows. The settlers who joined Pontiac were nearly all half-breeds or men mated with Indian wives. Others, such as Pierre Reaume and Louis Campau, believing their lives to be in danger on account of their loyalty to the new rulers, sought shelter in the fort.

By July 4 the Indians, under the direction of French allies, had strongly entrenched themselves and had begun a vigorous attack. But a force of about sixty men marched out from the fort and drove them from the position. In the retreat two Indians were killed, and one of the pursuing soldiers, who had been a prisoner among the Indians and had learned the ways of savage warfare, scalped one of the fallen braves. The victim proved to be a nephew of the chief of the Saginaw Chippewas, who now claimed life for life, and demanded that Captain Campbell should be given up to him. According to the *Pontiac Manuscript* Pontiac acquiesced, and the Saginaw chief killed Campbell 'with a blow of his tomahawk, and after cast him into the river.' Campbell's fellow-prisoner M'Dougall, along with two others, had escaped to the fort some days before.

The investment continued, although the attacks became less frequent. The schooners manoeuvring in the river poured broadsides into the Indian villages, battering down the flimsy wigwams. Pontiac moved his camp from the mouth of Parent's Creek to a position nearer Lake St Clair, out of range of their guns, and turned his thoughts to contrive some means of destroying the troublesome vessels. He had learned from the French of the attempt with fire-ships against the British fleet at Quebec, and made trial of a similar artifice. *Bateaux* were joined together, loaded with inflammable material, ignited, and sent on their mission; but these 'fireships' floated harmlessly past the schooners and burnt themselves out. Then for a week the Indians worked on the construction of a gigantic fire-raft, but nothing came of this ambitious scheme.

It soon appeared that Pontiac was beginning to lose his hold on the Indians. About the middle of July ambassadors from the Wyandots and Potawatomis came to the fort with an offer of peace, protesting, after the Indian manner, love and friendship for the British. After much parleying they surrendered their prisoners and plunder; but, soon after, a temptation irresistible to their treacherous natures offered itself, and they were again on the war-path.

Amherst at New York had at last been aroused to the danger; and Captain James Dalyell had set out from Fort Schlosser with twenty-two barges, carrying nearly three hundred men, with cannon and supplies, for the relief of Detroit. The expedition skirted the southern shore of Lake Erie until it reached Sandusky. The Wyandot villages here were found deserted. After destroying them Dalyell shaped his course for the Detroit River. Fortune favoured the expedition. Pontiac was either ignorant of its approach or unable to mature a plan to check its advance.

Through the darkness and fog of the night of July 28 the barges cautiously crept upstream, and when the morning sun of the 29th lifted the mists from the river they were in full view of the fort. Relief at last! The weary watching of months was soon to end. The band of the fort was assembled, and the martial airs of England floated on the morning breeze. Now it was that the Wyandots and Potawatomis, although so lately swearing friendship to the British, thought the opportunity too good to be lost. In passing their villages the barges were assailed by a musketry fire, which killed two and wounded thirteen of Dalyell's men. But the soldiers, with muskets and swivels, replied to the attack, and put the Indians to flight. Then the barges drew up before the fort to the welcome of the anxious watchers of Detroit.

The reinforcement was composed of men of the 55th and 8th regiments, and of twenty Rangers under Major Robert Rogers. Like their commander, Dalyell, many of them were experienced in Indian fighting and were eager to be at Pontiac and his warriors. Dalyell thought that Pontiac might be taken by surprise, and urged on Gladwyn the advisability of an immediate advance. To this Gladwyn was averse; but Dalyell was insistent, and won his point. By the following night all was in readiness. At two o'clock in the morning of the 31st the river gate was thrown open and about two hundred and fifty men filed out.

Heavy clouds hid both moon and stars, and the air was oppressively hot. The soldiers marched along the dusty road, guided by Bâby and St Martin, who had volunteered for the work. Not a sound save their own dull tramp broke the silence. On their right gleamed the calm river, and keeping pace with them were two large *bateaux* armed with swivels. Presently, as the troops passed the farmhouses, drowsy watch-dogs caught the sound of marching feet and barked furiously. Pontiac's camp, however, was still far away; this barking would not alarm the Indians. But the soldiers did not know that they had been betrayed by a spy of Pontiac's within the fort, nor did they suspect that snake-like eyes were even then watching their advance.

At length Parent's Creek was reached, where a narrow wooden bridge spanned the stream a few yards from its mouth. The advance-guard were half-way over the bridge, and the main body crowding after them, when, from a black ridge in front, the crackle of musketry arose, and half the advance-guard fell. The narrow stream ran red with their blood, and ever after this night it was known as Bloody Run. On the high ground to the north of the creek a barricade of cordwood had been erected, and behind this and behind barns and houses and fences, and in the cornfields and orchards, Indians were firing and yelling like demons.

The troops recoiled, but Dalyell rallied them; again, they crowded to the bridge. There was another volley and another pause. With reckless bravery the soldiers pressed across the narrow way and rushed to the spot where the musket-flashes were seen. They won the height, but not an Indian was there. The musket-flashes continued and war-whoops sounded from new shelters. The *bateaux* drew up alongside the bridge, and the dead and wounded were taken on board to be carried to the fort. It was useless to attempt to drive the shifty savages from their lairs, and so the retreat was sounded.

Captain Grant, in charge of the rear company, led his men back across the bridge while Dalyell covered the retreat; and now the fight took on a new aspect. As the soldiers retreated along the road leading to the fort, a destructive fire poured upon them from houses and barns, from behind fences, and from a newly dug cellar. With the river on their left, and with the enemy before and behind as well as on their right, they were in danger of being annihilated. Grant ordered his men to fix bayonets: a dash was made where the savages were thickest, and they were scattered. As the fire was renewed panic seized the troops. But Dalyell came up from the rear, and with shouts and threats and flat of sword restored order.

Day was breaking; but a thick fog hung over the scene, under cover of which the Indians continued the attack. The house of Jacques Campau, a trader, sheltered a number of Indians who were doing most destructive work. Rogers and a party of his Rangers attacked the house, and, pounding in the doors, drove out their assailants. From Campau's house Rogers covered the retreat of Grant's company, but was himself in turn besieged. By this time the armed *bateaux*, which had borne the dead and wounded to the fort, had returned, and, opening fire with their swivels on the Indians attacking Rogers, drove them off; the Rangers joined Grant's company, and all retreated for the fort.

The shattered remnant of Dalyell's confident forces arrived at Fort Detroit at eight in the morning, after six hours of marching and desperate battle, exhausted and crestfallen. Dalyell had been slain—an irreparable loss. The casualty list was twenty killed and forty-two wounded. The Indians had suffered but slightly. However, they gained but little permanent advantage from the victory, as the fort had still about three hundred effective men, with ample provisions and ammunition, and could defy assault and withstand a protracted siege.

In this fight Chippewas and Ottawas took the leading part. The Wyandots had, however, at the sound of firing crossed the river, and the Potawatomis also had joined in the combat, in spite of the truce so recently made with Gladwyn. At the Battle of Bloody Run at least eight hundred warriors were engaged in the endeavour to cut off Dalyell's men. There was rejoicing in the Indian villages, and more British scalps adorned the warriors' wigwams. Runners were sent out to the surrounding nations with news of the victory, and many recruits were added to Pontiac's forces.

The Fall of the Lesser Forts

While Fort Detroit was withstanding Pontiac's hordes, the smaller forts and blockhouses scattered throughout the hinterland were faring badly. On the southern shore of Lake Erie, almost directly south of the Detroit River, stood Fort Sandusky—a rude blockhouse surrounded by a stockade. Here were about a dozen men, commanded by Ensign Christopher Paully. The blockhouse could easily have been taken by assault; but such was not the method of the band of Wyandots in the neighbourhood. They preferred treachery, and, under the guise of friendship, determined to destroy the garrison with no risk to themselves.

On the morning of May 16 Paully was informed that seven Indians wished to confer with him. Four of these were members of the Wyandot tribe, and three belonged to Pontiac's band of Ottawas. The Wyandots were known to Paully, and as he had no news of the situation at Detroit, and no suspicion of danger to himself, he readily admitted them to his quarters. The Indians produced a *calumet* and handed it to Paully in token of friendship. As the pipe passed from lip to lip a warrior appeared at the door of the room and raised his arm. It was the signal for attack. Immediately Paully was seized by the Indians, two of whom had placed themselves on either side of him.

At the same moment a war-whoop rang out and firing began; and as Paully was rushed across the parade-ground he saw the bodies of several of his men, who had been treacherously slain. The sentry had been tomahawked as he stood at arms at the gate; and the sergeant of the little company was killed while working in the garden of the garrison outside the stockade.

When night fell Paully and two or three others, all that remained of the garrison, were placed in canoes, and these were headed for Detroit. As the prisoners looked back over the calm waters of Sandusky Bay, they saw the blockhouse burst into flames. Paully and his men were landed at the Ottawa camp, where a horde of howling Indians, including women and children, beat them and compelled them to dance and sing for the entertainment of the rabble. Preparations were made to torture Paully to death at the stake; but an old squaw, who had recently lost her husband, was attracted by the handsome, dark-skinned young ensign, and adopted him in place of her deceased warrior. Paully's hair was cut close; he was dipped into the stream to wash the white blood from his veins; and finally, he was dressed and painted as became an Ottawa brave.

News of the destruction of Fort Sandusky was brought to Gladwyn by a trader named La Brosse, a resident of Detroit, and a few days later a letter was received from Paully himself. For nearly two months Paully had to act the part of an Ottawa warrior. But early in July— Pontiac being in a state of great rage against the British—his squaw placed him in a farmhouse for safe keeping. In the confusion arising out of the attack on Fort Detroit on the 4th of the month, and the murder of Captain Campbell, he managed to escape, by the aid, it is said, of an Indian maiden. He was pursued to within musket-shot of the walls of Detroit. When he entered the fort, so much did he resemble an Indian that at first, he was not recognised.

The next fort to fall into the hands of the Indians was St Joseph, on the east shore of Lake Michigan, at the mouth of the St Joseph River. This was the most inaccessible of the posts on the Great Lakes. The garrison here lived lonely lives. Around them were thick forests and swamps, and in front the desolate waters of the sea-like lake. The Indians about St Joseph had long been under the influence of the French. This place had been visited by La Salle; and here in 1688, the Jesuit Allouez had established a mission. In 1763, the post was held

MAJOR ROBERT ROGERS

by Ensign Francis Schlosser and fourteen men. For months the little garrison had been without news from the east, when, on May 25, a party of Potawatomis from about Detroit arrived on a pretended visit to their relations living in the village at St Joseph, and asked permission to call on Schlosser. But before a meeting could be arranged, a French trader entered the fort and warned the *commandant* that the Potawatomis intended to destroy the garrison.

Schlosser at once ordered his sergeant to arm his men, and went among the French settlers seeking their aid. Even while he was addressing them a shrill death-cry rang out—the sentry at the gate had fallen a victim to the tomahawk of a savage. In an instant a howling mob of Potawatomis under their chief Washee were within the stockade. Eleven of the garrison were straightway put to death, and the fort was plundered. Schlosser and the three remaining members of his little band were taken to Detroit by some Foxes who were present with the Potawatomis. On June 10 Schlosser had the good fortune to be exchanged for two chiefs who were prisoners in Fort Detroit.

The Indians did not destroy Fort St Joseph, but left it in charge of the French under Louis Chevalier. Chevalier saved the lives of several British traders, and in every way behaved so admirably that at the close of the Indian War he was given a position of importance under the British, which position he held until the outbreak of the Revolutionary War.

We have seen that when Major Robert Rogers visited Detroit in 1760, one of the French forts first occupied was Miami, situated on the Maumee River, at the commencement of the portage to the Wabash, near the spot where Fort Wayne was afterwards built. At the time of the outbreak of the Pontiac War this fort was held by Ensign Robert Holmes and twelve men. Holmes knew that his position was critical. In 1762, he had reported that the Senecas, Shawnees, and Delawares were plotting to exterminate the British in the Indian country, and he was not surprised when, towards the end of May 1763, he was told by a French trader that Detroit was besieged by the Ottawa Confederacy.

But though Holmes was on the alert, and kept his men under arms, he was nevertheless to meet death and his fort was to be captured by treachery. In his desolate wilderness home, the young ensign seems to have lost his heart to a handsome young squaw living in the vicinity of the fort. On May 27, she visited him and begged him to accompany her on a mission of mercy—to help to save the life of a sick Indian woman. Having acted as physician to the Indians on former occasions,

Holmes thought the request a natural one. The young squaw led him to the Indian village, pointed out the wigwam where the woman was supposed to be, and then left him. As he was about to enter the wigwam two musket-shots rang out, and he fell dead. Three soldiers, who were outside the fort, rushed for the gate, but they were tomahawked before they could reach it.

The gate was immediately closed, and the nine soldiers within the fort made ready for resistance. With the Indians were two Frenchmen, Jacques Godfroy, whom we have met before as the ambassador to Pontiac in the opening days of the siege of Detroit, and one Miny Chesne, (the only recorded instance, except at Detroit, in which any French took part with the Indians in the capture of a fort. And both Godfroy and Miny Chesne had married Indian women); and they had an English prisoner, a trader named John Welsh, who had been captured and plundered at the mouth of the Maumee while on his way to Detroit.

The Frenchmen called on the garrison to surrender, pointing out how useless it would be to resist and how dreadful would be their fate if they were to slay any Indians. Without a leader, and surrounded as they were by a large band of savages, the men of the garrison saw that resistance would be of no avail. The gates were thrown open; the soldiers marched forth, and were immediately seized and bound; and the fort was looted. With Welsh the captives were taken to the Ottawa village at Detroit, where they arrived on June 4, and where Welsh and several of the soldiers were tortured to death.

A few miles south of the present city of Lafayette, on the southeast side of the Wabash, at the mouth of Wea Creek, stood the little wooden fort of Ouiatanon. It was connected with Fort Miami by a footpath through the forest. It was the most westerly of the British forts in the Ohio country, and might be said to be on the borderland of the territory along the Mississippi, which was still under the government of Louisiana. There was a considerable French settlement, and nearby was the principal village of the Weas, a subtribe of the Miami nation. The fort was guarded by the usual dozen of men, under the command of Lieutenant Edward Jenkins.

In March Jenkins had been warned that an Indian rising was imminent and that soon all the British in the hinterland would be prisoners. The French and Indians in this region were under the influence of the Mississippi officers and traders, who were, in Jenkins's words, 'eternally telling lies to the Indians,' leading them to believe that a great army would soon arrive to recover the forts. Towards the end of May ambassadors arrived at Ouiatanon, either from the Delawares or from Pontiac, bringing war-belts and instructions to the Weas to seize the fort. This, as usual, was achieved by treachery. Jenkins was invited to one of their cabins for a conference.

Totally unaware of the Pontiac conspiracy, or of the fall of St Joseph, Sandusky, or Miami, he accepted the invitation. While passing out of the fort he was seized and bound, and, when taken to the cabin, he saw there several of his soldiers, prisoners like himself. The remaining members of the garrison surrendered, knowing how useless it would be to resist, and under the threat that if one Indian were killed all the British would be put to death. It had been the original intention of the Indians to seize the fort and slaughter the garrison, but, less bloodthirsty than Pontiac's immediate followers, they were won to mercy by two traders, Maisonville and Lorain, who gave them presents on the condition that the garrison should be made prisoners instead of being slain. Jenkins and his men were to have been sent to the Mississippi, but their removal was delayed, and they were quartered on the French inhabitants, and kindly treated by both French and Indians until restored to freedom.

The capture of Forts Miami and Ouiatanon gave the Indians complete control of the route between the western end of Lake Erie and the rivers Ohio and Mississippi. The French traders, who had undoubtedly been instrumental in goading the Indians to hostilities, had now the trade of the Wabash and lower Ohio, and of the tributaries of both, in their own hands. No British trader could venture into the region with impunity; the few who attempted it were plundered and murdered.

The scene of hostilities now shifts to the north. Next to Detroit the most important fort on the Great Lakes west of Niagara was Michilimackinac, situated on the southern shore of the strait connecting Lakes Huron and Michigan. The officer there had supervision of the lesser forts at Sault Ste Marie, Green Bay, and St Joseph. At this time Sault Ste Marie was not occupied by troops. In the preceding winter Lieutenant Jamette had arrived to take command; but fire had broken out in his quarters and destroyed the post, and he and his men had gone back to Michilimackinac, where they still were when the Pontiac War broke out. There were two important Indian tribes in the vicinity of Michilimackinac, the Chippewas and the Ottawas. The Chippewas had populous villages on the island of Mackinaw and at

Thunder Bay on Lake Huron. They had as their hunting-grounds the eastern half of the peninsula which is now the state of Michigan. The Ottawas claimed as their territory the western half of the peninsula, and their chief village was L'Arbre Croche, where the venerable Jesuit priest, Father du Jaunay, had long conducted his mission.

The Indians about Michilimackinac had never taken kindly to the new occupants of the forts in their territory. When the trader Alexander Henry arrived there in 1761, he had found them decidedly hostile. On his journey up the Ottawa, he had been warned of the reception in store for him. At Michilimackinac he was waited on by a party of Chippewas headed by their chief, Minavavna, a remarkably sagacious Indian, known to the French as *Le Grand Sauteur*, whose village was situated at Thunder Bay.

This chief addressed Henry in most eloquent words, declaring that the Chippewas were the children of the French king, who was asleep, but who would shortly awaken and destroy his enemies. The king of England, he said, had entered into no treaty with the Chippewas and had sent them no presents: they were therefore still at war with him, and until he made such concessions, they must look upon the French king as their chief. 'But,' he continued, 'you come unarmed: sleep peacefully!' The pipe of peace was then passed to Henry. After smoking it he bestowed on the Indians some gifts, and they filed out of his presence.

Almost immediately on the departure of the Chippewas came some two hundred Ottawas demanding of Henry, and of several other British traders who were also there, ammunition, clothing, and other necessaries for their winter hunt, on credit until spring. The traders refused, and, when threatened by the Indians, they and their employees, some thirty in all, barricaded themselves in a house, and prepared to resist the demands by force of arms. Fortunately, at this critical moment word arrived of a strong British contingent that was approaching from Detroit to take over the fort, and the Ottawas hurriedly left for their villages.

For nearly two years the garrison at Michilimackinac lived in peace. In the spring of 1763, they were resting in a false security. Captain George Etherington, who was in command, heard that the Indians were on the warpath and that the fort was threatened; but he treated the report lightly. It is noteworthy, too, that Henry, who was in daily contact with the French settlers and Indians, and had his agents scattered throughout the Indian country, saw no cause for alarm. But it happened that towards the end of May news reached the Indians at Michilimackinac of the situation at Detroit, and with the news came a war-belt signifying that they were to destroy the British garrison. A crowd of Indians, chiefly Chippewas and Sacs, presently assembled at the post. This was a usual thing in spring, and would cause no suspicion.

The savages, however, had planned to attack the fort on June 4, the birthday of George III. The British were to celebrate the day by sports and feasting, and the Chippewas and Sacs asked to be allowed to entertain the officers with a game of lacrosse. Etherington expressed pleasure at the suggestion, and told the chiefs who waited on him that he would back his friends the Chippewas against their Sac opponents. On the morning of the 4th posts were set up on the wide plain behind the fort, and tribe was soon opposed to tribe. The warriors appeared on the field with *moccasined* feet, and otherwise naked save for breech-cloths. Hither and thither the ball was batted, thrown, and carried. Player pursued player, tripping, slashing, shouldering each other, and shouting in their excitement as command of the ball passed with the fortunes of the game from Chippewa to Sac and from Sac to Chippewa. Etherington and Lieutenant Leslie were standing near the gate, interested spectators of the game; and all about, and scattered throughout the fort, were squaws with stoical faces, each holding tight about her a gaudily coloured blanket.

The game was at its height, when a player threw the ball to a spot near the gate of the fort. There was a wild rush for it; and, as the gate was reached, lacrosse sticks were cast aside, the squaws threw open their blankets, and the players seized the tomahawks and knives held out in readiness to them. The shouts of play were changed to warwhoops. Instantly Etherington and Leslie were seized and hurried to a nearby wood. Into the fort the horde dashed. Here stood more squaws with weapons; and before the garrison had time to seize their arms, Lieutenant Jamette and fifteen soldiers were slain and scalped, and the rest made prisoners, while the French inhabitants stood by, viewing the tragedy with apparent indifference.

Etherington, Leslie, and the soldiers were held close prisoners. A day or two after the capture of the fort a Chippewa chief, *Le Grand Sable*, who had not been present at the massacre, returned from his wintering-ground. He entered a hut where a number of British soldiers were bound hand and foot, and brutally murdered five of them. The Ottawas, it will be noted, had taken no part in the capture of Michilimackinac. In fact, owing to the good offices of their priest, they acted towards the British as friends in need. A party of them from L'Arbre Croche presently arrived on the scene and prevented further massacre. Etherington and Leslie were taken from the hands of the Chippewas and removed to L'Arbre Croche.

From this place Etherington sent a message to Green Bay, ordering the *commandant* to abandon the fort there. He then wrote to Gladwyn at Detroit, giving an account of what had happened and asking aid. This message was carried to Detroit by Father du Jaunay, who made the journey in company with seven Ottawas and eight Chippewas commanded by Kinonchanek, a son of Minavavna. But, as we know, Gladwyn was himself in need of assistance, and could give none. The prisoners at L'Arbre Croche, however, were well treated, and finally taken to Montreal by way of the Ottawa River, under an escort of friendly Indians.

On the southern shore of Lake Erie, where the city of Erie now stands, was the fortified post of Presqu'isle, a stockaded fort with several substantial houses. It was considered a strong position, and its *commandant*, Ensign John Christie, had confidence that he could hold out against any number of Indians that might beset him. The news brought by Cuyler when he visited Presqu'isle, after the disaster at Point Pelée, put Christie on his guard. Presqu'isle had a blockhouse of unusual strength, but it was of wood, and inflammable. To guard against fire, there was left at the top of the building an opening through which water could be poured in any direction. The blockhouse stood on a tongue of land—on the one side a creek, on the other the lake. The most serious weakness of the position was that the banks of the creek and the lake rose in ridges to a considerable height, commanding the blockhouse and affording a convenient shelter for an attacking party within musket range.

Christie had twenty-four men, and believed that he had nothing to fear, when, on June 15, some two hundred Wyandots arrived in the vicinity., These Indians were soon on the ridges, assailing the blockhouse. Arrows tipped with burning tow and balls of blazing pitch rained upon the roof, and the utmost exertions of the garrison were needed to extinguish the fires. Soon the supply of water began to fail. There was a well nearby on the parade-ground, but this open space was subject to such a hot fire that no man would venture to cross it. A well was dug in the blockhouse, and the resistance continued. All day the attack was kept up, and during the night there was intermittent firing from the ridges.

Another day passed, and at night came a lull in the siege. A demand was made to surrender. An English soldier who had been adopted by the savages, and was aiding them in the attack, cried out that the destruction of the fort was inevitable, that in the morning it would be fired at the top and bottom, and that unless the garrison yielded, they would all be burnt to death. Christie asked till morning to consider; and, when morning came, he agreed to yield up the fort on condition that the garrison should be allowed to march to the next post. But as his men filed out, they were seized and bound, then cast into canoes and taken to Detroit. Their lives, however, were spared; and early in July, when the Wyandots made with Gladwyn the peace which they afterwards broke, Christie and a number of his men were the first prisoners given up.

A few miles inland, south of Presqu'isle, on the trade-route leading to Fort Pitt, was a rude blockhouse known as Le Boeuf. This post was at the end of the portage from Lake Erie, on Alleghany Creek, where the canoe navigation of the Ohio valley began. Here were stationed Ensign George Price and thirteen men. On June 18 a band of Indians arrived before Le Boeuf and attacked it with muskets and fire-arrows. The building was soon in flames. As the walls smoked and crackled the savages danced in wild glee before the gate, intending to shoot down the defenders as they came out. But there was a window at the rear of the blockhouse, through which the garrison escaped to the neighbouring forest. When night fell the party became separated. Some of them reached Fort Venango two days later, only to find it in ruins. Price and seven men laboriously toiled through the forest to Fort Pitt, where they arrived on June 26. Ultimately, all save two of the garrison of Fort Le Boeuf reached safety.

The circumstances attending the destruction of Fort Venango on June 20 are but vaguely known. This fort, situated near the site of the present city of Franklin, had long been a centre of Indian trade. In the days of the French occupation, it was known as Fort Machault. After the French abandoned the place in the summer of 1760, a new fort had been erected and named Venango. In 1763, there was a small garrison here under Lieutenant Gordon. For a time, all that was known of its fate was reported by the fugitives from Le Boeuf and a soldier named Gray, who had escaped from Presqu'isle. These fugitives had found Venango completely destroyed, and, in the ruins, the blackened bones of the garrison.

It was afterwards learned that the attacking Indians were Senecas, and that they had tortured the *commandant* to death over a slow fire, after compelling him to write down the reason for the attack. It was threefold: (1) the British charged exorbitant prices for powder, shot, and clothing; (2) when Indians were ill-treated by British soldiers, they could obtain no redress; (3) contrary to the wishes of the Indians, forts were being built in their country, and these could mean but one thing—the determination of the invaders to deprive them of their hunting-grounds.

With the fall of Presqu'isle, Le Boeuf, and Venango, the trade-route between Lake Erie and Fort Pitt was closed. Save for Detroit, Niagara, and Pitt, not a British fort remained in the great hinterland; and the soldiers at these three strong positions could leave the shelter of the palisades only at the risk of their lives. Meanwhile, the frontiers of the British settlements, as well as the forts, were being raided. Homes were burnt and the inmates massacred. Traders were plundered and slain. From the eastern slopes of the Alleghanies to the Mississippi no British life was safe.

The Relief of Fort Pitt

On the tongue of land at the confluence of the Monongahela and Alleghany Rivers stood Fort Pitt, on the site of the old French fort Duquesne. It was remote from any centre of population, but was favourably situated for defence, and so strongly garrisoned that those in charge of it had little to fear from any attempts of the Indians to capture it. Floods had recently destroyed part of the ramparts, but these had been repaired and a parapet of logs raised above them.

Captain Simeon Ecuyer, a Swiss soldier in the service of Great Britain and an officer of keen intelligence and tried courage, was in charge of Fort Pitt. He knew the Indians. He had quickly realised that danger threatened his wilderness post, and had left nothing undone to make it secure. On the fourth day of May, Ecuyer had written to Colonel Henry Bouquet, who was stationed at Philadelphia, saying that he had received word from Gladwyn that he 'was surrounded by rascals.' Ecuyer did not treat this alarm lightly. He not only repaired the ramparts and made them stronger, but also erected palisades within them to surround the dwellings. Everything near the fort that could give shelter to a lurking foe was levelled to the ground.

There were in Fort Pitt at this time about a hundred women and their children—families of settlers who had come to the fertile Ohio valley to take up homes. These were provided with shelter in houses

COLONEL HENRY BOUQUET

made shot-proof. Smallpox had broken out in the garrison, and a hospital was prepared under the drawbridge, where the patients in time of siege would be in no danger from musket-balls or arrows. But the best defence of Fort Pitt was the capacity of Ecuyer—brave, humorous, foresighted; a host in himself—giving courage to his men and making even the women and children think lightly of the power of the Indians.

It was nearly three weeks after the siege of Detroit had begun that the savages appeared in force about Fort Pitt. On May 27 a large band of Indians came down the Alleghany bearing packs of furs, in payment for which they demanded guns, knives, tomahawks, powder, and shot, and would take nothing else. Soon after their departure word was brought to Ecuyer of the murder of some traders and settlers not far from the fort. From that time until the beginning of August it was hazardous for anyone to venture outside the walls; but for nearly a month no attack was to be made on the fort itself. However, as news of the capture of the other forts reached the garrison, and as nearly all the messengers sent to the east were either slain or forced to return, it was evident that, in delaying the attack on Fort Pitt, the Indians were merely gathering strength for a supreme effort against the strongest position in the Indian territory.

On June 22 a large body of Indians assembled in the forest about the fort, and, creeping stealthily within range of its walls, opened fire from every side. It was the garrison's first experience of attack; some of the soldiers proved a trifle overbold, and two of them were killed. The firing, however, lasted but a short time. Ecuyer selected a spot where the smoke of the muskets was thickest, and threw shells from his howitzers into the midst of the warriors, scattering them in hurried flight. On the following day a party came within speaking distance, and their leader, Turtle's Heart, a Delaware chief, informed Ecuyer that all the western and northern forts had been cut off, and that a host of warriors were coming to destroy Fort Pitt and its garrison. He begged Ecuyer to withdraw the inmates of the fort while there was yet time. He would see to it that they were protected on their way to the eastern settlements.

He added that when the Ottawas and their allies arrived, all hope for the lives of the inhabitants of Fort Pitt would be at an end. All this Turtle's Heart told Ecuyer out of 'love for the British.' The British officer, with fine humour, thanked him for his consideration for the garrison, but told him that he could hold out against all the Indians in the woods. He could be as generous as Turtle's Heart, and so warned him that the British were coming to relieve Fort Pitt with six thousand men; that an army of three thousand was ascending the Great Lakes to punish the Ottawa Confederacy; and that still another force of three thousand had gone to the frontiers of Virginia.

'Therefore,' he said, 'take pity on your women and children, and get out of the way as soon as possible. We have told you this in confidence, out of our great solicitude, lest any of you should be hurt; and,' he added, 'we hope that you will not tell the other Indians, lest they should escape from our vengeance.'

The howitzers and the story of the approaching hosts had their effect, and the Indians vanished into the surrounding forest. For another month Fort Pitt had comparative peace, and the garrison patiently but watchfully awaited a relieving force which Amherst was sending. In the meantime, news came of the destruction of Presqu'isle, Le Boeuf, and Venango; and the fate of the garrisons, particularly at the last post, warned the inhabitants of Fort Pitt what they might expect if they should fall into the hands of the Indians.

On July 26 some Indian ambassadors, among them Turtle's Heart, came to the post with a flag of truce. They were loud in their protestations of friendship, and once more solicitous for the safety of the garrison. The Ottawas, they said, were coming in a vast horde, to 'seize and eat up everything' that came in their way. The garrison's only hope of escape would be to vacate the fort speedily and 'go home to their wives and children.' Ecuyer replied that he would never abandon his position 'as long as a white man lives in America.' He despised the Ottawas, he said, and was 'very much surprised at our brothers the Delawares for proposing to us to leave this place and go home. This is our home.' His humour was once more in evidence in the warning he gave the Indians against repeating their attack on the fort: 'I will throw bombshells, which will burst and blow you to atoms, and fire cannon among you, loaded with a whole bagful of bullets. Therefore take care, for I don't want to hurt you.'

The Indians now gave up all hope of capturing Fort Pitt by deception, and prepared to take it by assault. That very night they stole within range, dug shelter-pits in the banks of the Alleghany and Monongahela, and at daybreak began a vigorous attack on the garrison. Musket-balls came whistling over the ramparts and smote every point where a soldier showed himself. The shrieking balls and the wild war-whoops of the assailants greatly alarmed the women and children;

but never for a moment was the fort in real danger or did Ecuyer or his men fear disaster.

So carefully had the *commandant* seen to his defences, that, although hundreds of missiles fell within the confines of the fort, only one man was killed and only seven were wounded. Ecuyer himself was among the wounded: one of two arrows that fell within the fort had, to use his own words, 'the insolence to make free' with his 'left leg.' From July 27 to August 1 this horde of Delawares, Shawnees, Wyandots, and Mingoes kept up the attack. Then, without apparent cause, as suddenly as they had arrived, they all disappeared. To the garrison the relief from constant vigil, anxious days, and sleepless nights was most welcome.

The reason for this sudden relief was that the red men had learned of a rich prize for them, now approaching Fort Pitt. Bouquet, with a party of soldiers, was among the defiles of the Alleghanies. The fort could wait; the Indians would endeavour to annihilate Bouquet's force as they had annihilated Braddock's army in the same region eight years before; and if successful, they could then at their leisure return to Fort Pitt and starve it out or take it by assault.

In June, when Amherst had finally come to the conclusion that he had a real war on his hands—and had, as we have seen, dispatched Dalyell to Detroit—he had, at the same time, sent orders to Colonel Bouquet to get ready a force for the relief of Fort Pitt. Bouquet, like Ecuyer, was a Swiss soldier, and the best man in America for this particular task. After seven years' experience in border warfare, he was as skilled in woodcraft as the Indians themselves. He had now to lead a force over the road, two hundred odd miles long, which connected Fort Pitt with Carlisle, his point of departure in Pennsylvania; but every foot of the road was known to him.

In 1758, when serving under General Forbes, he had directed the construction of this road, and knew the strength of every fort and blockhouse on the way; even the rivers and creeks and morasses and defiles were familiar to him. Best of all, he had a courage and a military knowledge that inspired confidence in his men and officers. Cool, calculating, foreseeing, dauntlessly brave—there was not in the New World at this time a better soldier than this heroic Swiss.

Amherst was in a bad way for troops. The only available forces for the relief of Fort Pitt were 242 men of the 42nd Highlanders—the famous Black Watch—with 133 of the 77th (Montgomery's) Highlanders, and some Royal Americans. These, with a few volunteers, made up a contingent 550 strong. It was a force all too small for the task before it, and the majority of the soldiers had but recently arrived from the West Indies and were in wretched health.

Bouquet had sent instructions to Carlisle to have supplies ready for him and sufficient wagons assembled there for the expedition, but when he reached the place at the end of June, he found that nothing had been done. The frontier was in a state of paralysis from panic. Over the entire stretch of country from Fort Pitt the Indians were on the warpath. Every day brought tragic stories of the murder of settlers and the destruction of their homes. There was no safety outside the precincts of the feeble forts that dotted the Indian territory. Bouquet had hoped for help from the settlers and government of Pennsylvania; but the settlers thought only of immediate safety, and the government was criminally negligent in leaving the frontier of the state unprotected, and would vote neither men nor money for defence.

But they must be saved in spite of themselves. By energetic efforts, in eighteen days after his arrival at Carlisle, Bouquet was ready for the march. He began his campaign with a wise precaution. The last important fort on the road to Pitt was Ligonier, about one hundred and fifty miles from Carlisle. It would be necessary to use this post as a base; but it was beset by Indians and in danger of being captured. Lieutenant Archibald Blane in charge of it was making a gallant defence against a horde of savages. Bouquet, while waiting at Carlisle, engaged guides and sent in advance thirty Highlanders, carefully selected men, to strengthen the garrison under Blane. These, by keeping off the main trail and using every precaution, succeeded in reaching the fort without mishap.

Bouquet led his force westward. Sixty of his soldiers were so ill that they were unable to march and had to be carried in wagons. It was intended that the sick should take the place of the men now in Forts Bedford and Ligonier, and thus help to guard the rear. The road was found to be in frightful condition. The spring freshets had cut it up; deep gullies crossed the path; and the bridges over the streams had been in most cases washed away. As the little army advanced, panic-stricken settlers by the way told stories of the destruction of homes and the slaughter of friends. Fort Bedford, where Captain Lewis Ourry was in command, was reached on the 25th.

Here three days were spent, and thirty more guides were secured to serve as an advance-guard of scouts and give warning of the presence of enemies. Bouquet had tried his Highlanders at this work; but they were unfamiliar with the forest, and, as they invariably got lost, were of no value his scouts. Leaving his invalided officers and men at Bedford, Bouquet, with horses rested and men refreshed, pressed forward and arrived at Ligonier on August 2. Preparations had now to be made for the final dash to Fort Pitt, fifty odd miles away, over a path that was beset by savages, who also occupied all the important passes. It would be impossible to get through without a battle—a wilderness battle—and the thought of the Braddock disaster was in the minds of all.

But Bouquet was not a Braddock, and he was experienced in Indian warfare. To attempt to pass ambuscades with a long train of cumbersome wagons would be to invite disaster; so, he discarded his wagons and heavier stores, and having made ready three hundred and forty packhorses loaded with flour, he decided to set out from Ligonier on the 4th of August. It was planned to reach Bushy Creek—'Bushy Run,' as Bouquet called it—on the following day, and there rest and refresh horses and men. In the night a dash would be made through the dangerous defile at Turtle Creek; and, if the high broken country at this point could be passed without mishap, the rest of the way could be easily won.

At daylight the troops were up and off. It was an oppressively hot August morning, and no breath of wind stirred the forest. Over the rough road trudged the long line of sweltering men. In advance were the scouts; then followed several light companies of the Black Watch; then the main body of the little army; and in the rear came the toiling pack-horses. Until noon the soldiers marched, panting and tortured by mosquitoes, but buoyed up by the hope that at Bushy Run they would be able to quench their burning thirst and rest until nightfall. By one o'clock in the afternoon they had covered seventeen miles and were within a mile and a half of their objective point.

Suddenly in their front they heard the sharp reports of muskets; the firing grew in intensity: the advance-guard was evidently in contact with a considerable body of Indians. Two light companies were rushed forward to their support, and with fixed bayonets cleared the path. This, however, was but a temporary success. The Indians merely changed their position and appeared on the flanks in increased numbers. From the shelter of trees, the foe were creating havoc among the exposed troops, and a general charge was necessary. Highlanders and Royal Americans, acting under the directing eye of Bouquet, again drove the Indians back with the bayonet. Scarcely had this been accomplished when a fusillade was heard in the rear. The convoy was attacked, and it was necessary to fall back to its support.

Until nightfall, around a bit of elevated ground—called Edge Hill by Bouquet—on which the convoy was drawn up, the battle was waged. About the pack-horses and stores the soldiers valiantly fought for seven hours against their invisible foe. At length darkness fell, and the exhausted troops could take stock of their losses and snatch a brief, broken rest. In this day of battle two officers were killed and four wounded, and sixty of the rank and file were killed or wounded.

Flour-bags were piled in a circle, and within this the wounded were placed. Throughout the night a careful watch was kept; but the enemy made no attack during the darkness, merely firing an occasional shot and from time to time uttering defiant yells. They were confident that Bouquet's force would be an easy prey, and waited for daylight to renew the battle.

The soldiers had played a heroic part. Though unused to forest warfare, they had been cool as veterans in Indian fighting, and not a man had fired a shot without orders. But the bravest of them looked to the morning with dread. They had barely been able to hold their own on this day, and by morning the Indians would undoubtedly be greatly strengthened. The cries and moans of the wounded vividly reminded them of what had already happened. Besides, they were worn out with marching and fighting; worse than physical fatigue and more trying than the enemy's bullets was torturing thirst; and not a drop of water could be obtained at the place where they were hemmed in.

By the flickering light of a candle Bouquet penned one of the noblest letters ever written by a soldier in time of battle. He could hardly hope for success, and defeat meant the most horrible of deaths; but he had no craven spirit, and his report to Amherst was that of a true soldier—a man 'whose business it is to die.' After giving a detailed account of the occurrences leading up to this attack and a calm statement of the events of the day, and paying a tribute to his officers, whose conduct, he said, 'is much above my praise,' he added: 'Whatever our fate may be, I thought it necessary to give Your Excellency this information. . . . I fear unsurmountable difficulties in protecting and transporting our provisions, being already so much weakened by the loss in this day of men and horses.' Sending a messenger back with this dispatch, he set himself to plan for the morrow.

At daybreak from the surrounding wood the terrifying war-cries of the Indians fell on the ears of the troops. Slowly the shrill yells came nearer; the Indians were endeavouring to strike terror into the hearts of their foes before renewing the fight, knowing that troops in dread of death are already half beaten. When within five hundred yards of the centre of the camp the Indians began firing. The troops replied with great steadiness. This continued until ten in the morning. The wounded within the barricade lay listening to the sounds of battle, ever increasing in volume, and the fate of Braddock's men rose before them. It seemed certain that their sufferings must end in death—and what a death! The pack-horses, tethered at a little distance from the barricade, offered an easy target, against which the Indians soon directed their fire, and the piteous cries of the wounded animals added to the tumult of the battle. Some of the horses, maddened by wounds, broke their fastenings and galloped into the forest.

But the kilted Highlanders and the red-coated Royal Americans gallantly fought on. Their ranks were being thinned; the fatiguing work of the previous day was telling on them; their throats were parched and their tongues swollen for want of water. Bouquet surveyed the field. He saw his men weakening under the terrible strain, and realised that something must be done promptly. The Indians were each moment becoming bolder, pressing ever nearer and nearer.

Then he conceived one of the most brilliant movements known in Indian warfare. He ordered two companies, which were in the most exposed part of the field, to fall back as though retreating within the circle that defended the hill. At the same time the troops on the right and left opened their files, and, as if to cover the retreat, occupied the space vacated in a thinly extended line. The strategy worked even better than Bouquet had expected. The yelling Indians, eager for slaughter and believing that the entire command was at their mercy, rushed pell-mell from their shelter, firing sharp volleys into the protecting files. These were forced back, and the savages dashed forward for the barricade which sheltered the wounded.

Meanwhile the two companies had taken position on the right, and from a sheltering hill that concealed them from the enemy they poured an effective fire into the savages. The astonished Indians replied, but with little effect, and before they could reload the Highlanders were on them with the bayonet. The red men then saw that they had fallen into a trap, and turned to flee. But suddenly on their left two more companies rose from ambush and sent a storm of bullets into the retreating savages, while the Highlanders and Royal Americans dashed after them with fixed bayonets. The Indians at other parts of the circle, seeing their comrades in flight, scattered into the forest. The defiant war-cries ceased and the muskets were silent. The victory was complete: Bouquet had beaten the Indians in their own woods and at their own game. About sixty of the enemy lay dead and as many more wounded. In the two days of battle the British had fifty killed, sixty wounded, and five missing. It was a heavy price; but this victory broke the back of the Indian war.

Many horses had been killed or had strayed away, and it was impossible to transport all the stores to Fort Pitt. What could not be carried with the force was destroyed, and the victors moved on to Bushy Creek, at a slow pace on account of the wounded. No sooner had they pitched their tents at the creek than some of the enemy again appeared; the Highlanders, however, without waiting for the word of command, scattered them with the bayonet. On the following day the march began for Fort Pitt. Three days later, on August 10, the garrison of that fort heard the skirl of the bagpipes and the beat of the drum, and saw through the forest the plaids and plumes of the Highlanders and the red coats of the Royal Americans. The gate was thrown open, and the victors of Edge Hill marched in to the welcome of the men and women who for several months had had no news from their friends in the east.

Bouquet had been instructed to invade the Ohio country and teach the Shawnees and Delawares a lesson. But his men were worn out, half of them were unfit for service, and so deficient was he in horses and supplies that this task had to be abandoned for the present year.

Pennsylvania and Virginia rejoiced. This triumph meant much to them. Their borders would now be safe, but for occasional scalping parties. Amherst was delighted, and took to himself much of the credit of Bouquet's victory. He congratulated the noble Swiss officer on his victory over 'a band of savages that would have been very formidable against any troops but such as you had with you.' But it was not the troops that won the battle; it was Bouquet. In the hands of a Braddock, a Loudoun, an Abercromby, these war-worn veterans would have met a fate such as befell Braddock's troops. But Bouquet animated every man with his own spirit; he knew how to fight Indians; and at the critical moment—'the fatal five minutes between victory and defeat'—he proved himself the equal of any soldier who ever battled against the red men in North America.

DETROIT ONCE MORE

While Fort Pitt was holding out against the Ohio Indians and Bouquet was forcing his way through the defiles of the Alleghanies

LAKE ER

Miamis Fort

Maumee R.

Sandusky R.
180 Yards wide

Sandusky L.

Sandusky Ft.
Wyandot
Town

Junqueindundeh

Bald Eagle Cr.
80 Yards wide

Cayahoga R.

Ottawa
Cayah

Remains of a fort
built by the Ottawas

Miamis R. 25 Yards wide

6 Yards wide

8 Yards wide

Mohickon
John's Town

The Country from the Miamis Ft.
Small Creek to Sandusky and to the Lower
Shawneese Town is Level & Rich

Beaver Dams

Beav
at Tusca

Margrets Cr. 20 Yds
very Deep & Miry

20 Yards wide

100 Yards wide

Kill Bucks T.

Owls T.

10 Yards wide

Large Run
10 Yards wide
60 Yards wide

Whale Winans Cr.

10 Yards wide

Waukatatunukee T.

A Delaware T.

100 Yds
wide

20 Yards
wide

Spring

Licking Cr.
30 Yards wide
Beaver T.

New T.

New T.

New Town

10 Yards wide

Lick T.

New T.

Wills T.

Lower
Shawneese
Town

Lead Mine

Muskingum River

Sioto R.

Hockhocking R.

Passable with Canoes 40 Miles

Beaver Creek is laid down from o

Little
Hockhocking R.

This Part of the Ohio

Canhawa R.

BOUQUET'S ROUTES
1763 AND 1764
n old map by Thomas Hutchins

Scale of Miles

to its relief, Fort Detroit was still in a state of siege. The defeat of Dalyell's force at Bloody Run had given the Indians a greater degree of confidence. They had not dared, however, to make a general assault, but had merely kept the garrison aware of their presence by desultory and irritating attacks.

Nothing of importance took place until September 3. On this day the little *Gladwyn*, which had gone to the Niagara with dispatches, entered the Detroit River on her return trip. She was in charge of Captain Horst, who was assisted by Jacobs as mate, and a crew of ten men. There were likewise on board six Iroquois Indians. It was a calm morning; and as the vessel lay with idly flapping sails waiting for a wind, the Iroquois asked permission to stretch their limbs on shore.

Horst foolishly granted their request, and as soon as they had made a landing they disappeared into the forest, and no doubt hurried to Pontiac's warriors to let them know how weakly manned was the schooner. The weather continued calm, and by nightfall the *Gladwyn* was still nine miles below the fort. As darkness fell on that moonless night the captain, alarmed at the flight of the Iroquois, posted a careful guard and had his cannon at bow and stern made ready to resist attack. So dark was the night that it was impossible to discern objects at any distance. Along the black shore Indians were gathering, and soon a fleet of canoes containing over three hundred warriors was slowly and silently moving towards the becalmed *Gladwyn*.

So noiseless was their approach that they were within a few yards of the vessel before a watchful sentry, the boatswain, discerned them. At his warning cry the crew leapt to their quarters. The bow gun thundered out, and its flash gave the little band on the boat a momentary glimpse of a horde of painted enemies. There was no time to reload the gun. The canoes were all about the schooner, and yelling warriors were clambering over the stern and bow and swarming on the deck. The crew discharged their muskets into the savages, and then seized spears and hatchets and rushed madly at them, striking and stabbing—determined at least to sell their lives dearly.

For a moment the Indians in the black darkness shrank back from the fierce attack. But already Horst was killed and several of the crew were down with mortal wounds. The vessel seemed lost when Jacobs—a dare-devil seaman—now in command, ordered his men to blow up the vessel. A Wyandot brave with some knowledge of English caught the words and shouted a warning to his comrades. In an instant every warrior was over the side of the vessel, paddling or swimming to get to safety. When morning broke not an Indian was to be seen, and the little *Gladwyn* sailed in triumph to Fort Detroit. So greatly was the gallantry of her crew appreciated that Amherst had a special medal struck and given to each of the survivors.

Meanwhile, at Niagara, supplies were being conveyed over the portage between the lower landing (now Lewiston) and Fort Schlosser, in readiness for transport to the western posts. The Senecas claimed the territory about Niagara, and the invasion of their land had greatly irritated them. They particularly resented the act of certain squatters who, without their consent, had settled along the Niagara portage. Fort Niagara was too strong to be taken by assault; but the Senecas hoped, by biding their time, to strike a deadly blow against parties conveying goods over the portage. The opportunity came on September 14. On this day a sergeant and twenty-eight men were engaged in escorting down to the landing a wagon-train and packhorses which had gone up to Fort Schlosser the day before loaded with supplies.

The journey up the river had been successfully made, and the party were returning, off their guard and without the slightest thought of danger. But their every movement had been watched by Indian scouts; and, at the Devil's Hole, a short distance below the falls, five hundred warriors lay in ambush. Slowly the returning provision-train wound its way along the bank of the Niagara. On the right were high cliffs, thickly wooded; on the left a precipice, whose base was fretted by the furious river. In the ears of the soldiers and drivers sounded the thunderous roar of the mighty cataract.

As men and horses threaded their way past the Devil's Hole savage yells burst from the thick wood on their right, and simultaneously a fusillade from a hundred muskets. The terrified horses sprang over the cliffs, dragging wagons and drivers with them. When the smoke cleared and the savages rushed forward, not a living member of the escort nor a driver was to be seen. The leader of the escort, Philip Stedman, had grasped the critical character of the situation at the first outcry, and, putting spurs to his horse, had dashed into the bushes. A warrior had seized his rein; but Stedman had struck him down and galloped free for Fort Schlosser.

A drummer-boy, in terror of his life, had leapt over the cliff. By good fortune his drum-strap caught on the branch of a dense tree; here he remained suspended until the Indians left the spot, when he extricated himself. One of the teamsters also escaped. He was wounded, but managed to roll into the bushes, and found concealment in the thick undergrowth. The terrific musketry fire was heard at the lower landing, where a body of troops of the 60th and 80th regiments were encamped. The soldiers hastily armed themselves and in great disorder rushed to the aid of the convoy. But the Indians were not now at the Devil's Hole. The murderous work completed there, they had taken up a position in a thick wood half a mile farther down, where they silently waited. They had chosen well their place of concealment; and the soldiers in their excitement walked into the trap set for them. Suddenly the ominous war-cries broke out, and before the troops could turn to face the foe a storm of bullets had swept their left flank. Then the warriors dashed from their ambush, tomahawking the living and scalping both dead and dying. In a few minutes five officers and seventy-six of the rank and file were killed and eight wounded, and out of a force of over one hundred men only twenty escaped unhurt.

The news of this second disaster brought Major Wilkins up from Fort Niagara, with every available man, to chastise the Indians. But when Wilkins and his men arrived at the gruesome scene of the massacre not a red man was to be found. The Indians had disappeared into the forest, after having stripped their victims even of clothing. With a heavy heart the troops marched back to Niagara, mourning the loss of many gallant comrades. This was the greatest disaster, in loss of life, of the Pontiac War; but, like the defeat of Dalyell, it had little effect on the progress of the campaign. The Indians did not follow it up; with scalps and plunder they returned to their villages to exult in wild orgies over the victory.

Detroit was still besieged; but the Indians were beginning to weaken, and for the most part had given up hope of forcing the garrison to surrender. They had been depending almost wholly on the settlement for sustenance, and provisions were running low. Ammunition, too, was well-nigh exhausted. They had replenished their supply during the summer by the captures they had made, by the plundering of traders, and by purchase or gift from the French of the Mississippi. Now they had little hope of capturing more supply-boats; the traders were holding aloof; and, since the arrival of definite news of the surrender to Great Britain by France of the region east of the Mississippi, supplies from the French had been stopped. If the Indians were to escape starvation they must scatter to their hunting-grounds.

There was another reason why many of the chiefs deemed it wise to leave the vicinity of Detroit. They had learned that Major Wilkins was on his way from Niagara with a strong force and a fleet of *bateaux*

loaded with ammunition and supplies. So, early in October, the Potawatomis, Wyandots, and Chippewas held a council and concluded
to bury the hatchet and make peace with Gladwyn. On the 12th of
the month a delegation from these tribes came to the fort bearing a
pipe of peace. Gladwyn knew from experience how little they were
to be trusted, but he gave them a seemingly cordial welcome. A chief
named Wapocomoguth acted as spokesman, and stated that the tribes
represented regretted 'their bad conduct' and were ready to enter into
a treaty of peace.

Gladwyn replied that it was not in his power to grant peace to
Indians who without cause had attacked the troops of their father the
king of England; only the commander-in-chief could do that; but he
consented to a cessation of hostilities. He did this the more willingly
as the fort was short of food, and the truce would give him a chance
to lay in a fresh stock of provisions.

As the autumn frosts were colouring the maples with brilliant hues,
the Potawatomis, Wyandots, and Chippewas set out for fields where
game was plentiful; but for a time, Pontiac with his Ottawas remained,
threatening the garrison, and still strong in his determination to continue the siege. During the summer he had sent ambassadors to Fort
Chartres on the Mississippi asking aid in fighting what he asserted to
be the battle of the French traders. Towards the end of July, the messengers had returned with word from Neyon de Villiers, the commandant of Fort Chartres, saying that he must await more definite news as
to whether peace had been concluded between France and England.
Pontiac still hoped; and, after his allies had deserted, he waited at his
camp above Detroit for further word from Neyon.

On the last day of October Louis Césair Dequindre arrived at
Detroit from Fort Chartres, with the crushing answer that Neyon de
Villiers could give him no aid. England and France were at peace,
and Neyon advised the Ottawas—no doubt with reluctance, and only
because of the demand of Amherst—to bury the hatchet and give up
the useless contest. To continue the struggle for the present would be
vain. Pontiac, though enraged by the desertion of his allies, and by
what seemed to him the cowardly conduct of the French, determined
at once to accept the situation, sue for peace, and lay plans for future
action.

So far, he had been fighting ostensibly for the restoration of French
rule. In future, whatever scheme he might devise, his struggle must
be solely in the interests of the red man. Next day he sent a letter to

Gladwyn begging that the past might be forgotten. His young men, he said, had buried their hatchets, and he declared himself ready not only to make peace, but also to 'send to all the nations concerned in the war' telling them to cease hostilities. No trust could Gladwyn put in Pontiac's words; yet he assumed a friendly bearing towards the treacherous conspirator, who for nearly six months had given him no rest.

Gladwyn's views of the situation at this time are well shown in a report he made to Amherst. The Indians, he said, had lost many of their best warriors, and would not be likely again to show a united front. It was in this report that he made the suggestion, unique in warfare, of destroying the Indians by the free sale of rum to them, he wrote:

> If Your Excellency still intends to punish them further for their barbarities, it may easily be done without any expense to the Crown, by permitting a free sale of rum, which will destroy them more effectually than fire and sword.

He thought that the French had been the real plotters of the Indian war:

> I don't imagine there will be any danger of their (the Indians) breaking out again, provided some examples are made of our good friends, the French, who set them on.

Pontiac and his band of savages paddled southward for the Maumee, and spent the winter among the Indians along its upper waters. Again, he broke his plighted word and plotted a new confederacy, greater than the Three Fires, and sent messengers with *wampum* belts and red hatchets to all the tribes as far south as the mouth of the Mississippi and as far north as the Red River. But his glory had departed. He could call; but the warriors would not come when he summoned them.

Fort Detroit was freed from hostile Indians, and the soldiers could go to rest without expecting to hear the call to arms. But before the year closed it was to be the witness of still another tragedy. Two or three weeks after the massacre at the Devil's Hole, Major Wilkins with some six hundred troops started from Fort Schlosser with a fleet of *bateaux* for Detroit. No care seems to have been taken to send out scouts to learn if the forest bordering the river above the falls was free from Indians, and, as the *bateaux* were slowly making their way against the swift stream towards Lake Erie, they were savagely attacked from the western bank by Indians in such force that Wilkins was compelled to retreat to Fort Schlosser.

It was not until November that another attempt was made to send troops and provisions to Detroit. Early in this month Wilkins once more set out from Fort Schlosser, this time with forty-six *bateaux* heavily laden with troops, provisions, and ammunition. While they were in Lake Erie there arose one of the sudden storms so prevalent on the Great Lakes in autumn. Instead of creeping along the shore, the *bateaux* were in mid-lake, and before a landing could be made the gale was on them in all its fury.

There was a wild race for land; but the choppy, turbulent sea beat upon the boats, of which some were swamped and the crews plunged into the chilly waters. They were opposite a forbidding shore, called by Wilkins Long Beach, but there was no time to look for a harbour. An attempt was made to land, with disastrous results. In all sixteen boats were sunk; three officers, four sergeants, and sixty-three privates were drowned. The thirty *bateaux* brought ashore were in a sinking condition; half the provisions were lost and the remainder water-soaked. The journey to Detroit was out of the question. The few provisions saved would not last the remnant of Wilkins's own soldiers for a month, and the ammunition was almost entirely lost. Even if they succeeded in arriving safely at Detroit, they would only be an added burden to Gladwyn; and so, sick at heart from failure and the loss of comrades, the survivors beat their way back to the Niagara.

A week or two later a messenger arrived at Fort Detroit bearing news of the disaster. The scarcity of provisions at Detroit was such that Gladwyn decided to reduce his garrison. Keeping about two hundred men in the fort, he sent the rest to Niagara. Then the force remaining at Detroit braced themselves to endure a hard, lonely winter. Theirs was not a pleasant lot. Never was garrison duty enjoyable during winter in the northern parts of North America, but in previous winters at Detroit the friendly intercourse between the soldiers and the settlers had made the season not unbearable. Now, so many of the French had been sympathizers with the besieging Indians, and, indeed, active in aiding them, that the old relations could not be resumed. So, during this winter of 1763-64, the garrison for the most part held aloof from the French settlers, and performed their weary round of military duties, longing for spring and the sight of a relieving force.

WINDING UP THE INDIAN WAR

Amherst was weary of America. Early in the summer of 1763, he had asked to be relieved of his command; but it was not until October that General Thomas Gage, then in charge of the government of Montreal, was appointed to succeed him, and not until November 17, the day after Gage arrived in New York, that Amherst sailed for England. The new commander-in-chief was not as great a general as Amherst. It is doubtful if he could have planned and brought to a successful conclusion such campaigns as the siege of Louisbourg and the threefold march of 1760, on Montreal, which have given his predecessor a high place in the military history of North America.

But Gage was better suited for winding up the Indian war. He knew the value of the officers familiar with the Indian tribes, and was ready to act on their advice. Amherst had not done this, and his best officers were now anxious to resign. George Croghan had resigned as assistant superintendent of Indian Affairs, but was later induced by Gage to remain in office. Gladwyn was 'heartily wearied' of his command and hoped to 'be relieved soon'; Blane and Ourry were tired of their posts; and the brave Ecuyer was writing in despair:

> For God's sake, let me go and raise cabbages.

Bouquet, too, although determined to see the war to a conclusion, was not satisfied with the situation. Meanwhile, Sir William Johnson was not idle among the tribes of the Six Nations. The failure of Pontiac to reduce Fort Detroit and the victory of Bouquet at Edge Hill had convinced the Iroquois that ultimately the British would triumph, and, eager to be on the winning side, they consented to take the field against the Shawnees and Delawares. In the middle of February 1764, through Johnson's influence and by his aid, two hundred Tuscaroras and Oneidas, under a half-breed, Captain Montour, marched westward. Near the main branch of the Susquehanna, they surprised forty Delawares, on a scalping expedition against the British settlements, and made prisoners of the entire party.

A few weeks later a number of Mohawks led by Joseph Brant (Thayendanegea) put another band of Delawares to rout, killing their chief and taking three prisoners. These attacks of the Iroquois disheartened the Shawnees and Delawares and greatly alarmed the Senecas, who, trembling lest their own country should be laid waste, sent a deputation of four hundred of their chief men to Johnson Hall—Sir William Johnson's residence on the Mohawk—to sue for peace. It was agreed that the Senecas should at once stop all hostilities, never again take up arms against the British, deliver up all prisoners at Johnson Hall, cede to His Majesty the Niagara carrying-place, allow the free passage of troops through their country, renounce all intercourse with the Delawares and Shawnees, and assist the British in punishing them. Thus, early in 1764, through the energy and diplomacy of Sir William Johnson, the powerful Senecas were brought to terms.

With the opening of spring preparations began in earnest for a twofold invasion of the Indian country. One army was to proceed to Detroit by way of Niagara and the Lakes, and another from Fort Pitt was to take the field against the Delawares and the Shawnees. To Colonel John Bradstreet, who in 1758, had won distinction by his capture of Fort Frontenac, was assigned the command of the contingent that was to go to Detroit. Bradstreet was to punish the Wyandots of Sandusky, and likewise the members of the Ottawa Confederacy if he should find them hostile. He was also to relieve Gladwyn and re-garrison the forts captured by the Indians in 1763, Bradstreet left Albany in June with a large force of colonial troops and regulars, including three hundred French Canadians from the St Lawrence, whom Gage had thought it wise to have enlisted, in order to impress upon the Indians that they need no longer expect assistance from the French in their wars against the British.

To prepare the way for Bradstreet's arrival Sir William Johnson had gone in advance to Niagara, where he had called together ambassadors from all the tribes, not only from those that had taken part in the war, but from all within his jurisdiction. He had found a vast concourse of Indians awaiting him. The wigwams of over a thousand warriors dotted the low-lying land at the mouth of the river. In a few days the number had grown to two thousand—representatives of nations as far east as Nova Scotia, as far west as the Mississippi, and as far north as Hudson Bay.

Pontiac was absent, nor were there any Delaware, Shawnee, or Seneca ambassadors present. These were absent through dread; but later the Senecas sent deputies to ratify the treaty made with Johnson in April. When Bradstreet and his troops arrived, negotiations were in full swing. For nearly a month, councils were held, and at length all the chiefs present had entered into an alliance with the British. This accomplished, Johnson, on August 6, left Niagara for his home, while Bradstreet continued his journey towards Detroit.

Bradstreet halted at Presqu'isle. Here he was visited by pretended deputies from the Shawnees and Delawares, who ostensibly sought peace. He made a conditional treaty with them and agreed to meet them twenty-five days later at Sandusky, where they were to bring their British prisoners. From Presqu'isle he wrote to Bouquet at Fort Pitt, saying that it would be unnecessary to advance into the Delaware country, as the Delawares were now at peace. He also reported his success, as he considered it, to Gage, but Gage was not impressed: he disavowed the treaty and instructed Bouquet to continue his preparations. Continuing his journey, Bradstreet rested at Sandusky, where more Delawares waited on him and agreed to make peace. It was at this juncture that he sent Captain Thomas Morris on his ill-starred mission to the tribes of the Mississippi.

★★★★★★★★

Morris and his companions got no farther than the rapids of the Maumee, where they were seized, stripped of clothing, and threatened with death. Pontiac was now among the Miamis, still striving to get together a following to continue the war. The prisoners were taken to Pontiac's camp. But the Ottawa chief did not deem it wise to murder a British officer on this occasion, and Morris was released and forced to retrace his steps. He arrived at Detroit after the middle of September, only to find that Bradstreet had already departed. The story will be found in more detail in Parkman's *Conspiracy of Pontiac*.

★★★★★★★★

Bradstreet was at Detroit by August 26, and at last the worn-out garrison of the fort could rest after fifteen months of exacting duties. Calling the Indians to a council, Bradstreet entered into treaties with a number of chiefs, and pardoned several French settlers who had taken an active part with the Indians in the siege of Detroit. He then sent troops to occupy Michilimackinac, Green Bay, and Sault Ste Marie; and sailed for Sandusky to meet the Delawares and Shawnees, who had promised to bring in their prisoners. But none awaited him: the Indians had deliberately deceived him and were playing for time while they continued their attacks on the border settlers.

Here he received a letter from Gage ordering him to disregard the treaty he had made with the Delawares and to join Bouquet at Fort Pitt, an order which Bradstreet did not obey, making the excuse that the low state of the water in the rivers made impossible an advance to Fort Pitt. On October 18 he left Sandusky for Niagara, having accomplished nothing except occupation of the forts. Having already blundered hopelessly in dealing with the Indians, he was to blunder still further. On his way down Lake Erie he encamped one night, when storm threatened, on an exposed shore, and a gale from the north-east broke upon his camp and destroyed half his boats. Two hundred and eighty of his soldiers had to march overland to Niagara. Many of them perished; others, starved, exhausted, frost-bitten, came staggering in by twos and threes till near the end of December. The expedition was a fiasco. It blasted Bradstreet's reputation, and made the British name for a time contemptible among the Indians.

The other expedition from Fort Pitt has a different history. All through the summer Bouquet had been recruiting troops for the invasion of the Delaware country. The soldiers were slow in arriving, and it was not until the end of September that all was ready. Early in October Bouquet marched out of Fort Pitt with one thousand provincials and five hundred regulars. Grossing the Alleghany, he made his way in a northwesterly direction until Beaver Creek was reached, and then turned westward into the unbroken forest. The Indians of the Muskingum valley felt secure in their wilderness fastness. No white soldiers had ever penetrated to their country. To reach their villages dense woods had to be penetrated, treacherous marshes crossed, and numerous streams bridged or forded.

But by the middle of October Bouquet had led his army, without the loss of a man, into the heart of the Muskingum valley, and pitched his camp near an Indian village named Tuscarawa, from which the inhabitants had fled at his approach. The Delawares and Shawnees were terrified: the victor of Edge Hill was among them with an army strong enough to crush to atoms any war-party they could muster. They sent deputies to Bouquet. These at first assumed a haughty mien; but Bouquet sternly rebuked them and ordered them to meet him at the forks of the Muskingum, forty miles distant to the south-west, and to bring in all their prisoners.

By the beginning of November, the troops were at the appointed place, where they encamped. Bouquet then sent messengers to all the tribes telling them to bring thither all the captives without delay. Every white man, woman, and child in their hands, French or British, must be delivered up. After some hesitation the Indians made haste to obey. About two hundred captives were brought, and chiefs were left as hostages for the safe delivery of others still in the hands of distant tribes. So far Bouquet had been stern and unbending; he had reminded the Indians of their murder of settlers and of their black treachery regarding the garrisons, and hinted that except for the kindness of their British father they would be utterly destroyed. He now unbent and offered them a generous treaty, which was to be drawn up and arranged later by Sir William Johnson.

Bouquet then retraced his steps to Fort Pitt, and arrived there on November 28 with his long train of released captives. He had won a victory over the Indians greater than his triumph at Edge Hill, and all the greater in that it was achieved without striking a blow.

There was still, however, important work to be done before any guarantee of permanent peace in the hinterland was possible. On the eastern bank of the Mississippi, within the country ceded to England by the Treaty of Paris, was an important settlement over which the French flag still flew, and to which no British troops or traders had penetrated. It was a hotbed of conspiracy. Even while Bouquet was making peace with the tribes between the Ohio and Lake Erie, Pontiac and his agents were trying to make trouble for the British among the Indians of the Mississippi.

French settlement on the Mississippi began at the village of Kaskaskia, eighty-four miles north of the mouth of the Ohio. Six miles still farther north was Fort Chartres, a strongly built stone fort capable of accommodating three hundred men. From here, at some distance from the river, ran a road to Cahokia, a village situated nearly opposite the site of the present city of St Louis. The intervening country was settled by prosperous traders and planters who, including their four hundred negro slaves, numbered not less than two thousand. But when it was learned that all the territory east of the great river had been ceded to Britain, the settlers began to migrate to the opposite bank. The French here were hostile to the incoming British, and feared lest they might now lose the profitable trade with New Orleans. It was this region that Gage was determined to occupy.

Already an effort had been made to reach Fort Chartres. In February 1764, Major Arthur Loftus had set out from New Orleans with four hundred men; but, when about two hundred and forty miles north of his starting-point, his two leading boats were fired upon by Indians. Six men were killed and four wounded. To advance would mean the destruction of his entire company. Loftus returned to New Orleans, blaming the French officials for not supporting his enterprise, and indeed hinting that they were responsible for the attack. Some weeks later Captain Philip Pittman arrived at New Orleans with the intention of ascending the river; but reports of the enmity of the Indians to the British made him abandon the undertaking. So, at the beginning of 1765, the French flag still flew over Fort Chartres; and Saint-Ange, who had succeeded Neyon de Villiers as commandant of

St. Louis

Cahokia

Mill

Merimeg
River

A Spring

Road from Kaskaskias to Cahokia

FORTS & SETTLEMENTS
ON THE **MISSISSIPPI**
1764
From old map by
Thos Hutchins

Belle Fountain

Pond

River

Mississippi

St Philips

La Prairie de Roche River

Kaskaskias River

Indian Village

Fort Chartres

Old Wind Mill

Indian Village

Grist Mill

Old Fort

Kaskaskias Village

Scale of Miles

0   5   10   15   20

St Genivieve

The Saline

the fort, was praying that the British might soon arrive to relieve him from a position where he was being daily importuned by Pontiac or his emissaries for aid against what they called the common foe.

But, if the route to Fort Chartres by way of New Orleans was too dangerous, Bouquet had cleared the Ohio of enemies, and the country which Gage sought to occupy was now accessible by way of that river. As a preliminary step, George Croghan was sent in advance with presents for the Indians along the route. In May 1765 Croghan left Fort Pitt accompanied by a few soldiers and a number of friendly Shawnee and Delaware chiefs. Near the mouth of the Wabash a prowling band of Kickapoos attacked the party, killing several and making prisoners of the rest.

Croghan and his fellow-prisoners were taken to the French traders at Vincennes, where they were liberated. They then went to Ouiatanon, where Croghan held a council, and induced many chiefs to swear fealty to the British. After leaving Ouiatanon, Croghan had proceeded westward but a little way when he was met by Pontiac with a number of chiefs and warriors. At last, the arch-conspirator was ready to come to terms. The French on the Mississippi would give him no assistance. He realised now that his people were conquered, and before it was too late, he must make peace with his conquerors. Croghan had no further reason to continue his journey; so, accompanied by Pontiac, he went to Detroit.

Arriving there on August 17, he at once called a council of the tribes in the neighbourhood. At this council sat Pontiac, among chiefs whom he had led during the months of the siege of Detroit. But it was no longer the same Pontiac: his haughty, domineering spirit was broken; his hopes of an Indian empire were at an end. He said at this council:

> Father, I declare to all nations that I had made my peace with you before I came here; and I now deliver my pipe to Sir William Johnson, that he may know that I have made peace, and taken the king of England to be my father in the presence of all the nations now assembled.

He further agreed to visit Oswego in the spring to conclude a treaty with Sir William Johnson himself. The path was now clear for the advance of the troops to Fort Chartres. As soon as news of Croghan's success reached Fort Pitt, Captain Thomas Sterling, with one hundred and twenty men of the Black Watch, set out in boats for the Mississippi, arriving on October 9 at Fort Chartres, the first British troops to set foot in that country. Next day Saint-Ange handed the keys of the fort to Sterling, and the Union Jack was flung aloft. Thus, nearly three years after the signing of the Treaty of Paris, the *fleurs-de-lis* disappeared from the territory then known as Canada.

There is still to record the closing act in the public career of Pontiac. Sir William Johnson, fearing that the Ottawa chief might fail to keep his promise of visiting Oswego to ratify the treaty made with Croghan at Detroit, sent Hugh Crawford, in March 1766, with belts and messages to the chiefs of the Ottawa Confederacy. But Pontiac was already preparing for his journey eastward. Nothing in his life was more creditable than his bold determination to attend a council far from his hunting-ground, at which he would be surrounded by soldiers who had suffered treachery and cruelty at his hands—whose comrades he had tortured and murdered.

On July 23 there began at Oswego the grand council at which Sir William Johnson and Pontiac were the most conspicuous figures. For three days the ceremonies and speeches continued; and on the third day Pontiac rose in the assembly and made a promise that he was faithfully to keep:

> I take the Great Spirit to witness, that what I am going to say I am determined steadfastly to perform. . . . While I had the French king by the hand, I kept a fast hold of it; and now having you, father, by the hand, I shall do the same in conjunction with all the western nations in my district.

Before the council ended Johnson presented to each of the chiefs a silver medal engraved with the words:

> A pledge of peace and friendship with Great Britain, confirmed in 1766.

He also loaded Pontiac and his brother chiefs with presents; then, on the last day of July, the Indians scattered to their homes.

For three years Pontiac, like a restless spirit, moved from camp to camp and from hunting-ground to hunting-ground. There were outbreaks of hostilities in the Indian country, but in none of these did he take part. His name never appears in the records of those three years. His days of conspiracy were at an end. By many of the French and Indians he was distrusted as a pensioner of the British, and by the British traders and settlers he was hated for his past deeds. In 1769, he visited the Mississippi, and while at Cahokia he attended a drunken frolic held by some Indians. When he left the feast, stupid from the effects of rum, he was followed into the forest by a Kaskaskia Indian, probably bribed by a British trader. And as Pontiac lurched among the black shadows of the trees, his pursuer crept up behind him, and with a swift stroke of the tomahawk cleft his skull. Thus, by a treacherous blow ended the career of a warrior whose chief weapon had been treachery.

Milton Keynes UK
Ingram Content Group UK Ltd.
UKHW031002080824
1198UKWH00001B/5

9 781915 234018